Developing the
ICBM

INSTITUTE OF WAR AND PEACE STUDIES
of the School of International Affairs
of Columbia University

Developing the ICBM is one of a series of studies sponsored by the Institute of War and Peace Studies of Columbia University. Among those Institute studies also dealing with war, peace, and national security are *Defense and Diplomacy* by Alfred Vagts; *Man, the State and War* by Kenneth N. Waltz; *The Common Defense* by Samuel P. Huntington; *Changing Patterns of Military Politics* edited by Samuel P. Huntington; *Strategy, Politics, and Defense Budgets* by Warner R. Schilling, Paul Y. Hammond, and Glenn H. Snyder; *Stockpiling Strategic Materials* by Glenn H. Snyder; *The Politics of Military Unification* by Demetrios Caraley; *NATO and the Range of American Choice* by William T. R. Fox and Annette Baker Fox; *The Politics of Weapons Innovation: The Thor-Jupiter Controversy* by Michael H. Armacost; *The Politics of Policy Making in Defense and Foreign Affairs* by Roger Hilsman; *Inspection for Disarmament* edited by Seymour Melman; *To Move a Nation* by Roger Hilsman, jointly sponsored with the Washington Center of Foreign Policy Research, Johns Hopkins University, *Planning, Prediction and Policy-Making in Foreign Affairs* by Robert L. Rothstein; *The Origins of Peace* by Robert F. Randle; *European Security and the Atlantic System* edited by William T. R. Fox and Warner R. Schilling; *American Arms and a Changing Europe: Dilemmas of Deterrence and Disarmament* by Warner R. Schilling, William T. R. Fox, Catherine M. Kelleher, and Donald J. Puchala; *The Cold War Begins: Soviet-American Conflict Over Eastern Europe* by Lynn E. Davis; *The Crouching Future: International Politics and U. S. Foreign Policy—a Forecast* by Roger Hilsman; and *Germany and the Politics of Nuclear Weapons* by Catherine M. Kelleher.

DEVELOPING THE ICBM

A Study in Bureaucratic Politics

Edmund Beard

COLUMBIA UNIVERSITY PRESS
NEW YORK   1976

Edmund Beard is Assistant Professor in the Department of Politics, University of Massachusetts. As his doctoral dissertation, this book received the Bancroft Award from Columbia University.

Library of Congress Cataloging in Publication Data

Beard, Edmund; 1944–
   Developing the ICBM.

   Bibliography: p.
   Includes index.
      1. Intercontinental ballistic missiles. 2. United States—Military policy. 3. United States. Dept. of Defense. I. Title.
UG1312.I2B4   358'.17'540973   76–16037
ISBN 0–231–04012–1

COLUMBIA UNIVERSITY PRESS
New York   Guildford, Surrey

Copyright ©1976 by Columbia University Press

Printed in the United States of America

For Clare

Preface

IN WRITING THIS BOOK I have used extensively the voluminous (although often vague, superficial, or censored) Congressional hearings which were both a consequence and an integral part of the furor over the Sputnik launch. The most productive of the numerous hearings proved to be the *Study of Airpower,* conducted by the Air Force Subcommittee of the Senate Committee on Armed Services in 1956 under the chairmanship of Stuart Symington; the *Inquiry into Satellite and Missile Programs,* conducted by the Preparedness Investigating Subcommittee of the Senate Armed Services Committee in 1957 and 1958 under the chairmanship of Lyndon Johnson; and a series of hearings titled *Organization and Management of Missile Programs,* conducted by the Military Operations Subcommittee of the House Committee on Government Operations in 1959 and 1960 under the chairmanship of Chet Holifield.

Published reminiscences also proved productive. Such central figures as General Henry ("Hap") Arnold, Wernher von Braun, Theodore von Karman, Herbert York, General Bernard

Schriever, Trevor Gardner, and General Donald Putt, have published reports of varying usefulness. In addition, a wealth of secondary sources touch upon the ballistic missile development program.

I also interviewed many of the people involved. Usually, I was made welcome; the people interviewed were normally generous of both time and memory. The quality of their recollections did pose a problem, however. Interview information was most needed for the very earliest period of the study, before the 1954 speedup. After this period the available printed evidence is much more voluminous, largely because after 1954 much was being done and high-level attention was being directed to the ICBM.

However, my concern is precisely with the period before 1954, when little was happening, and there was not much to record. The problem was paralleled in the interviews. It was much easier for the people to recall what did take place than what did not—especially given the obvious fact that the years 1946 to 1953 are quite distant. This led to the added problem of my inadvertently putting dates, persons, or analysis into the mouths of those interviewed. Such "help" might be grasped either from sympathy for me, embarrassment over a seemingly faulty memory, a sense that what I said "sounds about right," or all three. Therefore, I have only included information derived from interviews when it can be supported by documents or when several people interviewed agreed.

Despite these sources, publication of my book in its present form would have been impossible without the Air Force's declassification policy. The Air Force (and probably the other services) feels undermanned and unequipped to undertake the continuing review and declassification of documents as it should be conducted. For this reason the Air Force Office of Information and the Office for Security Review within that division readily admits that enormous numbers of Air Force records remain under security classification for no valid reason.

This situation is exacerbated by a regulation that even minimally classified documents whose classifications include an "automatic declassification" provision (say, after twelve years)

cannot be declassified after the specified period without undergoing a formal review procedure. For instance, an interoffice
memo concerning public relations, dating from 1946 and originally classified "Confidential, automatic downgrade every three
years, declassify after twelve years," will still be classified and
unavailable to the public.

Recognizing the problem, the Air Force has developed a procedure whereby civilians without security clearance can undertake to accomplish the declassification. Briefly, the procedure is
to entertain applications from the public to be permitted access
to specified records. If the application is granted, the scholar (or
whoever) is then permitted to read and copy whatever he
wishes. All notes, however, must be left at the place of research
for delivery to the Air Force Office for Security Review. When
and if the notes are declassified, they are sent to the researcher
and are public, unclassified material.

There are several minor difficulties with the program. The
review of the original application may take an indefinite time and
averages perhaps six weeks. Review of the notes for possible
declassification is again an indefinite matter, and could take
months. During this time the researcher is left without the material he has so diligently copied.

Some persons may see a major difficulty, also. For some,
subjection to any kind of military security check or clearance
procedure may be distasteful even if the purpose is to accomplish the release of classified material. I felt some sympathy
for this position, but nevertheless used this opportunity. My
reasons were, first, that the military services do not provide
adequate personnel to maintain continuous up-to-date review of
the mountains of records constantly produced; researchers
might wish that they did, but wishing is not a particularly satisfying substitute for data. Second, the procedure is not designed to
foster classified studies or those based on classified material; its
purpose is the opposite—to provide a means for scholars to get
classified material unclassified for open publication. These
benefits seemed to outweigh by far any ideological or subjective
unease.

The Air Force personnel turned out to be quick and courteous in their handling of notes for this study. Furthermore, to the best of my memory (which must serve, as all original notes went to the Air Force), every note submitted was cleared and released, without deletion. Furthermore, certain notes came from documents as recent as 1958, which, given the common view of the military's security perceptions, is noteworthy. On the other hand, the Air Force wishes it emphasized that "the views expressed here are those of the author, and do not in any way imply endorsement of factual accuracy or opinion by the Department of Defense or any other person or agency of the Federal Government." I am glad to so emphasize.

Under this procedure, I undertook extensive research at the Historical Office at Air Force Systems Command, Andrews Air Force Base, Maryland; the National Archives in Washington; and the Air Force Archives at Maxwell Air Force Base, Montgomery, Alabama. I also used certain collections within the Library of Congress, but they did not prove so worthwhile. Although the general outline of the ICBM history could have been gleaned from the sources cited earlier, much of the fabric, and certainly the intimate detail, would not have been available. This is especially true for the important early years.

Author's Note

The Air Corps Act of July 2, 1926, changed the air arm's name from Air Service to Air Corps and created the office of Assistant Secretary of War to help promote military aeronautics. A reorganization that went into effect on March 1, 1935, created an Army General Headquarters Air Force on the same command level as the Air Corps, both Commanders reporting separately to the Chief of Staff, U.S. Army. A consolidation of these two agencies took place on March 1, 1939, when the GHQ Air Force was assigned the Chief of Air Corps. This situation ended November 19, 1940, when the GHQ Air Force was removed from the control of the Army Field Forces. On June 20, 1941, the Army Air Forces was created, combining the activities of the Air Force Combat Command (the old GHQ Air Force) and the Air Corps. General Henry H. Arnold, Chief of the Air

Corps and Deputy Chief of Staff, was placed in charge of the
new AAF. In 1942 three autonomous and co-equal commands—Army Air Forces, Army Ground Forces, and Services
of Supply—were established under the Chief of Staff, U.S.
Army. In 1943, Services of Supply was redesignated Army
Service Forces (see Monro MacCloskey, *The United States Air
Force* [New York: Frederick A. Praeger, 1967], pp. 19–36).
The Army Air Forces became the United States Air Force with
the signing of the National Security Act of September 15, 1947.
In the book I sometimes use "Air Force" for convenience in
discussing events that occurred before that date. In such cases
the reference is to the Army Air Forces.

Boston, Massachusetts   EDMUND BEARD
July 1976

Acknowledgments

I AM GRATEFUL to many people for their assistance. My Columbia dissertation sponsors, Warner R. Schilling and W. T. R. Fox, provided patient counsel, wise insight, and, not least, appropriate prodding. Bruce L. R. Smith was constantly receptive to my inquiries and offered many valuable suggestions. The late Dr. Donald McVeigh of the Air Force Systems Command gave helpful guidance in the intricacies of military research. Mr. William Cunliffe of the National Archives, Modern Military History Branch, was unfailingly courteous and helpful. The actual writing took place while I was a Brookings Institution Research Fellow. I made wide use of both Brookings facilities and personnel, but special thanks must go to Morton Halperin, Leon Sigal, Barry Blechman, Seyom Brown, Alton Quanbeck, and Leslie Gelb. My fellow Research Fellows, Ginger McMurtry and John Yochelson, were always ready with commiseration and suggestions of alternative careers. Four friends and colleagues, John Fullilove, Joel

Koblentz, Phillip Barber, and Thomas Bongiovanni, by their scholarly examples, kept me true to the task. My wife, Clare, left me alone and never read a word. To all of them I am deeply grateful.

E. B.

Contents

Developing the ICBM

Introduction

ON OCTOBER 4, 1957, the Soviet Union launched the first earth satellite, Sputnik 1. The much larger Sputnik 2 followed on November 3. These events caused an enormous shock in the United States, seeming as they did to herald the end of unquestioned American technological superiority.

Heightening the effect was the fact that the spectacular Soviet first came in an area intimately tied to military capabilities. If the Soviets had also solved the problems of guidance and reentry—and American research and development efforts to date gave no reason to assume that they had not—any spot in the United States might be vulnerable to a Soviet ICBM.

The Soviet leadership attempted to leave no doubts about the matter. In October of 1957, Soviet Premier Khrushchev told a visiting American newsman, ''I think I will not be revealing any military secrets if I tell you that we now have all the rockets we need: long-range rockets, intermediate-range rockets and close-range rockets."[1] Two months later Krushchev elaborated on his theme, announcing that, "We have developed an intercontinental ballistic missile with a hydrogen warhead."[2]

The effect in the United States was profound. A prolonged and bitter debate, which was to continue well into the following decade, immediately ensued. Charges were hurled at the Eisenhower Administration for supposedly having jeopardized the nation's security through excessive economy. Major inquiries were initiated in both houses of Congress. In the Senate, the Preparedness Investigating Subcommittee of the Committee on Armed Services under the chairmanship of Lyndon Johnson, Democrat of Texas, heard seventy witnesses and solicited voluminous supplementary evidence. In remarks initiating the hearings, Senator Johnson clearly outlined their impetus.

Our people have believed that in the field of scientific weapons and technology and science, that we were well ahead of Russia. With the launching of Sputniks I and II, and with the information at hand of Russia's strength, our supremacy and even our equality has been challenged.[3]

Although the Eisenhower Administration attempted to allay the fears that were apparent both throughout the American public and within the governing community, it was widely assumed that the Soviets were dangerously ahead. Administration officials generally agreed that there would be a numerical missile gap in the early 1960s, but they denied that this would produce a deterrence gap. Rather, the Administration consistently claimed that American strategic forces were too large and too varied to be eliminated by any Soviet attack utilizing whatever weapons. They just as consistently held that the potential numbers gap would not be so large as many critics were claiming. This issue remained in doubt, as the intelligence bases for most of the

---

[1] *New York Times,* October 10, 1957, p. 10.

[2] Quoted in Charles H. Donnelly, *The United States Guided Missile Program* (Washington, D.C.: Government Printing Office, 1959), p. 19.

[3] U.S. Congress, Senate Preparedness Investigating Subcommittee of the Committee on Armed Services, *Hearings, Inquiry into Satellite and Missile Programs,* 85th Congress, 1st and 2nd sessions, 1957 and 1958, pp. 1–2. Hereafter referred to as *Satellite and Missile Hearings.*

estimates being publicly bandied about were restricted. Further, the various arms of the national security establishment did not always agree. As one magazine put it, "It all boils down to a question of confidence in the one who makes the interpretation."[4]

The Administration position was not helped by evidence of its own apparent surprise. During the Johnson subcommittee hearings, the new Secretary of Defense, Neil McElroy, admitted that he was "very much surprised" by the Soviet accomplishment. At another point he acknowledged that "We are behind the Russians in missile and satellite development."[5] After CIA Director Allen Dulles had testified before the Senate, Senator Styles Bridges, Republican of New Hampshire and an administration supporter, reported hearing "very unpleasant information" that should "shock any complacency out of various officials and the American public."[6]

The charges against the Eisenhower Administration rapidly coalesced around a presumed "missile gap." This term was generally used to refer to a numerical disadvantage in ballistic missiles the United States would face in the early 1960s, although it also incorporated the somewhat different problem of the Soviet time lead in first acquisition of the ICBM. For example, Joseph Alsop predicted that through the first half of the 1960s the Soviet Union would hold a commanding lead over the United States in operational ballistic missiles, reaching as high as 1,500 versus 130 in 1963.[7]

Although there was disagreement about the exact figures, some version of this view was widely accepted. As late as 1960, no less an analyst than Henry A. Kissinger stated that

[4]"Debate over Missiles," *Commonweal*, 69 (February 20, 1959): 532. See also Roy E. Licklider, "The Missile Gap Controversy," *Political Science Quarterly*, 85, no. 4 (December 1970): 605–610.

[5]*Satellite and Missile Hearings* pp. 250, 198. McElroy had been nominated to succeed Charles Wilson in August 1957, and sworn in on October 9. McElroy's somewhat plaintive remark that "I suppose if I had been privy to the intelligence knowledge that had been around in the community, I would not have been so surprised," was not calculated to reassure an uneasy public. *Ibid.*, p. 250.

[6]*New York Times*, November 28, 1957, p. 1.

[7]*Washington Post*, October 7, 1959, p. A–17.

For all the heat of the controversy, it is important to note that there is no dispute about the missile gap as such. It is generally admitted that from 1961 until at least the end of 1964, the Soviet Union will possess more missiles than the United States.[8]

The "missile gap" haunted the Eisenhower Administration through the close of its term, and apparently played a significant role in the election of John Kennedy in 1960.[9]

Ironically, the great fears of missile inferiority proved unjustified. The Soviet Union never exploited its apparent opportunity to outproduce the United States in first generation ICBMs. Indeed, the Kennedy Administration moved quickly to reverse the situation and fully succeeded.

But I shall not focus here upon the ultimate resolution of the "missile gap." Rather, I shall deal with the events, decisions, and perceptions that led to the original situation of 1957. Although it later became apparent that the early Soviet ICBMs were not readily producible and were not good strategic weapons, it remains true that the Soviet Union had indeed "beaten" the United States to a vital weapon. As one knowledgeable observer has put it, "Beyond a doubt, the Soviet ICBM of 1957 both preceded in time and was of superior performance to its 1958 American counterpart."[10]

I shall demonstrate the process leading through the development of an American ICBM and describe why that weapon appeared when it did. By so doing, I hope to case new light on the interrelationship between technology, strategy, organization, and politics.

[8] Henry A. Kissinger, *The Necessity for Choice* (New York: Harper, 1961), p. 15.

[9] For a review of John Kennedy's use of the "missile gap" issue in criticism of the Republicans see Harland B. Moulton, "American Strategic Power: Two Decades of Nuclear Strategy and Weapon Systems, 1945–1965" (Ph. D. dissertation, University of Minnesota, 1969), pp. 150–55, 253–57. See also Edgar M. Bottome, *The Missile Gap: A Study of the Formulation of Military and Political Policy* (Rutherford, New Jersey: Fairleigh Dickinson University Press, 1971); and Licklider, "The Missile Gap Controversy," pp. 600–615.

[10] Warner R. Schilling, "The Politics of National Defense: Fiscal 1950," in Warner R. Schilling, Paul Y. Hammond, and Glenn H. Snyder, *Strategy, Politics, and Defense Budgets* (New York: Columbia University Press, 1962), p. 39.

A chronological pattern is necessary. The question of why the United States produced an ICBM when it did is by nature a matter of dates. Furthermore, if it is hypothesized that the political judgments and resulting decisions involved may have remained rigid while the technological or strategic elements of the issue evolved over time (and I do so hypothesize), it is important to proceed linearly and attempt first to illuminate and then to explain the process. Thus I shall follow the story of the American ICBM through a long pattern of disbelief, neglect, and delay—some of it apparently justified in the clear light of hindsight, some of it not.

In World War II, the Germans used ballistic missiles in the form of the V–2 rockets. Although the results appeared mixed, the weapons did cause considerable damage (not the least of which was psychological) to their target areas. Indeed, as eminent an observer as Dwight Eisenhower later stated that, "I feel sure that if [the Germans] had succeeded in using these weapons over a six-month period . . . OVERLORD might well have been written off."[11]

A top level scientific survey commissioned by the Air Force Chief of Staff, General Henry Arnold, concluded just after the war that long-range ballistic rockets were feasible. It added, however, that such weapons were not likely to be available until the distant future. For the present, Air Force attention should be devoted to manned aircraft and particularly toward the almost equally new jet airplanes. If any effort were to be devoted to long-range missiles, it should proceed cautiously by way of slower, less revolutionary, air-breathing vehicles.

This judgment led to emphasis upon the air-breathing Snark and Navaho—a priority that continued into the 1950s. A June 1947 Air Force report on missile development placed long-range, surface-to-surface missiles at the fourth level of priority and stressed missile types that could increase bomber and fighter capabilities. More important for the purposes of this study, ballistic rockets were excluded from the already down-

[11] Dwight D. Eisenhower, *Crusade in Europe* (Garden City, New York: Doubleday, 1948), p. 260.

played long-range efforts. Air Force Research on long-distance ballistic missiles was cancelled in 1947, not to be revived until 1951 and then only at a minimal level and under the influence of Korea-induced defense spending increases.

In August 1952, the Air Technical Intelligence Center sponsored a briefing concerning Soviet missile capabilities, and concluded that the Soviet program was similar to that of the United States and was moving through steps similar to the development of the Snark and Navaho. The rocket age was still considered far in the future.[12] This sense was reinforced in December of that year when an ad hoc committee of the Air Force Scientific Advisory Board recommended a slow pace of ballistic missile development.

Then in 1953–1954 a combination of factors caused an abrupt turnaround. These included technological developments, intelligence estimates, and most important, the infusion of new non–Air Force personnel who could recognize the first two elements and act on them outside of the prevailing cultural perspectives. The feat was not accomplished easily, however. Air staff resistance continued and helped contribute to a civilian decision to develop the ICBM outside of normal Air Force channels. A new organization and revolutionary management procedures were created, and the program was placed on a crash basis. By 1958 this effort had produced an ICBM. It was a year after Sputnik, however.

The Sputnik launch, and the ICBM capability it demonstrated, were of enormous symbolic importance. American international prestige and American domestic self-perception and self-confidence were strongly shaken. Although the change may have been primarily symbolic, something had been significantly altered. The United States was no longer seen, by other nations or by its own citizens, in quite the same light. In an area of great

---

[12]This judgment was later demonstrated not to be true. In actuality, a high level Soviet decision to pursue an intercontinental ballistic rocket had been made as early as 1947. [See G. A. Tokaty, "Soviet Rocket Technology," in Eugene M. Emme, ed., *The History of Rocket Technology* (Detroit: Wayne State University Press, 1964).]

potential significance, the United States was suddenly and demonstrably second.

In addition, one of the strongest fears underlying much of the "missile gap" scare was that the Soviet Union might be able, by taking advantage of its development lead, to gain a first-strike capability against the United States which could not be effectively answered. This advantage never materialized, in part because the Soviet Union chose not to build a fleet of the first-generation missiles. Nevertheless, until U–2 and other intelligence proved that no large Soviet deployments were taking place, this was a widely discussed threat. The Soviet leaders may, of course, never have contemplated such a first-strike action; more likely, they may have decided against wide deployment since the early weapons were not particularly effective. Another interpretation is that such "rational" arguments may not have played so large a role in the Soviet decisions as, for instance, the resistance of the established Armed Services to the enormous redirection of military spending into long-range missiles that such a deployment would have necessitated.

Regardless of the Soviet motives, it seems clear from both contemporary and later accounts of the "missile gap" period that the top American leadership originally shared to some extent the fear of a large early Soviet ICBM deployment and would have much preferred that the possibility not have arisen. Although the civilian Eisenhower Administration consistently held after Sputnik that no "deterrent gap" existed and that the nation was safe and secure, they did fear, until intelligence sources alleviated such worries, that the Soviets might push hard for a first-strike ballistic capability, and perhaps convince themselves they had it. Such a perception, even if incorrect, was nevertheless dangerous. Had the Soviets been tempted to employ a nuclear missile force, the results would have been catastrophic, regardless—indeed partly because of—any widespread American retaliation.

The Soviet first-generation ICBM fleet did not materialize. Any possibility of a "missile gap" was eliminated within a few years. Nevertheless, the American leaders, at the time of certain of the relevant decisions (particularly during the period 1950–1953) did not expect the Soviet Sputnik feat and would certainly not have chosen to run the risk of either a Soviet ICBM first-strike capability or the appearance of one. These attitudes, held by both the Truman and Eisenhower Administrations, are apparent in the public literature of the period and in later reminiscences. My examination is from the perspectives of those leaders. If they did not wish this situation to come about, and if it was not inevitable, why did it occur?

To answer this question, I shall discuss the perspectives and attitudes that governed the American ICBM effort, and then use the information to analyze the decisions made throughout the period and to speculate about how those decisions might have been different.

My opinion is that the United States could have developed an ICBM considerably earlier than it did but that such development was hindered by organizational structures and belief patterns that did not permit it. In its simplest form, the proposition could be that the Air Force was committed to manned aircraft, and particularly to manned bombers, and refused to change. Such a bald statement would not adequately describe the ICBM story, however, although in some ways it is quite true. Before the reversal and acceleration of 1954, the Air Force's stance toward ballistic missiles can best be characterized as neglect and indifference. This attitude was commonly associated with public judgments that the weapons were extremely unlikely if not impossible. Until late 1953, and despite the existence of contrary evidence and opinions, a general emphasis on manned bomber systems (or on missile types that did not threaten them) with a slow, conservative approach to ballistic missiles persisted within the Air Force. Contrary opinions were disregarded, contrary evidence dismissed. Men who had always flown and relied upon bombers found it hard, indeed almost impossible, to sense the revolutionary implications of ballistic missiles. Organizations that had been designed to advocate and maintain bombers continued to do so.

For much of the period there was no institutional lobby for

the competing missiles; even though the Air Research and Development Command—an organization that perceived missiles as a major area of responsibility—had been created in 1951, that agency remained for some years weaker and less influential than its peers. In addition, the ARDC birth was accompanied by friction and bitterness from the parent Air Materiel Command, a problem that persisted for several years.

Particularly relevant here is the "principle of least harm," which advocates the choice of that action "which appears to involve the least cost if the technical premise on which it is based proves to be wrong."[13] Some of the technological issues surrounding the ICBM were clearly uncertain during the late 1940s and early 1950s. One of the reasons, however, that they were so uncertain is that insufficient funds (and for some time no funds at all) were allocated to their solution. Perhaps the Air Force was sensible in not leaping headlong into ICBM production in 1950 or 1951. In any event, given the stringent budgets, such a course was impossible. On the other hand, ICBM development was of potentially very great significance. Thus, under the principle of least harm, a serious research and development program should have been directed at the ICBM in order to inspect the technological issues and attempt to prevent any unfortunate surprises. This was never adequately undertaken until 1954. Even after the large increases in defense spending occasioned by the Korean War, the ICBM was kept on a sputtering back burner until outside civilian dictate caused a reversal. The ICBM's neglect most surely would have continued longer than it did without this sudden civilian interposition. One result was that even with a crash program, an American ICBM was not available until 1958—a year after Sputnik.

[13]Warner R. Schilling, "Scientists, Foreign Policy, and Politics," in Robert Gilpin and Christopher Wright, eds., *Scientists and National Policy Making* (New York: Columbia University Press, 1964), p. 150. Schilling offers as an example of the "principle of least harm" the contention that "in World War II, given the American belief that the Germans were hard at work on an A-bomb, it seemed more sensible to spend $2 billion on the assumption that the bomb could be made, than to do little or nothing on the assumption that it could not." *Ibid.* See also Bernard Brodie, "Strategy as a Science," *World Politics,* 1 (July 1949): pp 467–88.

American national security policy clearly requires organizations capable of necessary change, innovation, and open-minded planning. If bureaucratic structures, organizational inertia, and individual bias or misperception affect the output and implementation of American defense policy, such influences should be recognized and, where possible, remedied.

The interrelation between technology and strategy must also be studied. Strategy will always be affected by available technology, but it may be wrong to allow current strategy to restrain or distort technology. On a more immediate level, weapons in hand may very well dictate the political or military options available in any given situation; they will certainly rule out some alternatives.

It is not my intention to present myself as a warmongerer. I most emphatically do not recommend that the military be provided with whatever weapons it requests, and the more technologically complicated the better. Quite the reverse, I suggest that the military may not be the best judges of what weapons are feasible or most useful (in terms of both cost and capability) despite their apparent expertise. Clausewitz is often quoted as teaching that war is too important to be left to generals. It may be just as true that technological exploration and weapons development choices may be too important to trust to the rigidities of bureaucratic routine or the vagaries of bureaucratic competition. At the least, major weapons choices ought to be reviewed like any other decision of political or strategic importance by informed persons as free as possible of ideological, doctrinal, or organizational blinders.

The term "bureaucratic politics" has come to define a distinct approach to decision-making analysis. Very briefly this approach holds that

the 'maker' of government policy is not one calculating decision-maker, but rather a conglomerate of large organizations and political actors who differ substantially about what their government should do on any particular issue and who compete in attempting to affect both governmental decisions and the actions of their government.[14]

[14] Graham Allison and Morton Halperin, "Bureaucratic Politics: A Paradigm and Some Policy Implications," *World Politics*, 24 (1971):42.

As Stanley Hoffmann has said, "Study of the way in which foreign policy is elaborated in the state reveals that to a considerable extent the goals are determined, not by calculations about the outside world, but by internal needs and bureaucratic politics.[15]"

This is not a new concept. Neither is it an altogether satisfying one. If the "bureaucratic politics" model is taken to state that organizations pursue organizational goals and that such pursuit alone determines foreign (or defense, or any other) policy, then the theory is clear. Unfortunately it is also incorrect. If the model says, on the other hand, that policies are influenced to a greater or lesser degree by organizational and personal interests, which operate generally within a broad set of shared images or constraints, the theory is probably irrefutable. It is also much less clear. Indeed, it has become all-inclusive—capable of explaining any policy, or for that matter any action, in retrospect.

Yet, the bureaucratic approach has clearly illuminated aspects of the decision-making process that have been misinterpreted or ignored in some of the traditional literature of state behavior. A particularly relevant example of "traditional" analysis, which assumes "rational," linear decision making, is to be found in an ambitious study of the weapons acquisition process. Merton Peck and Frederic Scherer have stated that "the thermonuclear breakthrough [occurring in 1953] was mainly responsible for the decision in 1954 to accelerate the Atlas development program."[16] However, other factors—including personnel changes, human temperament, and organizational self-interest—were at least as important, particularly in placing the decision in 1954.

I shall focus on the evolution of an issue within an organization and look down into the middle or lower levels of that entity. Instead of providing analysis of a major decision in terms of which actors participated, who was able to mobilize most support, who first got the attention of the powerful actors, who held

---

[15]Stanley Hoffmann, Foreword to Robert L. Rothstein, *Planning, Prediction, and Policymaking in Foreign Affairs* (Boston: Little, Brown, 1972), p. viii.

[16]Merton Peck and Frederic Scherer, *The Weapons Acquisition Process* (Cambridge: Harvard University Press, 1962), p. 229.

their favor or at least finally commanded it, and why, I shall instead spend much time discussing a non-issue.

For many years after World War II, intercontinental ballistic missiles were neglected and virtually ignored within the Air Force (and consequently more or less within the United States government). After the retirement of General Arnold in 1946, no powerful figure or group within the Air Force gave much consideration to long-range ballistic missile potentials until 1953. No important command or agency saw its function as their promotion. On the contrary, the Air Force structure was geared to concentrate on manned aircraft. Furthermore, the research and development arm of the Air Force was, until 1951, subordinated within an airplane-oriented command and thus both naturally and by orders followed that lead.

A major American redirection of effort to accelerate ballistic missile development did not occur until 1953–54, some seven years after the Soviet Union had initiated such a program. The reasons for the later American lag in ICBM attainment will be seen to lie in these years. They will consequently be studied at length. This approach differs significantly from the more usual concentration upon the pulling and hauling attendant upon a major decision. The latter moments are usually marked by the participation of those occupying the highest positions in the government. I hope to cast light on what happens before this point.

The date of arrival of an issue for high-level action can be as important as its resolution. Indeed, in the case of ballistic missiles, this might well have been the case. Yet, an issue may be invisible not because it is irrelevant or impractical, but simply because it hasn't been brought up to the "visible" level. And this lack of visibility may be due not to its unimportance, but rather to an organization's failure to provide important information for the busy, often harried top figures. Government leaders cannot be expected to keep abreast of all developments on their own, and I shall provide a detailed review of what happens before a major decision. This period may well shape the timing of the large decision as well as its nature. It should be examined more often.

A difficulty I encountered was in the evaluation of the technological arguments that took place—particularly when one group was claiming a certain technique was possible while another was maintaining the opposite. In these cases, however, the significant factor was usually the existence of expert opinion that something was possible, while those in authority refused to consider it. A point that will be made often here is not that a potentially valuable weapon was easily available at any given date, but rather that some able persons thought so and that, regardless, funds were not provided even to inspect the matter.

This last point underscores the difficulty of working on a period in which "nothing" happens. In my analysis of what takes place within the middle levels of an organization before an issue reaches a "decision" stage, I was at times disconcerted to be able to record so little activity, even when the lack of activity was precisely the point I was demonstrating.

One excellent study of the weapons innovation process opens with the dictum that "The process by which strategy, defense budgets, and weapons policies are conceived and implemented cannot be more accurately described than political in the most fundamental sense of the term."[17]

The evidence gathered in a review of the ICBM development certainly supports this observation. The same work, however, adds that

The disposition to innovate [is not] generally inhibited by a technically illiterate and conservative military leadership. Having witnessed the decisive impact of novel weapons on the battlefield in World War II, and having been entrusted with the responsibility for maintaining a continuing deterrence, generals and admirals have been transformed "from being the most traditional element in any national society—hanging on to their horses, or their sailing ships, for as long as possible —into the boldest innovators."[18]

My results cast some doubt upon this last judgment.

[17]Armacost, Michael H. *The Politics of Weapons Innovation: The Thor-Jupiter Controversy* (New York: Columbia University Press, 1969), p. 2.
[18]*Ibid.* The quoted portion is from Alastair Buchan, "The Age of Insecurity," *Encounter*, 20 (June 1963):5.

1

The Advent of
Guided Missiles and
of Military Rivalry
over Them

IN NINETEENTH-CENTURY AMERICA, there had been little active interest in the use of missiles for military purposes. This is not to say that the United States was totally inexperienced in the field of military rocketry. During the War of 1812, rockets developed by William Congreve were used by the British to burn Washington. These same rockets found a place in the American National Anthem after Francis Scott Key saw them used against Fort McHenry at Baltimore.

Soon after the United States entered World War I, the Army Air Service looked into the possibility of developing powered, remotely controlled, flying weapons. Tests of preset flying bombs (which could not be guided after launch) were conducted

by the Air Service in 1918 and 1919. C. F. Kettering, E. A.
Sperry of Sperry Gyroscope Co., and Orville Wright assisted in
the development and test of these missiles. One Air Service
Officer closely involved in this project was Colonel Henry H.
Arnold, later to become Chief of Staff of the Army Air Forces.[1]

While no Air Service guided missile entered combat during
World War I, testing continued throughout the war and after its
conclusion. In 1923 the Chief of the Air Service Engineering
Division called for development of radio controls for the "torpedo airplane," and funds were forthcoming in 1924. Although a
series of successful tests took place during the 1920s, by 1932
the project was deemed unnecessary and wasteful, and funding
was halted. No further work was conducted until 1938, when the
Army Air Corps Engineering Division reopened the "torpedo
airplane." At that time military characteristics were designated
and a design competition instituted, but no adequate design was
ever submitted.[2]

Outside of the armed services, the situation was much the
same. Dr. Robert H. Goddard had experimented extensively
with various rocket techniques since the early part of the century. There is little evidence that Goddard contemplated the use
of rocket-propelled bombardment weapons. His interest was
exoatmospheric research, and development of vehicles to support such research. He was the first to employ gyroscopes for
rocket guidance; he demonstrated that rockets would operate in
a vacuum; he employed movable exhaust vanes; and he worked
with staged rockets. In any event his work aroused little interest
in the United States, something his reticent personality did little
to change.[3] However, Goddard's work was appreciated elsewhere, particularly in Germany. The German V–1 and V–2
employed during World War II owed much to his concepts.

[1] Henry Arnold, *Global Mission* (New York: Harper, 1949), pp. 74–76.

[2] The above historical review is drawn almost in total from Mary R. Self,
History of the Development of Guided Missiles, 1946–1950 (Historical Office,
Air Materiel Command, 1951), pp. 1–3.

[3] Goddard's papers have only recently been published. See Esther C. Goddard, ed. with Edward Pendray, *The Papers of Robert H. Goddard, 1882–1945*,
Vols. 1, 2, 3 (New York: McGraw-Hill, 1970).

Wernher von Braun has stated that "everything we know we learned from him."[4]

Dr. Theodore von Karman, then Director of the Guggenheim Aeronautical Laboratory at the California Institute of Technology, started another noteworthy rocket research project. The first federal contract for rocket research in the United States was granted in 1939 to the Guggenheim Laboratory to undertake studies for the Army Air Forces, including rocket-assisted take-offs for aircraft. The name given to these rockets was JATO (jet-assisted takeoff) because "the word 'rocket' was of such bad repute that [we] felt it advisable to drop the use of the word. It did not return to our vocabulary until several years later."[5]

In addition to JATO experiments, the American Armed Services attempted development during World War II of remote controlled bomber aircraft or drones, glide bombs, vertical control bombs, glide torpedoes, and other projects.[6] Within the Army Air Forces, responsibility for guided missile development was assigned early in World War II to the Materiel Division of the Assistant Chief of Air Staff (Materiel and Services). Responsibility was then delegated to the Special Weapons group of the Materiel Command, located at Wright Field, Dayton, Ohio. By 1942 the Air Communications Officer in the headquarters of the Army Air Forces had become interested in the guided missile projects because of their coordination with developments in electronics. The Air Communications Officer wished to see greater emphasis placed upon the missile projects, and felt that such emphasis was unlikely under the present organizational arrangements. Air Communications felt that the Special Weap-

[4]Quoted in Stanley Ulanoff, *Illustrated Guide to U.S. Missiles and Rockets* (New York: Doubleday, 1959), p. 7.

[5]Frank J. Malina, "Origins and First Decade of the Jet Propulsion Laboratory" in Eugene M. Emme, ed., *History of Rocket Technology*. In 1944, the C. I. T. Rocket Research Project became the Jet Propulsion Laboratory. See also Loyd S. Swenson, James Grimwood, and Charles Alexander, *This New Ocean: A History of Project Mercury* (Washington, D.C.: Government Printing Office, 1966), pp. 15–16, for a brief history of these developments.

[6]Mary Self, pp. 3–4.

ons group at Wright Field did not possess adequate authority within the Air Force hierarchy to promote the missiles projects properly. There was a further belief that the Assistant Chief of the Air Staff (Materiel and Services) was too interested in what he considered the more important and pressing problems of aircraft development and production to bother with the guided missiles program. Consequently, the Air Communications Officer prepared a staff study for the Assistant Chief of the Air Staff (Plans) urging the appointment of a single office within the Air Forces headquarters to have overall authority for the guided missiles program. The Air Communications Office was suggested. This study was vigorously opposed by the Materiel Command at Wright Field, who claimed that they were doing an adequate and indeed commendable job in a very difficult area. The Special Weapons Project at Wright Field was suggested as the most sensible choice to oversee the Air Forces guided missile program because of its long experience and demonstrated expertise in the area of air weapons development.

The decision resolving this conflict perhaps demonstrated the correctness of the Air Communications Officer's original fears concerning the lack of organizational clout of the Special Weapons group and the less than total interest of the Assistant Chief of Staff (Materiel and Services). In September 1943, the ACO was designated the responsible agency for "monitoring, coordinating, and expediting" the guided missiles program. The Office of the ACO "seemed to be the most logical place for the guided missile responsibility. Controllable or guided missiles were nothing more than radio-controlled miniature aircraft at the start of the war and no operational difficulties were anticipated."[7]

The September 1943 decision was not permanent, however. Several agencies complained that the assignment of guided missiles responsibility to the Air Communications Officer was out of normal channels and tended toward confusion and a blur-

[7] Much of the above story, and the final quoted line, can be found in History of the Guided Missiles Division, AC/AS–3, June 1946. File "History." Box "Guided Missiles History." HQ USAF, DSC/D, GM Branch, National Archives.

ring of accepted organizational functions. The Assistant Chief of the Air Staff (Operations, Commitments, and Requirements) (AC/AS [OCR]) appears to have led the continuing complaints. He seems to have felt that the Air Communications Officer was a particularly inappropriate choice to have authority over guided missile projects. This opposition proved effective, and early in 1945 an office instruction from headquarters greatly reduced the authority of the ACO. Much of the guided missiles responsibility was, by this directive, transferred to the AC/AS (OCR). The Air Communications Officer was to continue overall monitoring of all communications aspects of the missiles program.[8]

The simple act of transfer of missiles responsibility back into more normal organizational routines seems to have satisfied the AC/AS (OCR), as the program was not then given high priority or particular attention in its new home. Having gained control of the missiles program, the AC/AS (OCR) proceeded to delegate it to the Bombardment Branch of the Requirements Division, where it was subordinated to the more pressing needs of the air offensive in the European and Pacific theaters.

The January 1945 action in effect returned guided missiles development to the same channels as aircraft. As a result of this directive three organizations were left in control of the missile program: the Assistant Chief of Air Staff (Materiel and Services); the Air Communications Officer; and the AC/AS (OCR). The latter was the "office of primary interest in this headquarters in the guided missiles program."[9]

The jurisdictional conflict over the guided missiles program was now at least partially tempered. Criticism about the slow rate of development of and lack of enthusiasm for guided missiles continued to be heard (often from the recently dispossessed Air Communications Officer) but generally such criticism originated in the lower levels of the AAF hierarchy and it seldom rose above its origins. Missiles responsibility at headquarters continued at a low level of priority in the Bombardment Branch.

The Germans' partial success in development and use of

[8]*Ibid.*

[9]Memo, Brigadier General F. H. Smith, Jr., DC/AS, to Chief Management Control, Dec. 28, 1944. Quoted in Self, p. 17.

rockets began, however, to worry some elements of the Air Staff and to intrigue others. The German activities created renewed interest in guided missiles and led to further discussion of the possible need for a more authoritative location for missile projects. There was also discussion of which service agency was to gain operational control of guided missiles. A decision in October 1944 had sought to postpone the latter issue.

The progress in research and development of long-range guided missiles does not yet enable us to form a clear-cut understanding of the ultimate tactical employment of these weapons, and therefore not yet warranted is a specific assignment in every case of such missiles to exclusive employment by any one arm or service.[10]

It was recognized that because the arm or service which developed a particular weapon was in a strong position to claim its operational employment, the assignment of operational control of these weapons might therefore settle the question of their research and development. Throughout the spring and summer of 1945, the AC/AS (OCR) actively sought official designation as the responsible agency for operational employment of guided missiles.

Several attempts at the operational assignment of missiles within the Army Air Forces and between that arm and the Army Ground Forces during early 1945 were severely criticized. The difficulties in reaching an acceptable compromise resulted in another decision to postpone the decision.

It is believed that decision on the overall assignment of operational employment of guided missiles should be withheld. The development, characteristics, control and capabilities of these missiles have not developed to the point where definite assignment of the operational employment to a major command can be determined without the possibility of jeopardizing future development.

The memorandum . . . of 2 October 1944 to the three major com-

[10]Memo, Lt. General Jospeh T. McNarney, Deputy Chief of Staff, to Commanding General, Army Air Forces, October 2, 1944. File 319.1. Box 408 "War Dept. GM Policies." HQ USAF, DCS/O, Assistant for GM, National Archives.

mands, subject 'Guided Missiles,' assigning responsibilities for research and development, remains in effect.[11]

Despite this directive, the AC/AS (OCR) continued to press the issue. One effort to solidify this office's position in the guided missiles field was the creation late in 1945 of a guided missiles division within its organization. The new division was given responsibility for monitoring all operational phases of the guided missiles program—including military characteristics, numerical requirements, testing, organization, and acquisition and training of personnel.[12]

The confusion and often conflict evident within the Army Air Forces over the assignment of responsibility was paralleled within the War Department as a whole. Both the Army Air Forces and the Army Service Forces were involved in guided missile development during the war, and both branches felt they should be granted the main responsibility in this area.

Similarly, just as there were attempts throughout the war to bring more order and coherence into the missile programs within the Army Air Forces, so were there efforts to improve coordination between the Army Air and Service forces. Extensive studies were made beginning early in the war. These efforts finally resulted in a formal delineation of responsibilities within the War Department. This directive took the form of the earlier cited memo of October 2, 1944, signed by Lt. General Joseph T. McNarney, the Deputy Chief of Staff of the Army.

Stating that "it is essential that Research and Development in the long-range guided missile field continue toward ultimate production of some usable weapons which can be evaluated with respect to our strategy and our existing weapons," McNarney directed:

[11]Memo for the Assistant Chief of Staff, G–3, from Brigadier General H. I. Hodes, Assistant Deputy Chief of Staff, June 21, 1945. File 319.1. Box 408. HQ USAF, DCS/O, Assistant for GM, National Archives.

[12]The above developments can be found in greater detail in *History of the Guided Missiles Division, AC/AS–3,* File "History." Box "Guided Missiles History." HQ USAF, DCS/D, GM Branch, National Archives.

a. That the Commanding General, Army Air Forces, have research and development responsibility, including designation of military characteristics, for all guided or homing missiles dropped or launched from aircraft.

b. That the Commanding General, Army Air Forces, have research and development responsibility for all guided or homing missiles launched from the ground which depend for sustenance primarily on the lift of aerodynamic forces.

c. That the Commanding General, Army Service Forces, have research and development responsibility for guided or homing missiles launched from the ground which depend for sustenance primarily on momentum of the missile.[13]

Under the terms of this directive the development of ballistic missiles would fall under the responsibility of the Army Ground Forces. Despite this directive (and as had been the case within the Army Air Forces singly) the conflict for primary responsibility in guided missiles development continued between the Army Service Forces, represented by the Ordnance Command, and the air arm. Much of the continuing friction arose out of Air Forces' beliefs that the Ordnance Command was overstepping its delegated area of cognizance and in general evading the intent of the McNarney memo.

On September 6, 1945, the AAF, in a memo circulated at War Department headquarters, attempted to garner the guided missiles program on the basis of experience and expertise.

the AAF was the only agency of the allied powers to use guided missiles operationally in World War II. Radio controlled conventional type bombs were employed, as well as remotely controlled bombers equipped as robot missiles and glider bombs controlled by television and radio. The experience gained from the operational use of these weapons has given us a basis on which to plan for new types of guided missiles which are expected to play such a vital part in any wars of the future.[14]

This memo was followed by several others, as elements of the Air Forces became increasingly unhappy with the apparent incursions of the Ordnance Command into AAF territory. The

[13]Joseph T. McNarney, Deputy Chief of Staff, Memo to the Commanding General, Army Air Forces, October 2, 1944.
[14]Quoted in Self, p. 10.

problems grew primarily out of the fact that the Ordnance Command was undertaking developments in many areas of the guided missile field, including relatively long-range models. This was done while the Ordnance Command continued to pay lip service to the McNarney directive, not by emphasis on ballistic missiles but rather by such devices as referring to what appeared to Air Forces observers to be wings, as fins. Another memo in October of 1945 made clear the Air Forces' argument.

the assignment of army guided missiles development responsibility in the 2 October 1944 memorandum, resulted in widely differing interpretations by the Army Service Forces and the Army Air Forces. Ordnance is increasingly entering into the field of aeronautics on their Guided Missiles program.[15]

This memo included an urgent request for clarification of the McNarney division of responsibility directive.

Army Air Forces' complaints about encroachment by the Ordnance Department continued during the latter part of 1945 and into early 1946, quite possibly prodded by demobilization and the increased jealousy over organizational "turf" in a shrinking arena. By January 1946, the Air Forces' resentment had progressed to the point of calling the Ordnance Department's infringement upon AAF guided missile authority a "flagrant violation" of the terms of the McNarney directive. To bolster their case, the Air Forces at this time suggested that an Air Forces "missile" with a range of at least one thousand miles be fired by August 1946.[16]

Perhaps worrying that if AAF complaints continued at a high enough decibel level they might finally be satisfied, the Ordnance Department got into the act in January 1946 with a request of its own for revision of the McNarney directive—only in this case with further responsibility in the missiles field coming to it.

[15]Quoted in *ibid.*

[16]*Ibid.*, p. 11. This desire resulted in the "automatic" flight of a B–29 which was subsequently widely proclaimed as the dawn of an ability to construct long-range cruise missiles. The later difficulties in the cruise missile programs showed it to have been nothing of the sort.

It should be noted that by January 1946 there had been important organizational changes within the Army Air Forces. In September 1945, Franklin Collbohm of the Douglas Aircraft Company came to the AAF with a proposal for a long-term basic research project in the field of intercontinental air warfare, including in particular guided missiles. The Douglas proposal had grown out of Collbohm's wartime association with Dr. Edward L. Bowles, special consultant to General Arnold. Bowles and his associates had gradually conceived of a joint industry–government planning group to coordinate scientific and technological development with long-range strategic planning. The idea of contracting with a private organization for this purpose had apparently taken form in midsummer 1945.[17]

Donald Douglas was apparently quite interested personally in the project. The new organization was to be separate from Douglas's existing research and engineering division. It seems clear that at this time Collbohm and some of the individuals with whom he spoke in the War Department were quite aware of the potential importance to this field of the recently demonstrated atomic bomb. At any rate, Collbohm's proposal met with favorable response from General Arnold and also from Secretary of War Patterson.[18]

One problem that faced members of the Air Staff who were brought into the discussion of the Douglas Project was that there was no office within the Air Staff that seemed particularly suited to direct or oversee this kind of program. The normal procurement pattern involved the setting of a requirement which was then fulfilled by the Air Materiel Command at Wright Field. This procedure entailed very tight control by the AMC over its contractors, with specific directions made as to what these contractors were to produce. The Douglas idea proposed to reverse this process. As envisioned, it would involve broad basic research designed to see what might be done. General Arnold was a strong supporter of this approach. But to oversee this kind of

[17]See Bruce L. R. Smith, *The RAND Corporation* (Cambridge: Harvard University Press, 1966), pp. 30–65.
[18]Interview with Frank Collbohm.

project and ensure that it did not fall under the domination of the traditional "requirements" approach championed by the Wright Field Materiel Command, it was felt that a new staff agency was needed. The result was creation of a Deputy Chief of Air Staff for Research and Development.[19] General Norstad, Assistant Chief of Air Staff (Plans), appears to have favored the establishment of this office, not least because one of its purposes would be to ensure that the Plans division gained a greater voice in research and development. By the same token, the Materiel Command raised strong objections to the entire Douglas proposal. There were complaints that the proposal would bring civilians into the area of military planning, and that civilians could hardly be expected to know as well as the military itself what the military needed. It was also felt that contractors should be employed simply to produce what the military requested and not to tell the armed services what they ought to be doing. The Materiel Command also felt the new Office of Deputy Chief of Staff (R&D) was intruding into its own responsibilities.

General Curtis E. LeMay had been appointed to head the R&D office when it came into being on December 5, 1945. The Air Materiel Command was obliged to take its objections to the Douglas project to him. Since one main impetus to the creation of LeMay's office had been the need to oversee and coordinate the Douglas Project and any others like it, LeMay declined to cancel it.[20]

On a broader level, however, LeMay's office was not granted any specific directive assigning it responsibility for the Air Forces' guided missiles program. Therefore, the struggle for control continued. The Guided Missiles division of A–3 (the new designation for Assistant Chief of Staff, Operations, Commitments, and Requirements) and the research and engineering division of A–4 (Assistant Chief of Staff, Materiel and Services)

[19]Smith, p. 45.

[20]The account of the genesis of the RAND Project and the creation of the Office of DCAS/R&D has been drawn from T. von Karman, *The Wind and Beyond*, p. 302; Bruce L. R. Smith, *The RAND Corporation*, pp. 30–65; interview with Frank Collbohm; and interview with General Curtis E. LeMay, USAF (Ret.)

both continued to claim to be the obvious choice for assignment of primary interest in guided missiles. The latter office strengthened its case by citing both the need and its own readiness to work closely with General LeMay's new office.[21] For his part, General LeMay, who in his role as Air Forces' representative in inter-service R&D disputes was complaining that there was "no integrated program" in the missiles field and that direction from the Joint Chiefs was inadequate,[22] also suggested the need within the Air Forces to "get thinking started on the matter of getting this guided missiles business headed up by one outfit."[23]

By this point the dispute over missiles control was reaching such proportions that some new attempt at settlement had become necessary. In February 1946, the Commanding Generals of the Army Air Forces, the Army Service Forces, and the Army Ground Forces were directed to review the terms of the October 2, 1944, memo. In particular, they were requested to suggest modifications in assignments of responsibility which could be expected to better coordinate the War Department's postwar missiles program and eliminate unnecessary duplication.[24] Indicating the two levels of conflict, the February 1946 memo directed that attention be given to assignment of responsibilities

a. As between the War and Navy Departments
b. Within the War Department as between the Army Air Forces, the Army Services Forces, and the Army Ground Forces.[25]

The Navy Department was asked to conduct a parallel review of its missiles program. This request was contained in a letter from General Eisenhower, Army Chief of Staff, to Admiral Nimitz on or about March 1. It was hoped that through such

[21]Self, p. 18.
[22]Hanson Baldwin, *New York Times,* May 12, 1946, p. 1.
[23]Quoted in Self, p. 18.
[24]Self, p. 12.
[25]Memorandum for the Commanding Generals, Army Air Forces, Army Service Forces, Army Ground Forces, from H. I. Hodes, Assistant Deputy Chief of Staff, February 13, 1946. File 319.1. Box 408. HQ USAF, DCS/O, Assistant for GM, National Archives.

review unnecessary duplication could be avoided. Eisenhower told Nimitz he intended to ask the Guided Missiles Committee, under the Joint Chiefs of Staff, to resolve any differences. This was a subcommittee of the Joint New Weapons and Equipment Committee with the function of appraising possible targets, recommending relative emphasis and priority among the guided missile programs of the different services, and finally recommending a national program for the development of guided missiles.[26]

In January of 1946, before the February review noted above, the Army Air Forces had forwarded to General Eisenhower a "Statement of Mission and Responsibilities of the Air Forces." This statement noted that in accomplishing the common mission of the armed forces "to maintain the security of the United States and to uphold and advance its national policies and interests . . . the Army Air Forces executes those military operations that are normally performed through the medium of air." It then further stated that the Army Air Forces is responsible for: "The research, development, and procurement of missiles (and related equipment) that use the air as a medium and are controlled or guided after launching, and the maintenance and operation of these weapons to perform the normal functions of the Army Air Forces."[27]

General Eisenhower responded in a memorandum of January 26, 1946, to General Spaatz; he generally approved of the statement, but there was one problem area.

Regarding paragraph k, the operational assignment of guided missiles has not been settled. Until research and development of these weapons has progressed further, I believe no definite decision should be made as to which component is given operational assignment.

[26]Self, p. 12. Also History of the Guided Missile Division. AC/AS-3. File "History." Box "Guided Missiles History." HQ USAF, DCS/D, GM Branch, National Archives. A committee had been formed by the Navy Department in late 1944 to look into the present status and probable future development of guided missiles. A report was completed in May of 1945, which recommended continued attention to missiles, particularly for naval defense and as an adjunct to naval aircraft.

[27]Statement of Missions and Responsibilities of the Air Force, Jan., 1946. File 319.1. Box 408. HQ USAF, DCS/O, Assistant for GM, National Archives.

At this time I suggest paragraph *k* be reworded substantially as follows:

(1) The research, development, and procurement of pilotless aircraft (and related equipment) other than those peculiar to the launching from naval aircraft or from naval vessels. (Pilotless aircraft comprises all air-launched guided missiles and those missiles which depend primarily for sustenance on aerodynamic forces.)

(2) The maintenance and operational employment of guided missiles which may be assigned to the Army Air Forces for this purpose by higher authority.[28]

In accordance with the February 13, 1946, request for a review of the October 1944 McNarney directive, the AAF produced a "Proposed Policy on Research and Development of Guided Missiles." It recommended that the McNarney memo be rescinded and a new directive be issued, to include the following instructions:

a. The Commanding General, Army Air Forces, is responsible for the initiation of military characteristics for (1) all guided or homing missiles dropped or launched from aircraft, (2) all guided or homing missiles to be used as strategic weapons, and (3) all guided or homing missiles launched from the ground for the interception of enemy aircraft or guided missiles.

b. The Army Ground Forces are responsible for the initiation of military characteristics for, (1) all guided or homing missiles of a tactical utility, (2) all tactical or anti-aircraft type missiles not requiring guidance in flight.

c. The Commanding General, Army Air Forces, is assigned the research and development responsibilities for all guided or homing missiles controllable in flight.

d. The Commanding General, Army Service Forces, is assigned research and development responsibilities for those missiles which are tactical in nature and do not require guidance after launching.[29]

Members of the Army Air Forces were aware of other possible arrangements for the coordination of U.S. missile programs. An inter-office memo at Air Forces Headquarters in March 1946 noted that

[28]Memorandum for Dwight D. Eisenhower to General Spaatz, January 26, 1946, *ibid.,* National Archives.

[29]AAF Proposed Policy on Research and Development of Guided Missiles, *ibid.,* National Archives.

In view of the increasing importance of guided missiles, pilotless aircraft and associated materiel, it is felt that present organizations and the
lines of cognizance, cutting both vertically and horizontally, through
various components and through entire organizations and major commands, should be re-examined.[30]

This memo continued by outlining alternative arrangements,
including:

a. A single government agency similar in scope to the Manhattan Dis-
trict with exclusive control over research, development, production,
and operational application.
b. A less inclusive organization but organized at the War Department
level to include all War Department guided missile activity.
c. A single command within the Air Forces with sole cognizance of all
guided missile activity within the Air Forces.[31]

The first two options were not apt to excite great enthusiasm
within the Army Air Forces. Option A, a Manhattan project
approach, risked taking guided missiles development out of the
hands of the armed services, thus undermining the authority and
control of its own functions granted to the military. Option B, a
unified missiles organization at the War Department level, was
not much more appealing. This was a period in which the Air
Force's drive for autonomy was at its height. Furthermore, the
Air Force saw its most important mission as long-range strategic
bombardment—a mission that had been of great importance in
World War II, if not to the degree sometimes claimed by its
most enthusiastic advocates. With the advent of nuclear
weapons, any shortcomings appeared to be eliminated. A War
Department agency above the Air Forces, with control of the
missiles program, was precisely the kind of loss of responsibility
the AAF wanted to avoid. Keeping the long-range strategic
bombardment role within the Air Forces was deemed vital. This

---

[30]Memo from Brigadier General R. C. Coupland, AC/AS-4 to AC/AS-3,
Guided Missiles Division, dated March 6, 1946. File "AAF GM Policy
1946." Box "A-7 Catapults." HQ USAF, DCS/D, GM Branch, National
Archives.
[31]*Ibid.*

meant maintaining control of weapons capable of performing it, including missiles.[32]

Following AAF submission of its "Proposed Policy on Research and Development of Guided Missiles," another memo on the subject was sent to the Deputy Chief of Staff by General Spaatz on March 4, 1946. This memo was routed to the New Development Division of Army Ordnance, which prepared a revision that was resubmitted to the Army Air Forces. The response of the AAF was that the revision did not remedy the fault of the October 2, 1944, directive in that "no clearly defined dividing line was made in the responsibility of development between the Ordnance Department and the Army Air Forces."[33]

Clearly, the positions of the Air Forces and the Army remained in conflict. The recommendations of the various armed services had been requested by the end of February 1946 in order that the Guided Missiles Committee could have them in hand for use in its preparation of a "National Program for Guided Missiles." This report was completed on March 23, 1946. Despite its name it did not lay out a formal program of development. It listed several types of missiles as ultimate objectives, including those for long-range area attacks and precision attacks at short, middle, and long ranges. It also noted the need for defensive missiles to be employed against modern aircraft and future missiles. These were only ultimate objectives. The "National Program" emphasized basic research. The Guided Missiles Committee noted that practical development

[32]An excellent review of Air Force attitudes during the drive for autonomy and Air Force strategies toward attaining that end can be found in Demetrios Caraley, *The Politics of Military Unification* (New York: Columbia University Press, 1966). Air Force emphasis on strategic bombardment was brought out clearly in the struggle a few years later with the Navy, which focused on the B–36 bomber and proposed Navy "supercarriers." Paul Y. Hammond, "Supercarriers and B–36 Bombers: Appropriations, Strategy, and Politics," in Harold Stein, ed., *American Civil–Military Decisions* (Birmingham: University of Alabama Press, 1963), pp. 465–564.

[33]Memo from AFDRE–3 (AC/AS–4), General Crawford, to Commanding General, AAF, dated March 26, 1946, subject, "Policy in R&D of Guided Missiles." File "AAF GM Policy 1946." Box "A–7 Catapults." HQ USAF, DCS/D, GM Branch, National Archives.

was clearly the most expensive aspect of the program and consequently recommended that it not be rushed. "Sound knowledge" arising out of basic research was to be sought first. The desirability of competition was recognized and some duplication of effort was deemed valuable. Prompt and complete exchange of scientific and technical information was directed, but the means by which this was to be effected was left to future interservice consultation. Groups were to be established within each service to provide continual staff study of the strategic and tactical roles of guided missiles and all related problem areas, such as logistics, organization, training, and intelligence.[34]

Clearly, this "National Program" had not dealt firmly with the issues in conflict. The "National Program" was not a program at all, but simply a recommendation of continued basic research in the guided missiles field coupled with several calls for full interservice consultation and cooperation. The document skirted the most troublesome areas of interservice competition over control of the various missile programs by stating that competition was healthy and even duplication was valuable. A situation that had been unsatisfactory for more than a year continued.

In the face of continued inability to arrive at a satisfactory delegation of responsibility, General LeMay called a conference of the interested agencies for March 25, 1946. Personnel from Army Air Forces, Army Ground Forces, the Army Ordnance Department, and the Chief of Staff's office were in attendance. The meeting proved fruitless. Ordnance was unwilling to give up the development of missiles that could be maneuvered in flight. The Army Air Forces were equally indisposed to concede that Army Ordnance should be in the development of maneuverable missiles since these weapons would require use of autopilots, remote control devices, and wings, "all of which have been and should continue to come under AAF cogni-

---

[34]Memorandum for the Secretary of War, Secretary of the Navy, from Admiral W. D. Leahy, for the Joint Chiefs of Staff. Dated 23 March 1946. Contained in document collection appended to J. Allen Neal, *The Development of the Navaho Guided Missile: 1945–1953* (Historical Branch, Wright Air Development Center, ARDC, 1956).

zance."[35] Again it is interesting to note that the original October 1944 assignment of responsibilities had assigned ballistic missiles (not cited by name, but these are vehicles "which depend for sustenance primarily on momentum of the missile") to the Army Service Forces. The Army wished to pursue missiles of the V–1, winged flying bomb type, however, and the Air Force wanted to prevent this. Hence the argument. Ballistic missiles were generally neglected throughout the controversy.

The Air Forces' argument was spelled out in a memo to General Spaatz, reviewing the abortive conference.

AAF feels development of all guided missiles which are controlled when in flight should be assigned to AAF for following reasons:

1. Eliminates the infringement of other services into the aerodynamic field.

2. Places developmental responsibility with service having the basic know-how in development of aircraft.

3. Permits a gradual transition of the aircraft industry from piloted to pilotless aircraft or missiles, should pilotless aircraft progress to a point of replacement of the conventional military aircraft.

4. Permits the aircraft industry to continue to look to one service for its contracts and contacts.

5. Eliminates the current frantic inter-service competitive efforts, which competition, though healthful, will inevitably get out of control, and result, not only in a waste of money, but an unnecessary overloading of the qualified industry, with a strong possibility of delay in reaching the ultimate solution.[36]

This summary memo concluded by noting a major related fear held by the Air Forces—that squabbling within the War Department might open the way to another competition.

It is essential that the Army Ordnance Department and the AAF come to a unified opinion on the allocation of development responsibility for guided missiles for the reason that if we are divided within the War Department, our efforts to convince the Navy that they should limit their development as stated above loses its effectiveness. This lack of a unified stand can only result eventually in the Navy continuing their present parallel development program which may result in the Navy gaining control of the entire guided missiles development field.[37]

[35]Memo from General Crawford, to Commanding General, AAF, March 26, 1946.
[36]Ibid.
[37]Ibid.

The problem with the Air Force approach was that the Army, represented by Army Ordnance, was strongly interested in maintaining as flexible options as possible. This meant keeping a hand in the development of long-range guided missiles. If the claims of the most enthusiastic strategic bombardment and missile advocates were ever even partially validated, there might in fact be only limited use for a large Army trained and equipped in the conventional fashion—hard as this might be to conceive.[38]

Long-range missiles viewed as artillery, on the other hand, would preserve a major army role in a future war, whatever its nature. But the AAF, while attempting to limit intra–War Department squabbling and to enlist Army support against the Navy missile programs, was also interested in restricting Army activity in this area, particularly at the strategic ranges. An Air Force memo at the time is indicative of that service's thinking.

Would it not be wise at this time to include as a part of our 70-group Peace-time Air Force and also in our mobilized Air Force a certain number of strategic missile groups. Admittedly, we do not know the composition of a guided missile launching force; however, we could show these without a troop basis at this time, just to indicate progressive thinking and the AAF interest in taking a major part in the lightning warfare of the future. If we do not do this the Artillery may beat us to the punch.[39]

The Navy and the Army, as they soon realized, were natural allies in this contest. For the Army, an alliance with the Air Force view would only ensure that the Army would lose. Support of the Navy call for equal developmental opportunities for

[38] Despite the conclusion of the United States Strategic Bombing Survey that "Allied air power was decisive in the war in Western Europe," the results of World War II strategic bombing were inconclusive. Airpower coupled with ordinary high explosives was extremely expensive and its results uncertain. The advent of nuclear weapons, however, seemed to many people to dispel any doubts about the efficacy of strategic bombardment. For a concise survey of World War II bombardment and the influence of the atomic bomb on postwar American strategic thinking, see Harland B. Moulton, "American Strategic Power: Two Decades of Nuclear Strategy and Weapon Systems, 1945–1965" (Ph.D. dissertation, University of Minnesota, 1969), pp. 1–14. See also Bernard Brodie, *Strategy in the Missile Age* (Princeton: Princeton University Press, 1959), pp. 107–44.

[39] Memo, Colonel Sims to General Eaker, January 2, 1946. File 145.86–19. Historical Archives, Maxwell AFB, Montgomery, Alabama.

all services, in line with their individual needs, was much more attractive.

The pressures for some sort of formal distribution of the missile programs continued unabated during the spring and summer. In fact, the struggle became noisy enough to surface in the public press. On May 10, 1946, at White Sands Proving Ground, Las Cruces, New Mexico, a captured German V–2 was for the first time fired successfully. This event occasioned a front-page article by Hanson Baldwin in the *New York Times* (May 12, 1946) headed "Rocket Program Splits Services; Army Air Forces Seeking Control." The tests at White Sands were conducted by the Army Ordnance Department. Much of the needed instrumentation, however, was provided by the Army Air Forces and the Navy. Furthermore, technical aid and direction was provided by personnel from all three services.

In Baldwin's words, the service struggle, and particularly "the frank and outspoken effort of the Army Air Forces to secure sole, or at least dominating, control of the long-range missile program," provided a "somewhat somber background" to the success of the firing. Another dark cloud was "the knowledge that the Germans—and perhaps other nations—were far ahead of us in giant rocket development." Baldwin viewed the struggle, in which he saw the Army Ordnance Department, Signal Corps, and other nonflying Army agencies siding with the Navy against the Army Air Forces, as a result of two similar "fear psychoses." For some time the most outspoken members of the Army Air Forces had been saying that the usefulness of the Navy in any future war—particularly with the advent of atomic weapons—would be greatly restricted. For example, an Air Forces memo in July 1946 noted "the current frantic interservice competitive efforts" and then observed "It is apparent that the navy is doing all within its power to gain preeminence in the guided missiles field, as they see in it a means for the navy to continue to be a major operational service in the next war instead of being reduced to the minor functions of supplying carrier based air power and limited surface surveillance." The memo then concluded, "It is known that the navy dept. is taking steps to set up a strongly unified navy program. It is therefore essential that the war department do likewise."[40]

Hanson Baldwin also saw the Navy's interest in long-range missiles as insurance that they would stay in the strategic field and maintain a place of importance in the American Defense Establishment. Baldwin observed, however, that the Air Forces also felt some of the same fear psychosis. General Arnold had already said that World War II might be the last war of the pilots, implying that pilotless missiles or rockets would replace them.[41] In Baldwin's estimation, such a statement "had had a great effect on Air Force thinking."

Before the White Sands test, General LeMay had asked for $200–$300 million for establishment of a huge Army Air Force Missile Development Center.[42] The Air Forces claimed that it was wasteful and foolish to maintain a Navy missile development center at Inyokern, California, the Army Ordnance base at White Sands, and the Air Forces missile development test center at Wendover, Utah, in addition to several other smaller missile research and proving projects throughout the country. It would be far more efficient and profitable to combine these scattered efforts in one main center to be controlled by the Air Forces.[43] The Air Force approach was strongly opposed by the

[40] Prepared briefing for General Aurand (Chief of Research, War Dept. General Staff.) July 12, 1946. File "Guided Missile Policy 1946–48. From Higher Authority." Box "GM Policy." HQ USAF, DCS/D, GM Branch, National Archives.

[41] General H. H. Arnold, "Third Report of the Commanding General of the Army Air Forces," in Walter Millis, ed., *American Military Thought* (Indianapolis: Bobbs-Merrill, 1966), pp. 445–59.

[42] *New York Times,* May 12, 1946, p. 19.

[43] One specific reason given for the creation of a large new center was the relatively inadequate wind tunnel facilities existing in the United States at that time. Theodore von Karman relates that the genesis of the new installation, to be known as the Center for Supersonic and Pilotless Aircraft Development, occurred in a 1945 memo from Frank Wattendorf to von Karman. Wattendorf had recently visited the huge wind tunnel in Ofstal, Austria, and had been greatly impressed with the potential of the facility, which had no comparison in the United States. Referring to the name chosen for the new center, von Karman relates, "we used the term 'pilotless aircraft' to cover all types of missiles, so as to prevent the project from falling into the hands of the Army, from which the Air Force was about to separate." Von Karman notes that opposition de-

Navy and the nonflying services of the Army, who, as Hanson
Baldwin noted, "seem to be cooperating in the missile project
with excellent teamwork. . . . And . . . who get along together
much better, at least in the missile field, than do the Army Air
Forces and the rest of the Army."[44] The Navy and Army Ordnance (the leader of the intra–War Department opposition to the
Air Forces' claims on long-range missiles) position was that
such large sums of money would be better spent on many basic
research grants to universities and other institutions and to improvement of existing facilities. These services maintained that
duplication of effort at the early stages of research was the best
way to achieve maximum and early results, as had long been
proved in industrial practice.

The Hanson Baldwin front page *New York Times* article is an
indication both of the extent of the conflict and its intensity. The
article was implicitly opposed to the Air Force position. The
possible importance of public support and the influence of the
press in molding that support was recognized by both sides. In
the larger struggle over unification of the armed services, public
opinion was eagerly sought and may have had a significant effect
on the debate within Congress. Despite some disagreement over
exactly where public opinion lay and what its effect might be,
favorable publicity for one's position was universally deemed
better than unfavorable publicity or silence while one's opponents received good notices. The V–2 launching on May 10,
1946, from the Army testing grounds and the resultant publicity
was a coup for the Army. The Air Force immediately began
plans for a similar but larger show of Air Force missiles and
techniques to be held at Wendover Field. That the purpose of

veloped from the aircraft industry, who wanted the government to spend money
on airplanes, not research facilities. The Arnold Engineering Development
Center (as it was ultimately named) was finally built near Tullahoma, Tennessee,
on the site of an old World War II camp. It was dedicated by President Truman
in 1952. This center, however, did little toward advancing the purpose of undercutting or taking over the Navy and Army long-range guided missile projects. It
was provided for by Congress in 1947, but as an addition to the programs of the
three services, not as their substitute. Theodore von Karman, with Lee Edson,
The Wind and Beyond, (Boston: Little, Brown, 1967), pp. 298–300.

[44]*New York Times,* May 12, 1946, p. 1.

this show was publicity and not simply scientific experiment is made clear in a memo sent in July 1946 from the Research and Development Division of the AC/AS–4 to the Commanding General of the Air Materiel Command at Wright Field.

In order to obtain necessary support from the American public for continuance of the AAF Guided Missile Program, it has been considered necessary to make as complete and spectacular display of AAF Guided Missiles as possible for use by: "newspapers, broadcasting, news reels, congressmen." . . . It is imperative that the demonstration referred to above be carried on during the fall of this year, 1946.[45]

Much of the Air Force–Army Ordnance–Navy missile dispute had been couched in almost philosophical argument about the most efficient approach to research and development. Hanson Baldwin's talk of fear psychoses points up another side to the question. The underlying assumptions and fears motivating the Air Forces' position were clearly set forth in a memo sent from General LeMay's office to General Spaatz in late September 1946.

The AAF [guided missiles] program covers the needs of the whole Army, while that of Ordnance is restricted to part of Army Ground Forces' needs.

At the outset it was recognized that Ordnance was entering the field early and aggressively to antedate AAF competition, so that the 2 October 1944 directive was proposed and written by the AAF with intent to eliminate destructive competition, and to limit the Ordnance Department to non-aerodynamic missiles.

. . . The great criticism of the AAF proposal to do all guided missiles development is the danger of a monopoly leading AAF to complacency.

. . . One very serious reason for not giving ground is the stated opinion of Army Ground Forces that AGF should operate its own guided missiles, close support aircraft, and strategic bombardment aircraft, classing all these as extensions of artillery. It is fairly certain that if development of missiles is turned over to Ordnance, operation will be done by Army Ground Forces, and it will be only a short and logical

[45]Memo from General Crawford, R&D Div., AC/AS-4, to Commanding General, AMC, Wright Field, dated July 29, 1946. Subject: "Wendover Show." File "GM Public Relations, 1946–48." Box "GM Program Progress Rpt." HQ USAF, DCS/D, GM Branch, National Archives.

step from this to operation of support and strategic aircraft by AGF. Further, General Aurand's [Director of R&D, Army General Staff] expressed policy of entire separation of development service from using arm will then either turn Air Materiel Command into another Army Technical Service, or incorporate AMC bodily into the Ordnance Department. General Aurand has already informally proposed the former.

. . . Our best course seems to be to follow through our previous requests for assignment of all guided missiles, driving at economy and clear, workable directives, making it plain that our ultimate aim is to better prepare the U.S. for the war which is sure to come.[46]

There are a number of interesting points in this memo. The "great criticism" (presumably from outside the Air Force) of the Air Force proposal for control of all guided missiles research and development being "the danger of monopoly leading AAF to complacency" will be developed later. It is important to note here, however, the fears expressed by General LeMay that the Army Ground Forces, if granted operational control of missiles through delegation from Army Ordnance, might proceed to operation of support and strategic aircraft. Indeed, this would be "only a short and logical step." Thus he feared the Air Forces might lose control of a weapon (or weapons) that could ultimately replace manned aircraft (and consequently the need for the "manned" element) as well as control of major portions of their functions in the immediate and interim period. The essence of the Air Forces' doctrine was strategic bombardment. Tactical support of ground troops was another important function not only because the role was vital to the effectiveness of these ground troops, but also because flying airplanes, particularly from land bases, is the Air Forces' job. Once ground forces were given the right to fly tactical support, it might prove very difficult to restrict their range of operations.[47]

[46]Memo from General LeMay, DCAS, R&D, to General Spaatz, dated 20 September 1946. File "AAF, GM Policy, 1946." Box "A-7 Catapults." HQ USAF, DCS/D, GM Branch, National Archives.

[47]Notice, for instance, the continuing battle between the Army and the Air Force over close-in tactical battle support and troop carriers—areas which the Army consistently feels the Air Force neglects. Notice also the Army restriction in the area of fixed wing aircraft to various small utility and artillery observation planes. In a 1967 signed agreement, the Army turned over its fleet of C–7

General LeMay concluded with several observations about the importance of missile and rocket development to the long-term future of what would soon be the independent Air Force.

The present situation with regard to guided missiles in Europe, with Russia, England, and France all hiring German engineers and pressing development energetically, with the Russian reopening of Peenemunde and Nordhausen, with Russian missiles seen in Sweden, makes it absolutely imperative that the U.S. press guided missiles development with maximum energy.

. . . The long-range future of the AAF lies in the field of guided missiles. Atomic propulsion may not be usable in manned aircraft in the near future, nor can accurate placement of atomic warheads be done without sacrifice of the crews. In acceleration, temperature, endurance, multiplicity of functions, courage, and many other pilot requirements, we are reaching human limits. Machines have greater endurance, will stand more severe ambient conditions, will perform more functions accurately, will dive into targets without hesitation. The AAF *must* go to guided missiles for the initial heavy casualty phases of future wars.[48]

Evidence is available that fears of imperialistic fellow services were also present in Navy thinking. In June 1946 Navy Commander James Scott in a lecture at the Navy Bureau of Ordnance noted "The recently announced determination by the Army Air Forces to overall responsibility and control of the national Guided Missiles." He then continued, "There is no place in their program for development of guided missiles by any other service agency. . . . The Army Air Forces have deliberately delayed the [Navy] Bureau of Aeronautics' entire Pt. Magu project by stalling tactics."[49]

Admiral Gallery, Admiral Radford's Deputy for Guided Missiles and a major supporter of the Navy Guided Missiles program, visited Wright Field in January 1947. By this time, further action had been taken to resolve the guided missile controversy

transport aircraft to the Air Force in exchange for the right to employ helicopter gunships. Subsequently, the Army has consistently lobbied the Air Force to develop a newer, better transport vehicle, which the Army feels the Air Force has been neglecting.

[48] Memo from LeMay to Spaatz, 20 September 1946. Emphasis in original.

[49] Quoted in, "Memo for Record," Dec. 4, 1946. Written by M.F. Cooper, Chief, Guided Missiles Branch. File "History." Box "Guided Missile History." HQ USAF, DCS/D, GM Branch, National Archives.

within the War Department between the AAF and the rest of the Army. This War Department action had not resolved the controversy with the Navy, as a record of Gallery's visit to Wright Field makes clear.

Finally, Admiral Gallery told Colonel Price that the attempts over the past two months to get together on common characteristics have been delayed by the Navy because of their fear that once a set of common military characteristics are agreed upon between the W. D. [War Department] and the Navy, the Navy is afraid that the W. D. will use these common characteristics as an argument for stepping in and taking over the Navy's guided missile program.

. . . Admiral Gallery indicated that the Navy would be most receptive to a truce between the W. D. and the Navy on guided missiles, and that they would be willing to put down on paper their policy that they would not attempt to try to take from the W. D. any of the W. D. guided missile program if they could get a similar written agreement on the part of the W. D. that they would not attempt to take the Navy's guided missile program from the Navy and consolidate the two programs into one national program.[50]

The extent of the mutual suspicions is revealed in an Air Force observer's evaluation of the Navy offer.

there may be more to this than meets the eye in that it is a wonderful tool for the Navy to use in arguing against unification because if we can get together on a common meeting ground on an item as controversial as guided missile development, it weakens our case for unification of the services. Another possible pitfall is that should we accept the written statement from the Navy or should they accept one from us agreeing that we could not aspire to take over the other's guided missile responsibilities, that agreement would last only as long as the people who made it remained in command, and the service gullible enough to continue operation on the basis that they were secure and would not be gobbled up by the other service, might some day wake up to find that they had no guided missile program left.[51]

[50]Memo for Record. Written by M. F. Cooper, Guided Missiles Branch, dated January 8, 1947, subject, "Recent Navy Attitude." File "History." Box "Guided Missile History." HQ USAF, DCS/D, GM Branch, National Archives.

[51]*Ibid.* The competition between the Air Force and the Navy was particularly bitter and was evident well before the 1949 "Revolt of the Admirals" occasioned by the cancellation of the Navy supercarrier. Before the end of World War II, General LeMay had been quoted to the effect that B–29s had rendered

Phrases like "guillible enough to continue operation on this basis," and "gobbled up by the other service" indicate clearly the problems involved in effecting a settlement with the Navy. Projected difficulties in communication, the creation of trust, and enforcement all are evident. Now that a degree of accord had been reached within the War Department, however, there were many advantages to arriving at a mutually satisfactory settlement which would allow each service to continue its own programs without fear of undercutting by a rival service. The problem was, of course, in reaching an acceptable division of authority. The Air Force was primarily interested in maintaining the strategic role against all competitors. If the Navy would agree to limit itself to a series of short-range offensive and defensive guided missiles designed to bolster traditional Navy operations at sea, that would be fine. Indeed, if that was Admiral Gallery's offer, then, in the words of the memo quoted at length just above, "It appears to this office very desirable if we could get together with the Navy on this basis."

No agreement was reached at this time, however. The issue of control of research and development—and particularly of operational employment of long-range guided missiles—continued to generate conflict. Reviews were undertaken at various levels of the Air Staff throughout the summer. Surveys of the positions of the several services continued to appear, some at the request of the Air Staff and others as unsolicited representations.

In September 1946, General LeMay set forth the Air Forces' position in a memo to the Assistant Secretary of War (Air), in which he outlined four principal aims of the Army Air Forces in regard to guided missile responsibility. These four aims were:

1. To fill AAF needs for aero-dynamic missiles.
2. To fill the needs of Army ground forces and other agencies for missiles controlled in flight.

carriers obsolete. In early 1946 the Commanding General of the Army Air Force, General Carl Spaatz, asked the question, "Why should we have a Navy at all?" and implicitly answered it himself with the observation that, "There are no enemies for it to fight except apparently the Army Air Force." Both cited in Huntington, *The Common Defense*, p. 369.

3. To have the 2 October 1944 directive revised to assign responsibility for research and development of all missiles requiring guidance in flight to the AAF who will, in turn, rely upon the facilities of other Technical Services for the development of components. . . .

4. To allow no exceptions to the principles of the desired revised directive, without approval of the War Department Director of Research and Development.[52]

This position continued to be opposed by the Navy and Army Ordnance on the grounds that guided missiles were too new a subject yet to be sensibly assigned to a particular service. Each service should rather be free to develop missiles according to their own needs. The Ground Forces ought to develop both antiaircraft (and antimissile) weapons and new artillery weapons. To assign an arbitrary limit to the range of artillery would unnecessarily handicap the Army both in operations and in the continuing development of new weapons, which is a part of its job in maintaining the national security. The same arguments were applied to the Navy and its program of missiles to be launched from ships.

At this stage there were Navy and Army Ground Forces' plans for the Navy to join in the development of White Sands as a major test area for short- and medium-range missiles, and for Army Ordnance and the Signal Corps to participate in the development of long-range missiles at a naval proving ground.[53]

The Army Air Forces had been invited to participate in both these programs, but given the AAF's primary interest in excluding the rival services from the long-range strategic bombardment role, this offer was unlikely to be appreciated.[54] The Navy and Army Ordnance and the Army Signal Corps, however, professed themselves very well satisfied with the arrangements. To

[52]Memo, General LeMay, DC/S for R&D, to Asst. Secretary of War (Air), Sept. 3, 1946. Quoted in Self, p. 14.

[53]See Hanson Baldwin, in the *New York Times,* May 12, 1946, p. 1.

[54]Army Ordnance was to all intents and purposes a division of a rival service. The unification of the armed services, and the attendant creation of the United States Air Force as a third service equal to the Navy and the Army, was well under way. That Air officers tended to think of themselves as members of a separate service is well illustrated by the conflict described here.

the AAF's complaints that there was no adequate coordination or integration of the missile programs, they replied that their coordination was in fact excellent and that they were profiting thereby much more than they would have individually.[55]

This continuing conflict, particularly that within the War Department, demanded settlement. A decision was made and its terms spelled out in a memo of October 7, 1946, from Brigadier General H. I. Hodes, the Assistant Deputy Chief of Staff. The memo, rescinding the memorandum of October 2, 1944, held:

In order to attain the most efficient utilization of scientific talent and engineering facilities, the following policies are announced to govern research and development activities pertaining to guided missiles:

1. The Commanding General, Army Air Forces, is responsible for the research and development activities pertaining to guided missiles. This is to include corresponding countermeasures, as well as related and associated items of equipment.

2. In carrying out this responsibility, the Commanding General, Army Air Forces, will effect maximum ultilization of existing personnel and facilities, both within and without the War Department, by calling upon other developing agencies to perform tasks for which they are best qualified.

3. The Director of Research and Development, War Department General Staff, in the manner provided by existing procedures, will determine both as to present and future activities which projects are to be classified as guided missiles projects.[56]

This new directive referred only to responsibility for research and development. Assignment of operational responsibility for guided missiles remained an open question to be determined at a later date. The directive was announced at a press conference on October 8, 1946, by the Assistant Secretary of War (Air), Stuart Symington.[57]

[55]Baldwin, *New York Times,* May 12, 1946, p. 1.

[56]Memo to Commanding General AAF, Commanding General AGF, Chiefs of All Technical Services, signed General H. I. Hodes, Assistant Deputy Chief of Staff, by order of the Secretary of War. File 319.1. Box 408. HQ USAF, DCS/O, Assistant for GM, National Archives.

[57]Copies of the directives governing implementation can be found in a press package prepared for General LeMay in late 1946 for use in outlining the AAF's new responsibility in guided missiles R&D. Box 408, HQ USAF, DCS/O, Assistant for GM, National Archives.

By assigning the Army guided missiles R&D projects to the Army Air Forces, this new directive took a large step toward resolving the intra–War Department struggle. Within a year, however, the Unification Act, which created an independent Air Force, had reopened the entire question. Once again protracted and sometimes heated negotiations were instituted, primarily at the insistence of the Army. The issue was again settled, at least in a formal sense, on July 19, 1948, when the Air Force was relieved of the responsibility for the Army guided missiles research and development programs. One of the elements of this agreement was that development of tactical guided missiles was assigned to the Army and strategic missiles to the Air Force. This division reflected the Air Force's interest in maintaining responsibility for the strategic role. The boundaries of "tactical" and "strategic" were not specifically defined, however. Conflict over the entire question of research and operational control of guided missiles, range limitations to be allowed the Army and Navy, and, indeed, the nature of the weapons and their planned employment, was to continue for at least a decade and at times to grow even more heated.

2

Postwar
Air Force Missiles
Policy Is Set

ON AUGUST 7, 1945, President Harry S. Truman returned to Washington from the Potsdam Conference. The next afternoon a message was sent from the President to the Secretary of War, which contained the following instructions:

It is vital to the welfare of our people that this nation maintain development work and the nucleus of a producing aircraft industry capable of rapid expansion to keep the peace and meet any emergency. I therefore request that your office in conjunction with the Secretary of the Navy, the Director of the Budget, and the Director of the Office of War Mobilization and Reconversion, act immediately in preparing estimates for presentation to the Congress for legislation that will permit the letting of contracts for the continued production, immediately following V–J day, of an adequate number of advanced and developmental aircraft.[1]

[1]Letter, President Truman to Secretary of War, *et al.*, August 8, 1945. Quoted in Ethel M. De Haven, *Aerospace—The Evolution of USAF Weapons Acquisition Policy, 1945–1961* (DCAS Historical Office, June 1962).

On August 6, 1945, an atomic bomb had been dropped on Hiroshima, Japan; the next day another atomic device exploded over Nagasaki. The Army Air Forces hierarchy thus naturally felt the President's directive confirmed their own belief that air power was and would continue to be the most important element in the nation's defense. The Air Technical Service Command (during August 1944 the Air Service Command and the Materiel Command merged to form the Air Technical Service Command), with the support of the Air Staff, considered the directive to be clear authority to make superiority of air weapons a primary postwar objective.[2]

The fiscal 1946 research and development budget was larger than any in the past. Coupled with the Presidential support for "developmental aircraft" and the von Karman survey of rocket technology, the budget provided the basis for a comprehensive approach to guided missile development. By this time the Air Forces had already experimented with copies of the German V weapons. After the V–1 (a winged, pulse-jet, flying bomb) exploded in London on June 13, 1944, the Materiel Command of the Army Air Forces asked American manufacturers to design a similar weapon. By mid July a sample V–1 was available, and in less than six months, more than a half dozen flying bomb projects were underway.

The first V–2 ballistic rocket exploded in Paris September 6, 1944. Two days later a V–2 struck London. These events prompted another call from the Air Technical Service Command for a similar American weapon. No immediate response was forthcoming.[3] A year later, in the fall of 1945, the Air Staff approved expansion of the Air Forces' guided missiles program. The Air Technical Service Command was directed to undertake a review both of current missile capabilities and of prospects after a projected two-year research and development period.[4]

[2] De Haven, *Aerospace,* p. 2.

[3] U.S. Congress, House, Committee on Science and Astronautics, *A Chronology of Missile and Astronautic Events,* 87th Congress, 1st Session, 1961, p. 7. This source includes a summary of the total V-weapons launched, the number successful, and the resultant damage.

[4] De Haven, *Aerospace,* p. 8. The information was for use by the JCS Guided Missiles Committee in preparing a "National Program for Guided Missiles." This document is discussed in chapter 1.

At this date guided missiles development had been noticeably denigrated by the Air Technical Service Command, an agency that was primarily in the airplane business. No strong missile advocate held a position of authority in the command. Consequently, the resulting study was sometimes contradictory, sometimes implicitly opposed to missile development. In general, missile programs, particularly in the longer ranges, were judged very difficult and expensive, while at the same time few funds were requested for their support.[5]

The office of Assistant Chief of Air Staff (Materiel and Services) was, on the other hand, more interested and was consequently engaged in a jurisdictional battle over the control of the guided missiles program. General Crawford, head of the Research and Development Division in that office, also appears to have been personally enthusiastic about the prospects for guided missiles. His response to the Air Technical Service Command study was quite critical:

1. The distribution of "desired" funds between various classes of missiles does not appear to be in accordance with the priorities assigned, particularly of the ground-to-ground missiles.

2. No allocation of funds is shown for countermeasures or offensive and defensive control centers.

3. No allocation of funds is shown for aerodynamic research for guided missiles. . . .

4. In "future planned expenditures" it appears a mistake to have the scale of planned effort tapering downward. . . .

5. The statement that "no long-range development of air-to-air pilotless aircraft is contemplated at the present time" appears shortsighted.

6. The mention . . . of the "vast amount of basic long-term research" to be done is in contrast with the zero allocation of funds for aerodynamic research and lack of indication of action to secure research and development of warheads, fuzing, and launching devices.

Delays in actual contract development and placement were also noted unfavorably:

[5] Memo from General A. R. Crawford, Research and Engineering, AC/AS-4, to Air Technical Service Command, November 8, 1945. Titled "Information for Joint Chiefs of Staff Guided Missile Committee." File "AAF–G.M. Progress Report." Box "Defense Systems." HQ USAF, DCS/D, GM Branch, National Archives.

The existence of no contracts for the postwar guided missiles program, and the apparent lack of a coordinated plan for executing in proper order the various phases of the program are indications of unsatisfactory progress in this extremely important field. On 12 April 1945, seven months ago, the Air Technical Service Command was notified of this program; yet today, there is little prospect of letting contracts for development before January or February 1946. More energetic prosecution of the Guided Missiles program is desired.[6]

The optimistic expectations of the Air Staff Office of Research and Development in contrast to those of the Air Technical Service Command can also be seen in a memo sent a week later from the former office to the Strategy Section of the Office of the Chief of Staff:

The future guided missiles development program is expected to change comparatively frequently and radically as development progress is made in the highly developmental fields of: supersonic propulsion and airframe design, warheads and fuzing, remote and self-navigation, control systems, and launching systems.[7]

The extent of the development problems and the difficulties apt to be encountered were recognized. Nevertheless, the R&D office was obviously optimistic about the chances of ultimate success and merely foresaw a good deal of necessary hard work, which would prove profitable. This outlook was cogently expressed in an appendix to the memo quoted above:

The guided missiles program, as a whole, is now crossing the very difficult hurdle from subsonic to supersonic speeds. Much could be done in the subsonic field in the next two to three years, but since there appears to be no urgency for interim development in that time period, there will be few subsonic missile developments. It will probably be *at least* three to five years before supersonic missiles become available for operational use. Considerable research and development will have to be done in supersonic control, supersonic propulsion, and supersonic aerodynamics and long-range self-guided or remotely guided navigation before the desired characteristics will be possible. Decided advances

[6]*Ibid.*
[7]Memo, General Crawford, to Chief of Staff, att. Strategy Section, Operations Division. Dated November 16, 1945. Subject: "AAF Guided Missile Development." Box "Guided Missiles Committee." HQ USAF, DCS/D, GM Branch, National Archives.

are anticipated, however, before that time in the fields of basic research and component development. The extent and expediency of research and development of both subsonic and supersonic missiles obviously depends on adequate funds.[8]

Sensing the interest at the Air Staff level, the Air Technical Services Command, on October 31, 1945, had distributed letters to seventeen companies throughout the aircraft industry inviting proposals on a ten-year program of research and development leading to practical designs of ground-to-ground pilotless aircraft. The projects were grouped in four categories by range —from 20 miles to 5,000 miles.[9]

The end of hostilities had presented the aircraft manufacturers with the prospect of greatly lowered production schedules and consequent retrenchment. Although missiles were not particularly highly thought of by airplane builders at the time,[10] contracts of any nature were welcome in a period of lowering demand, and the companies responded favorably. The fiscal 1946 guided missiles program within the Army Air Forces included 26 different projects. These represented only the projects contracted for by the Army Air Forces through the close of Fiscal Year 1946. Within both the War Department and the Navy Department, the total spent on missiles research and development had reached approximately $50 million.[11]

By February 1946, six major aircraft companies (North

[8]*Ibid.* Emphasis in original.

[9]John L. Chapman, *Atlas: The Story of a Missile* (New York: Harper and Brothers, 1960), p. 27. See also: U.S. Congress, House, Committee on Government Operations, Military Operations Subcommittee, *Hearings, Organization and Management of Missile Programs,* 86th Congress, 1st Session, 1959, pp. 4–5. Hereafter referred to as *Organization and Management Hearings.*

[10]Theodore von Karman, *The Wind and Beyond,* p. 239. In discussing his hopes in 1946 for a new "pilotless aircraft" research center, von Karman says, "Opposition developed among some industrialists. Dutch Kindleberger, President of North American Aviation, didn't like the idea of the government's spending money on research facilities instead of on planes. . . . Kindleberger was representing a point of view of some important businessmen of the time. They understood products like an airplane, but they were not yet attuned to the coming research revolution."

[11]Memo, General Crawford, Research and Engineering Division, AC/AS–4 to AC/AS–4, February 23, 1946. Quoted in Self, p. 40.

American Aviation, The Glenn L. Martin Co., Curtiss-Wright, Republic Aviation, Northrop Aircraft, and Consolidated Vultee) had begun work on surface-to-surface missiles. The projects included a 500-mile subsonic aircraft, a 500-mile supersonic winged rocket, two 1,500-mile missiles including a supersonic ramjet, and two missiles of 5,000-mile range. The last were a supersonic turbojet vehicle and a supersonic ballistic rocket.[12]

The 5,000-mile ballistic rocket was proposed by the Consolidated Vultee Aircraft Corporation (Convair), which was at that time producing the B–36. Convair had, as early as May 1945, expressed interest in long-range rockets. The corporation's Vultee Field Division, at Downey, California, had earlier been involved in the short-range navy rocket-powered missile, Lark.[13] By January 1946 the division had produced two study designs of 5,000-mile missiles: a subsonic, winged, jet-powered missile and a supersonic, ballistic rocket. Convair proposed a research contract to determine the relative merits of the two designs. This proposal was accepted by the Air Force in April 1946, when the company received a one-year study contract for $1.4 million. The project was labeled MX–774.

Northrop Aircraft, Inc. had also been invited to submit ground-to-ground guided missile research proposals. Northrop responded with a proposed design for a 5,000-mile supersonic missile utilizing turbojet propulsion. On February 18, 1946, the engineering division of the Air Technical Service Command recommended that Northrop's proposal be accepted. The following month the War Department approved a letter contract. Although the formal contract was not signed until early 1947, work was begun earlier. Both the subsonic and supersonic designs were pursued under the Project name, MX–775.[14]

[12] De Haven, *Aerospace,* p. 8. Also, letter from Maj. General B. W. Chidlaw, AMC, to Commanding General, Army Air Forces, att'n. AC/AS–4. May 2, 1947. In Document Collection appended to De Haven study.

[13] Interview, William Patterson, who was an engineer closely involved with the rocket project at Convair at the time.

[14] Robert L. Perry, *The Development of the Snark Guided Missile, 1945–1953.* Historical Branch, Office of Information Services, WADC, ARDC. January 1956. In March 1946, the Air Technical Service Command, which had incorporated the earlier Materiel Command, became the Air Materiel Command.

The proposals from Northrop and Convair constituted the whole of the Air Force programs in very long-range (5,000-mile) guided missiles. These were complemented by two air-to-air fighter-launched missiles, two air-to-air bomber-launched missiles, three air-to-surface missiles of varying ranges up to 300 miles, a surface-to-air antiaircraft missile, a surface-to-air anti-rocket missile, and the surface-to-surface 500-mile and 1,500-mile missiles noted earlier.[15]

An idea of the expectations of some of the Air Forces' personnel involved in the guided missiles development program at this point can be gleaned from a memo sent from the Chief of the Guided Missile Branch of the Deputy Chief of Staff (Development) to a new member of the scientific liaison section of the Assistant Chief of Air Staff (Materiel and Services). The memo's purpose was to acquaint the recipient with the history of Air Force missile work and current prospects. Observing that "it was not until the Japanese surrender in August 1945 that any serious action was taken" in terms of a "long-term guided missiles program," the memo cited three principal aims of the present program:

1. Defense of the U.S. and its overseas bases against attack from the air, including improved versions of present-day aircraft and missiles.
2. Missiles for strategic offensive use, to cover ranges up to at least 5,000 miles and to supplement or, insofar as is economically possible, to replace the work of the present strategic bomber.
3. Missiles for tactical offensive use; for short-range operation and for direct support of ground armies.

From this memo it can again be seen that some members of the Air Forces involved in the guided missiles program were favorably disposed to the new weapons and, indeed, expected

[15]See letter of May 2, 1947, from General B. W. Chidlaw, Deputy Commanding General, Engineering Division, Air Materiel Command, to the Commanding General, Army Air Forces, attention AC/AS–4, in De Haven Document Collection. See also, Letter from Engineering Division, AMC, to North American Aviation, April 25, 1946. Copy in Document Collection appended to J. Allen Neal, *The Development of the Navaho Guided Missile: 1945–1953*. Historical Branch. Office of Information Services, WADC, ARDC. January 1956. Documents collected in chronological order.

that someday they would fulfill many of the functions of the manned strategic bomber. The predicted budgetary allocations included in the memo confirm this.

. . . The following figures will give an idea of the extent of the current and planned guided missiles development program:

AAF Fiscal Year 1945—Budget for GM, $3,747,124 or 2.63% [of the R&D budget]

AAF Fiscal Year 1946—Budget for GM, $28,837,185 or 14.6% [of the R&D budget]

AAF Fiscal Year 1947—Budget for GM, $75,681,900 or 34.4% [of the R&D budget]

AAF Fiscal Year 1948—Contemplated budget for GM, $83,500,000.[16]

Such a program called for an enormous increase in spending for guided missiles, both in total amount and in percentage of the budget. These figures also assumed a rising total allocation for research and development. These expectations were to be disappointed.

The six companies with contracts for ground-to-ground guided missiles research (ranges from 175 miles to 5,000 miles) were asked to prepare evaluative studies to be ready during the last quarter of fiscal year 1947. By May of 1947, however, the funding bubble had burst. The country was interested in returning to peacetime pursuits; military spending was no longer popular.[17] Budget cuts and retrenchment became the rule in planning, and research and development was expected (indeed ordered) to contribute its share.

There had, of course, been some warnings of what was to come. The "National Program" of the JCS Guided Missiles

[16]Memo from Col. Cooper, Chief, Guided Missiles Branch, DCAS/D, to Col. B. A. Schriever, Scientific Liaison Section, AC/AS–4, June 7, 1946, Titled, "Review of Postwar R&D Aims of AAF in Guided Missiles." File "AAF, G.M. Policy 1946." Box "A–7 Catapults." HQ USAF, DCS/D, GM Branch, National Archives.

[17]A discussion of the interaction between the national mood and national military planning after the Second World War can be found in Samuel P. Huntington, *The Common Defense* (New York: Columbia University Press, 1961), pp. 14–47. See also testimony of Dr. Wernher von Braun, U.S. Congress, Senate, Committee on Armed Services, *Hearings, Inquiry into Satellite and Missile Programs,* 85th Congress, 1st and 2nd Sessions, 1958, p. 584.

Committee had been conservative in terms of finances. Emphasis had been placed on further "basic information." "Practical development" was not to be "pushed ahead of sound knowledge." Furthermore, professional military men might have been expected to understand one very normal consequence of the termination of hostilities—a cutback in funds coupled with a lessened interest in the financial welfare of the military.

The extent of the imposed research and development budget cuts—both in immediate and projected funds—was significant. The figures were spelled out in a memo to the Air Force information office in the spring of 1947:

Our best estimate . . . was that the AAF R&D expenditure should rise from its average annual war-time figure of approximately $200,000,000 to an annual expenditure of $272,000,000 for each of the fiscal years from 1946 to 1951, inclusive. Hereafter, it was felt that the annual cost could drop gradually until, after 1956, it could level out at about $150,000,000 annually. Many factors have developed to modify our wartime planning but the general picture of *requirements* remains the same. The AAF received $200,000,000 from Congress for R&D in FY 1946. In FY 1947 it received $185,000,000 which subsequently was reduced to $110,000,000. Money for AAF R&D for 1948 has not yet been appropriated, but the AAF has defended a budget of but $147,000,000 for this purpose. If it receives all the money it has asked of Congress, the amount will be only slightly more than half the planned figure.[18]

The original fiscal year 1947 budget for guided-missile development was approximately $29 million. In December 1946, this budget was cut to $22 million. The cut forced cancellation of 11 of the then currently planned 28 guided missile projects.[19] The projects to be dropped were determined by a recommendation from the Air Materiel Command, which was approved by the Air Staff in late December 1946. Among the projects cancelled were the Convair subsonic, jet-powered, surface-to-surface missile and the similar subsonic project of the Northrop

[18]Memo from General LeMay, Deputy Chief of Staff, R&D, to Director of Information, Information Division. April 11, 1947. File 168.64–47, Pt. 1, 1945–1947. Historical Archives, Maxwell Air Force Base.
[19]Mary Self, p. 42.

Company. The supersonic Northrop and Convair projects were continued.[20]

This action allowed Convair to concentrate on its ballistic design, which was the model favored by that company's development engineers. (A "ballistic" missile is guided at the outset of its flight, but approaches its target as a free falling object.) Convair was informed, however, that funds for Project MX–774, which were originally expected to finance the project only slightly over a year, would have to be stretched out, requiring a slowdown in the project planning.[21]

These reductions did not prove adequate to meet the new R&D budget limitations. In May 1947, Air Force Headquarters was informed of the necessity for further missile project cancellations:

The Air Materiel Command and AAF missile contractors have for the past six months been carrying on detailed studies of the probable cost of developing guided missiles. From these studies the conclusion must be drawn that the AAF program, while desirable and technically sound, is considerably over-expanded if we are to carry it on with a budget approximating $22 million a year. There is attached as Exhibit "B" the financial details of a development program through F.Y. 1953. This exhibit shows conclusively that the AAF program must be drastically cut.[22]

Determination of which projects were to be eliminated was again initiated by the Air Materiel Command's Engineering Division. The decision at Wright Field was that with a fixed and limited amount of development money, "we should concentrate on those missiles which show the greatest promise of early tactical availability."[23] The newly recommended program would lower the total number of Air Forces guided missile projects

[20]Memo from General Grandison Gardner, Deputy Assistant, Chief of Air Staff–4, to Commanding General, Air Materiel Command, May 19, 1947. Document collection appended to Perry, *The Development of the Snark*.

[21]Letter to author from Karel Bossart, Chief Convair engineer for Project MX–774. See also Chapman, *Atlas*, p. 35.

[22]Letter of May 12, 1947, from General Chidlaw, Engineering, AMC, to Commanding General, Army Air Forces, attention AC/AS–4. DeHaven Document Collection.

[23]*Ibid.*

from the seventeen left after the December cuts, to twelve. The remaining projects were to be:

1. Air-to-air fighter-launched missile.
2. Air-to-air bomber-launched missile.
3. Air-to-surface missile, 100-mile range.
4. Air-to-surface missile, 300-mile range.
5. Surface-to-air missile, antiaircraft.
6. Surface-to-air missile, antirocket.
   a. University of Michigan prolonged study at $1 million a year.
   b. General Electric prolonged study at $500,000 a year.
7. Surface-to-surface missile, 500-mile range.
   a. Subsonic aircraft (Martin).
   b. Supersonic winged rocket (North American).
8. Surface-to-surface missile, 1,500-mile range (North American, probably ramjet).
9. Surface-to-surface missile, 5,000-mile range.
   a. Supersonic turbojet (Northrop).
   b. North American 5,000-mile supersonic missile (probably ramjet).

The missile programs suggested for cancellation were:

1. Air-to-air fighter-launched
2. Air-to-air bomber-launched
3. Air-to-surface underwater target
4. Surface-to-surface missile, 1,500 mile-range
5. Surface-to-surface missile, 5,000 mile-range Consolidated Vultee rocket.[24]

As was noted above, the Air Materiel Command based these decisions on the prospects for early tactical availability. For this reason, in addition to the proposed cancellations, funds for the two surface-to-air antirocket projects were greatly reduced.

The most important item in this proposed restructuring of the Air Forces missiles program was the cancellation of Convair's Project MX–774. This 5,000-mile ballistic rocket was the only

---

[24]*Ibid.* A ramjet is a jet engine in which the air is continuously compressed by being rammed into the open front end.

very long-range surface-to-surface rocket program in the Air Force's inventory, and its cancellation left North American's 500-mile winged project as the only remaining rocket. This missile was also soon cancelled.

The letter containing the proposed new program stated that the MX–774 had been cancelled because it "does not promise any tangible results in the next eight to ten years." In an appendix to the letter, the reasons behind this decision were explored more fully:

As a result of studies to date, it is now believed that we should not at this time expend funds on the development of a 5,000-mile rocket, for two principal reasons. First, the specific impulse of fuels which are available or promise to become available is too low. Oxygen and Alcohol are the best fuels available today and have a specific impulse of 225. The Consolidated two-stage rocket is designed around a fuel with a specific impulse of 425, with the result that when the Consolidated 5,000-mile rocket is loaded with real fuel, *i.e.,* oxygen and alcohol, it will have a range of only 1,500 miles. . . . The development program would cost $47 million to complete. It does not seem wise to continue this development until such time as fuels of high specific impulse are definitely going to be available.

The second reason is the problem of re-entry temperature. It is certain that a rocket of this range and of necessity high speed, would encounter very serious temperature difficulties on re-entry into the earth's atmosphere. It seems equally certain that a long series of costly experiments would be required by Consolidated to arrive at the design of a missile which would be satisfactorily insulated against high temperatures, inasmuch as so little is presently known about the properties of the upper air and heat transfer at the required missile speeds and altitudes.[25]

The Air Materiel Command suggested activating instead, on a

[25]*Ibid.* In the late 1950s, and particularly after the demonstration of Soviet ICBM capability in 1957 with the launching of Sputnik, the Convair rocket cancellation was given much scrutiny by congressional investigators. Later explanations of the 1947 action centered primarily on the high atomic warhead weights and low yields available at that time. See testimony of General Bernard A. Schriever, U.S. Congress, Senate, Committee on Armed Services, Subcommittee on the Air Force, *Hearings, Study of Airpower,* 84th Congress, Second Session, p. 1156; and testimony of Air Secretary James H. Douglas, *Hearings, Inquiry into Satellite and Missile Programs,* p. 848; and *Hearings, Organization and Management of Missile Programs,* p. 5. It is interesting that the arguments advanced in the late 1950s were not those which dictated the recommendations of the Air Materiel Command engineers working on the original project. After

very low priority basis, a 5,000-mile missile project at North American. This project was to rank below the 500-mile and 1,500-mile North American programs and was not to compromise development of either. It was projected that the 5,000-mile missile "would amount to little more than a thorough study for some time to come"; $500,000 would be provided for the project in fiscal year 1948, and the sum would increase to $1 million in fiscal year 1950 and would not rise above this figure "until some time subsequent to FY 1954."[26]

The result of the above reasoning was to cancel the most unusual 5,000-mile missile (which also promised by far the greatest operational capabilities if successful), and to place the second most technologically innovative 5,000-mile missile "on a low priority basis," which would amount to little more than a study project "for some time to come." The other 5,000-mile missile suggested for retention was the supersonic turbojet vehicle to be built by Northrop, whose history will be discussed below.

This program reduction had been necessitated by communications from the Air Staff to the effect that budget reductions in guided-missile research and development were mandatory. The programs chosen for elimination were the result of determinations made by the Air Materiel Command. These recommendations were received at Air Force Headquarters in May 1947. In June the Air Staff completed an evaluation of the guided-missile program in the context of the operational requirements of the Air Force during the next ten years.[27] The purpose of the Air

the resurrection of a long-range ballistic missile in the early 1950s, however, warhead weight and yield figures were used by the Air Staff planners to support demands for extremely high accuracy and other performance standards. This pattern long marked the ballistic missile program. The increasingly false nature of the warhead argument and the existence of important barriers to the long-range ballistic missile program other than the limits of technology will be demonstrated later in the study.

[26]Letter, Crawford, AMC, to HQ, USAF, May 12, 1947.

[27]The following discussion, and the quotes, are derived from a memorandum for the Commanding General, Army Air Forces, from General Thomas S. Power, Deputy Assistant Chief of Air Staff Operations, Commitments and Requirements. Dated June 12, 1947. File 319.1. Box 408. HQ USAF, DCS/O, Assistant for GM, National Archives.

Staff Review was to determine an order of priority for the development of guided missiles in the light of the reduced budget then available and likely to continue. The priority policy being determined was meant to establish the "general trend" of the guided-missile programs. The chosen program was based on a number of assumptions, both about the nature of likely technological developments during the approaching decade and the capabilities of potential enemies. This procedure, of course, opened the study to the possible risk that the reasoning might prove incorrect because of limits imposed on the discussion. As it happened, one major assumption did have determining influence on the conclusions reached. The Air Staff review stated that

a. For the next ten years, at least, the subsonic bomber will be the only means available for the delivery of long-range (1,000 miles and over) air bombardment.

Despite the belief that only manned bombers could perform the long-range bombardment function over the coming decade, their job was not deemed easy.

b. Such bombers will require air-to-surface guided missiles and may require greatly improved defensive armament in order to deliver attacks against defended targets.

This statement demonstrates a significant recognition by the Air Staff that the conventional role of the bomber—that of flying over a target and dropping its bombload more or less vertically (except for the force of inertia) would increasingly be jeopardized. Bomber-launched guided missiles were expected to be necessary, and even with them the risks to the attacking forces might be great. The threat from defended targets would be strong because of the increasing likelihood of effective surface-to-air antiaircraft missiles. It was expected that by 1952 surface-to-air missiles with ranges up to 50 miles would have attained high efficiency against subsonic attackers, whether bombers or missiles. With present and likely aircraft, "it will be disastrous for subsonic vehicles to attempt penetration of such defense."

A third assumption underlying the ordering of Air Forces guided missiles development in 1947 involved the question of what forces might be used against the United States in a future conflict.

c. Within the next ten years, a potential enemy of the U. S. will have a maximum capability of attacking the U. S. with conventional bombers and guided missiles.

This statement is not exactly clear. If the "guided missiles" mentioned refer to land-launched, and thus intercontinental, missiles (assuming that an attack was unlikely to come from North America), then this sentence could be read as either a seeming contradiction to the first assumption, or an admission that a potential enemy might within the decade have a valuable weapon that the United States would not possess. Of course, the more likely explanation is simply that these "guided missiles" were expected to be similar to the bomber-launched air-to-surface missiles which would be required in the American arsenal according to the second assumption. Whether this was the case, however, is left unclear by the fourth and last assumption.

d. The U.S. has at present no means with which to detect and intercept a supersonic guided missile, such as the V–2 or an air-launched missile.

This is an interesting admission, since it could have important consequences for the security of the nation if a potential opponent in a future war were to develop such weapons. One solution, of course, is that if such developments are deemed extremely unlikely throughout the period covered by the review at hand, the problem is similarly lessened. And if the problem doesn't exist, then there is no need to rank projects designed to counter it particularly high. The results of these assumptions are easily predicted. If long-range surface-to-surface missiles are not apt to be operationally available and viable during the period under review, then their development should have a low priority. And if such weapons are ruled out, then weapons to oppose them should also have low priority.

This reasoning was hindered by the recognized "fact" that area bombardment with supersonic missiles of the V–2 type at ranges up to 250 miles was possible at that time by both the United States and other nations. However, the function of the Air Force (both in its own and civilian eyes) was primarily offensive, able to inflict heavy (theoretically incapacitating) damage to the industrial heart of an enemy. The intent of the Air Force was to hurt an opponent so badly in his own economic (and perhaps also population) centers that he would neither want nor be able to continue fighting. Defensive activities were not central to the Air Force's conception of itself:

The list of facts and assumptions led to certain conclusions. For the next ten years, long-range air bombardment would be effected by means of subsonic bombers only. Supersonic air-to-surface guided missiles with ranges of at least 100 miles were required at present and would be mandatory by 1952; these weapons should carry both atomic and nonatomic warheads, and would be used against land- and water-borne targets. Greatly improved defensive armament for bombers was required; the air-to-air bomber-launched guided missile should proceed as a high priority. The need was urgent for the early development of surface-to-air guided missiles to be employed against attacking bombers of up to sonic speeds, and detection devices for such bombers should also be pushed. Also of urgency was the early development of the means to detect and destroy enemy supersonic guided missiles (surface-to-surface and air-to-surface). Operational air-to-air fighter-launched missiles were required by 1952. The early perfection of high-accuracy, supersonic surface-to-surface guided missiles was necessary; these missiles, with ranges up to 1,000 miles, would be employed for coast defense, and tactical and strategic land bombardment. Finally, "although there is little likelihood that they will be operationally available prior to 1957," research and development of long-range supersonic surface-to-surface missiles should proceed "at the maximum rate"; such weapons should have a range of up to 10,000 miles, and should have the capability of carrying either conventional or atomic warheads.

This last statement fit the policy that the atomic bomb was to be a "special purpose" weapon. There was an overall Air Force operational requirement for the ability to deliver "many bombs with 500–3,000 pound non-atomic warheads."

A final conclusion was to prove quite interesting in light of the subsequent history of the Air Force's guided missile programs. It was determined that "there is no operational requirement for subsonic surface-to-surface guided missiles, other than missile aircraft (drone) types."

The result of these determinations was that guided missiles were recommended for development in the following general order of priority:

1. Bomber-launched air-to-air and air-to-surface missiles.
2. Surface-to-surface missile, 150-mile range.
3. Surface-to-air missiles, with associated means to detect enemy aircraft and missiles, and fighter-launched air-to-air missiles.
4. Long-range surface-to-surface missiles.
5. Interim air-to-surface missiles.[28]

The memo with this ordering was sent to the Chief of Staff on June 12, 1947. It was approved by General Vandenberg as official Air Force policy on June 18, 1947.

As was evident in the reasoning and final recommendations of the Air Staff review of the guided missiles program discussed here, interest in the ballistic missile project was not particularly strong. This is demonstrated by a revealing exchange which took place in 1958 between Senator Stuart Symington and Thomas G. Lanphier, Jr., during the Senate Armed Services Committee's inquiry into the U.S. missiles programs. Mr. Lanphier, then Vice President of the Convair Division of General Dynamics Corp., had served as special assistant to Symington while the latter was Secretary of the Air Force in the late 1940s. The discussion refers to the 1947 cancellation of the MX–774 ballistic missile:

[28]Memo for the Commanding General from Thomas S. Power, June 12, 1947.

LANPHIER: Senator, the fact is, in those days, and for a long time thereafter, the ballistic missile was not considered above the rank of majors and colonels, except among the Germans in the Army where they were pressing for it.

SYMINGTON: Do you think these were the reasons that the head of the OSRD, Dr. Vannevar Bush, was opposed to the ballistic missile?

LANPHIER: I assume so. In those days you were not opposed to it. Nobody was proposing it very strongly, but I remember he made a statement very much adverse to it.

SYMINGTON: Probably the matter was not even brought up to the then Chief of Staff?

LANPHIER: That is right.

SYMINGTON: Because it was in such a research study position; is that correct?

LANPHIER: Yes, sir. As Mr. Dempsey testified earlier, in those days the RDB adjudicated on the lower levels, and if it did not get above them, it never got to anybody at the Secretary's level, and this one never got above them.[29]

To the recollection of the chief Convair project MX–774 engineer, no specific technical directions or even design suggestions were ever received from the Air Force. While this might have indicated a commendable willingness by the Air Force to give the contractor flexibility in design research, evidence that disinterest may have also played a part lies in the fact that the Air Force project officers who were assigned to the study contract were, in the words of the same Convair engineer, "from the lowest echelons." Furthermore, during the period of the MX–774 project life (late 1946 to late 1948), the visits of the project officers to the Convair plant could be "counted on the fingers of one hand." Beyond that, the Air Force sent an observer to each of three test launches conducted at the White Sands missile range.[30]

Frank Davis, an assistant to the chief engineer at Convair's Downey plant, had been sent to Washington in the spring of 1947 to attempt to counter widespread talk in Air Force circles that the MX–774 project should be cancelled because its concepts were far beyond practicability. Davis was told during this

[29]*Hearings, Inquiry into Satellite and Missile Programs,* p. 1876.
[30]Letter to author from Karel Bossart.

visit that scientists advising both the Army and the Navy felt that guided missiles at even a 3,000-mile range were at least twenty-five years in the future.[31]

Although project MX–774 was cancelled in the summer of 1947, provision was made for Convair to use whatever MX–774 funds remained to complete and fly several test missiles. The first MX–774 was finished by the late fall of 1947. Static test firings took place in late 1947 and the spring of 1948. These tests were completed by the end of May 1948. The missile was then transported to the White Sands proving ground in New Mexico, arriving there on June 7, 1948. After preparations were completed, launches were attempted on June 28 and 29, but were prevented by minor technical problems. The first MX–774 launch finally took place on July 14. It ended in failure when the missile's engines cut off soon after takeoff and the vehicle crashed and exploded. The missile reached an altitude of approximately 6,200 feet and flew less than a minute.

The second MX–774 test vehicle was launched at White Sands on September 27, 1948. This missile also experienced engine failure, although slightly later than the first. It too crashed and exploded. The third and final MX–774 test vehicle was launched on December 2, 1948. The result was the same. After fifty-one seconds of flight, the missile's engines experienced premature burnout, and the missile crashed. Thus, by the end of 1948, the only long-range ballistic missile project in the United States had been cancelled and all test vehicles had been expended in unsuccessful experimental launches.

Despite the failure of the test launches, Project MX–774 produced some valuable results. Convair engineers had incorporated into the missile several new features, which would prove valuable in later programs. These included swiveling engines, several innovations in fuel tank design, and a separating nose cone. The swiveling concept was developed by Karel Bossart to deal with the major problem of control of the direction of a rocket's flight. Existing procedures involved placing movable

---

[31]Chapman, *Atlas*, p. 56. The most prominent of these scientists was Dr. Vannevar Bush, whose viewpoint will be discussed at length below.

vanes in the rocket's exhaust stream, which acted like a ship's rudder (or, in this case, rudders). This was the system employed in the V–2. It was not particularly satisfactory, however, because the vanes restricted exhaust flow, thereby cutting the thrust of the engine, sometimes by as much as 17 percent.[32]

The four engines of the MX–774 were instead placed on swivel mounts, which would allow each engine to pivot in one direction during the rocket's flight. This idea was forerunner to the gimballed engines (movable in any direction) which were later to be widely incorporated. At the time Bossart thought he was the first to attempt this idea, but the concept had actually been considered by the Germans in connection with the V–2, and later abandoned for technical reasons peculiar to their design.

Convair's fuel tank concepts were among their most revolutionary ideas and probably met with considerable opposition for that reason. Fuel for the V–2 had consisted of liquid oxygen and alcohol. Each substance was contained in one of two separate metal containers inside the metal outer walls of the rocket. Airplanes had originally been built in this fashion, but later were built without separate internal tanks; the fuel was simply held within the outer skin of the airplane, thereby providing greater fuel capacity and less weight. Convair decided to incorporate this feature in the design of the MX–774. The result has been described as "a flying propellant tank which had a power plant at its rear and a package of instruments at its front."[33] A single interior barrier separated the two fuel components.

A second innovation involving fuel caused the greatest debate. Nitrogen gas was used in the MX–774 design to help push the two fuel components out of their storage areas for engine consumption. The Convair engineers decided to use the nitrogen for a second purpose—to support the outer walls of the rocket. The body of the V–2 had been stabilized and held in shape by internal metal supports. The Convair engineers reasoned that

[32]*Ibid.*, pp. 32–34.
[33]*Ibid.*, p. 32.

the pressure of the nitrogen could accomplish the same purpose. The result was an airframe that was basically an aluminum balloon whose paper-thin walls could not support themselves. The nitrogen pressing against the walls stiffened them adequately while saving the weight of the metal supports. Because of the weight reductions accomplished by the Convair designers, the MX–774's airframe-to-propellant weight ratio was approximately three times better than that of the V–2.[34]

A final important difference between the Convair MX–774 and the V–2 was a separable warhead. The V–2 had been designed to reenter the atmosphere and impact whole, which required that the whole missile be built to withstand the considerable heat of reentry. The Convair designers decided to build a weapon in which the warhead would separate from the remainder of the missile body after engine burnout. In this way heat protection would be necessary only on the warhead. The rest of the missile could simply burn up in reentry. This innovation resulted again in weight savings.

Despite the Air Force's cancellation of Project MX–774, the Convair engineers who had been involved in it were highly optimistic about the future of long-range ballistic missiles. Several of them, led by Karel Bossart, convinced their superiors at Convair that ICBMs had a likely future. Convair accordingly decided to continue a small ICBM research program at its own expense for the 1949–50 period.[35]

During this two-year period, studies were conducted at Convair on airframe design, propellants, guidance, reentry, and other matters. Contact was maintained with the Air Force in continuing attempts to reinstate Air Force funding for the project. One Convair proposal was to build a number of MX–774 test vehicles for use by the Air Force in training personnel. It was also suggested that these missiles could be used in high-altitude research.

In response to this approach, supplemental funds were made

[34]This figure, as well as a general description of the process, can be found in *ibid.*, pp. 32–33.

[35]Letter to author from Karel Bossart.

available by the Air Force for fiscal year 1948 to procure fifteen training missiles. The cost was to be $1.5 million.[36] This high-altitude function, however, competed with the Viking high-altitude research program about to be undertaken by the Navy. The Viking rocket project had already been approved by the Defense Department's Research and Development Board, and it would not permit duplicate research programs of this nature.[37] A special subcommittee was appointed by the Guided Missiles Committee of the Research and Development Board to examine missile requirements for upper-atmosphere research. The group recommended that the Navy Viking missile be used for this purpose.[38]

Dr. Marcus O'Day, who had been in charge of the Air Force's upper air rocket research program in the late 1940s, has stated that he was favorably impressed with the Convair design and felt that "this rocket was ideal for the type of upper-atmospheric experiments in our program." Furthermore, he had been able to convince his superiors in the Air Materiel Command to give their support to the Convair rocket, with the result, as noted above, that funds had been earmarked for this purpose. However, the competition between the MX–774 upper

[36]Letter of September 29, 1948, from Lieutenant General H. A. Craig, DCS/M, to Commanding General, AMC. Cited in Self, p. 93.

[37]Testimony of James R. Dempsey, General Dynamics Corp. (which now includes Convair Aviation), *Hearings, Inquiry into Satellite and Missile Programs,* p. 1872.

[38]The Viking rocket was conceived in 1946. Launchings began in 1949, with the last Viking firing taking place in 1954. Two of the Vikings were used as test vehicles for Vanguard, which began development in 1954–55. The final Vanguard was fired in 1959. In all, fourteen Vikings were launched, nine of them successfully in that they reached altitudes useful for upper atmosphere research. Only three Vanguards out of twelve were successful. Naval interest in the Viking was hardly stronger than that of the Air Force in the MX–774. "There were only twelve men of the Viking launch crew. The Martin Company, which built the rocket, had no more than about two dozen engineers involved in the design. There were never more than about fifty men involved in building the vehicle, and we had to borrow these from other projects because Viking didn't have enough production to hold them permanently. Finally the government project group consisted of two men at first and was never more than four." Milton V. Rosen, speech, American Institute of Aeronautics and Astronautics Meeting, October 28, 1971, Washington, D.C., Panel on Rocketry in the 1950s. See also Milton V. Rosen, *The Viking Rocket Story* (New York: Harper, 1955).

air research function and the Viking project produced, in Dr. O'Day's words, a "bitter struggle" within the Research and Development Board in 1949 "with the result that the Navy was able to get a decision through the board to cancel the contract for the Convair missile." Dr. O'Day summed up his recollection of the MX–774 cancellation by observing that "this particular development is a very good example of how deleterious has been the intense inter-service rivalry" in the missile field.[39]

An Air Force review of the MX–774 program in early 1949 indicated that $1.5 million would be needed to continue the project. An appeal was made to Assistant Secretary of the Air Force, Arthur Barrows, for these additional funds. This request was refused.[40] In the Air Force view the procurement of MX–774 missiles for operational launching and handling training only was not justified in the light of their "high cost."[41] Accordingly, the MX–774 was again cancelled.

It must be noted here that the general denigration of long-range missiles in comparison to manned bombers—and the selection of air-breathing missiles over the ballistic models within the reduced program—had strong civilian scientific support. Late in 1944 General Arnold asked Dr. Theodore von Karman, now with the California Institute of Technology, to head a study of the present and future capabilities of the Air Force.[42]

[39] Letter dated December 1, 1957, from Dr. Marcus O'Day, Rocket and Satellite Research Panel, to Edwin L. Weisl, Special Counsel to Senate Preparedness Investigating Subcommittee of the Senate Committee on Armed Services. Printed as Exhibit A–22, in *Hearings, Inquiry into Satellite and Missile Programs,* pp. 2121–22.

[40] Letter from Donald L. Putt, USAF (ret.) to author. General Putt was in 1949 Director of Research and Development, office of the Deputy Chief of Staff, Materiel, HQ USAF. He was later Commander of the Air Research and Development Command and Deputy Chief of Staff, Development.

[41] Memo dated March 29, 1949, from General William Richardson, Chairman of Guided Missiles Group, to Deputy Chief of Staff, Operations. File "P 180–49." Box 120. HQ USAF, DCS/O, Assistant for GM, National Archives.

See also testimony of James R. Dempsey, Manager of Astronautics Division, General Dynamics Corporation. *Hearings, Inquiry into Satellite and Missile Programs,* p. 1872; and letter from Brigadier General A. A. Ressler, Jr., office of the DCS/M, April 4, 1949, cited in Self, p. 93.

[42] H. H. Arnold, *Global Mission,* pp. 532–33.

The panel created in response surveyed wartime achievements in aeronautics and rocketry, and visited Germany in the process. After concluding his German tour, von Karman met with Arnold in Paris in July 1945, while the General was en route to the Potsdam Conference. Arnold asked for a written summary of the findings on German developments. Von Karman returned to Washington and produced a secret study entitled *Where We Stand*. This report attempted to estimate United States potentials in areas such as propulsion and guidance and in defensive measures against possible future enemy capabilities.[43]

After completing this interim report of findings, von Karman returned to Europe to seek further technical information on German advances in aeronautics, including the concept of the transoceanic rocket, the great A–10, designed to fly from Berlin to New York. Von Karman stayed in Europe during September and October of 1945, and conducted further investigations. During this time Arnold, in Washington, suffered a heart attack. The General was apparently eager to see a final report, complete with recommendations, and his illness increased his sense of urgency.

Von Karman returned to Washington in October and set to work on the final report. By December, a preliminary draft had been completed. Titled *Toward New Horizons,* the report was classified and not publicly released until 1960. In his memoirs, von Karman stressed the prescience of the report in the field of guided missiles, citing as one key finding that "present technical competence could build ballistic missiles of 6,000-mile range, enough to blitz any country of the world from bases in any other country."

The fact that the V–2 was designed to have a range of only two hundred miles, and did not have much accuracy in hitting targets across the English Channel, made most people think of the V–2 as just a nuisance weapon. Even the Germans thought so, which accounts for the initial V, meaning vengeance. But because we could foresee the possibility of rocket multistaging, we were able to describe the potential of long-range intercontinental missiles capable of bringing atomic destruction

[43]von Karman, *The Wind and Beyond,* p. 289; Swenson, et al. *This New Ocean,* p. 517.

to the United States from six thousand miles away. Missile testing stations—at New Mexico and Cape Canaveral—came indirectly out of these concepts. All this brought a new dimension to warfare and to international relations. . . .

We examined the thrust capabilities of rockets and concluded that it was perfectly feasible to send up an artificial satellite, which would orbit the earth. We did not, however, give consideration to the military potential of such a satellite.[44]

There appears to be a bit of retrospective selective perception at work here, however. The von Karman panel's report did give significant credit to German rocketry accomplishments, but its conclusions were somewhat different from what von Karman has suggested. In the panel's view, the key to "air supremacy" lay in jet propulsion (which, of course, was also quite a new field).[45] Their report recommended an emphasis on jet-powered manned aircraft. Long-range ballistic missiles should be pursued through development of air-breathing, pilotless aircraft.[46] This was precisely the course chosen by the Air Force.

Another very important influence on the Air Force development program was Dr. Vannevar Bush. In December of 1945, while testifying before the special Senate Committee on Atomic Energy, Bush, then head of the Office of Scientific Research and Development, declared:

We have plenty enough to think about that as [sic] very definite and very realistic—enough so that we don't need to step out into some of these borderlines, which seem to me more or less fantastic. Let me say this: There has been a great deal said about a 3,000-mile high-angle rocket.

[44]*Ibid.,* pp. 289, 293.

[45]Nine months before Pearl Harbor, Vannevar Bush, Chairman of the National Advisory Committee for Aeronautics, had appointed a Special Committee on Jet Propulsion. Until then, there had been scant interest in jet propulsion either in NACA, the military services, or the aircraft industry. In the words of the historians of Project Mercury, "there had been little active disagreement with the conclusion reached in 1923 by Edgar Buckingham of the Bureau of Standards: 'Propulsion by the reaction of a simple jet cannot complete [sic] in any respect, with air screw propulsion at such flying speeds as are now in prospect.' " See Swenson, et al., *This New Ocean,* p. 9. This attitude was to change during the course of World War II.

[46]*This New Ocean,* p. 517. See also Army Air Forces Scientific Advisory Group, *Toward New Horizons: A Report to General of the Army H. H. Arnold* (Washington D.C., 1945).

In my opinion such a thing is impossible and will be impossible for many years. The people who have been writing these things that annoy me have been talking about a 3,000-mile high-angle rocket shot from one continent to another carrying an atomic bomb, and so directed as to be a precise weapon which would land on a certain target such as this city.

I say technically I don't think anybody in the world knows how to do such a thing, and I feel confident it will not be done for a very long period of time to come. I think we can leave that out of our thinking. I wish the American public would leave that out of their thinking.[47]

Bush developed his argument at greater length in his 1949 book *Modern Arms and Free Men,* although he also qualified the argument in significant ways. No longer did Bush claim that no one in the world knew how to build a rocket that could fly 3,000 miles with an atomic bomb and land on a city. On the contrary, he granted the feasibility of constructing such a missile, but discounted it as utterly foolish because of cost.

We have already stated that a rocket can be made to fly far if one disregards costs. . . . It could then hit a target, perhaps within ten miles, perhaps even within a mile or two if all went very well indeed. . . . In other words, great range and payload can be attained at very great cost. If we are content to pay millions of dollars for a single shot at a distant target, it can be done in this way for any stated distance.

Cost was the determining factor. And the cost of this kind of weapon would be "astronomical."

As a means of carrying high explosive, or any toxic substitute therefor, it is a fantastic proposal. It would never stand the test of cost analysis. If we employed it in quantity, we would be economically exhausted long before the enemy.[48]

Dr. Bush's argument is directed specifically against conventional bombardment, but he also discounted the use of rockets for delivery of atomic weapons owing to the scarcity of atomic bombs and their great cost. Because of these factors, "one does not trust them to a highly complex and possibly erratic carrier

[47]Vannevar Bush, quoted in *Hearings, Inquiry into Satellite and Missile Programs,* pp. 822–23.

[48]Vannevar Bush, *Modern Arms and Free Men* (Cambridge: M.I.T. Press, 1968), pp. 85–86.

of inherently low precision, for lack of precision decidedly increases such costs."[49] Bush's position was supported by a well known authority on air power, Major Alexander P. de Seversky. In 1947, de Seversky denied the possibility of very-long-range missiles and concluded that bombardment missiles should only be used to further the offensive potential of air-planes. Short-range missiles were not apt to be useful because bases for these weapons located close to a potential enemy "will be untenable." Missiles launched from the safety of the American continent, on the other hand, will never make it to an enemy's territory. "Nor will we be able to launch them from our mainland, due to lack of range. Delivery by aircraft, therefore, appears the only solution."[50]

There were, of course, many persons offering opinions counter to these. Vannevar Bush himself explained that his discussion of the unlikelihood of efficient long-range rockets in *Modern Arms and Free Men* was occasioned by the number of commentators who had persistently predicted a coming age of long-range rocket warfare. Discussion of whether there are soon to be high-trajectory guided missiles spanning thousands of miles and hitting precise targets is pertinent, explained Bush, only

because some eminent military men, exhilarated perhaps by a short immersion in matters scientific, have publicly asserted that there are. We have been regaled by scary articles, complete with maps and diagrams, implying that soon we are thus all to be exterminated, or that we are to employ these devilish devices to exterminate someone else. We even have the exposition of missiles fired so fast that they leave the earth and proceed about it indefinitely as satellites, like the moon, for some vaguely specified military purposes.[51]

Bush's statements were contrary to predictions being voiced at that time by General Arnold, whom Bush likely had in mind. Arnold, it will be recalled, had requested the von Karman report on German technological advances. In his "Third Report of the

[49]*Ibid.*, p. 87.

[50]Major Alexander P. de Seversky, "A Lecture on Air Power," *Air University Quarterly Review*, 1 (Winter 1947):27.

[51]Vannevar Bush, *Modern Arms and Free Men*, p. 85.

Commanding General of the Army Air Forces," released in late 1945, General Arnold observed:

National safety would be endangered by an Air Force whose doctrines and techniques are tied solely to the equipment and processes of the moment. Present equipment is but a step in progress, and any Air Force which does not keep its doctrines ahead of its equipment, and its vision far into the future, can only delude the nation into a false sense of security. . . .

Improvements in aerodynamics, propulsion, and electronic control will enable unmanned devices to transport means of destruction to targets at distances up to many thousands of miles. However, until such time as guided missiles are so developed that there is no further need for manned aircraft, research in the field of "conventional" aircraft of improved design must be vigorously pursued. . . .

Today, our Army Air Forces are the recognized masters of strategic bombing. Until others can match the present efficiency of our own anti-aircraft defenses, we can run a large air operation for the sole purpose of delivering one or two atomic bombs. . . .

When improved anti-aircraft defenses make this trip impracticable, we should be ready with a weapon of the general type of the German V–2 rocket, having greatly improved range and precision, and launched from great distances. V–2 is ideally suited to deliver atomic explosives, because effective defense against it would prove extremely difficult.[52]

Having thus quite explicitly endorsed the future of intercontinental ballistic missiles in the Air Force, General Arnold proceeded to discuss weapons-delivery vehicles of even more advanced concept:

If defenses which can cope even with such a 3,000-mile-per-hour projectile are developed, we must be ready to launch such projectiles nearer the target, to give them a shorter time of flight, and make them harder to detect and destroy. We must be ready to launch them from unexpected directions. This can be done from true space ships, capable of operating outside the earth's atmosphere. The design of such a ship is all but practicable today; research will unquestionably bring it into being within the foreseeable future.[53]

The men who followed Arnold were not, however, so intrigued by missiles as he had been. Research and development

[52]Report of General Henry H. Arnold, "Air Power and the Future," in Walter Mills, ed., *American Military Thought* (New York: Bobbs-Merrill, 1966), pp. 449, 453, 455.

[53]*Ibid.*, p. 455.

projects in these areas were approved as long as they weren't too costly and as long as funds were readily available. When the time of budgetary squeeze arrived, manned bombers seemed much more important. Even General Arnold had seen long-range missiles as weapons of the future. In the same report quoted at length above, General Arnold had stated:

The only known effective means of delivering atomic bombs in their present stage of development is the very heavy bomber, and that is certain of success only when the user has air superiority. For the moment at least, absolute air superiority in being at all times, combined with the best anti-aircraft ground devices, is the only form of defense that offers any security whatever, and it must continue to be an essential part of our security program for a long time to come.[54]

If Arnold recognized the vital importance of maintaining "absolute air superiority in being at all times," it was hardly surprising that his less imaginative fellow officers would stress the B–36 and then the B–52 over uncertain missile projects.

Here again the newness of even jet aircraft should be stressed. Jets were seen as the weapons of the future; long-range rockets were considered pure dreaming. The Strategic Air Command came into being in the spring of 1946. The first two air forces assigned the new Command were hardly overpowering. Between them they constituted only nine bombardment groups and two fighter groups. Only three of the 600 aircraft were jet planes. By the end of 1947, SAC had grown to sixteen bombardment and five fighter groups, but few units were fully operational. In 1948 SAC received its first postwar bombers, including the huge B–36s. The B–36 was an enormous improvement over the wartime B–29s and B–17s, but it was still a propeller aircraft. The jet-powered strategic bomber was the primary goal of the Air Force.

In addition, if an Air Officer preferred manned aircraft to "Buck Rogers" missiles, it was easy to single out Dr. Bush's explicit statements and ignore contrary opinion. As Senator Stuart Symington was to say much later in discussing the decisions taken throughout this period, "At the time Dr. Bush was

[54]*Ibid.*, p. 456.

probably the most prominent scientist in the United States."[55] Of perhaps even greater importance, Bush, at the time *Modern Arms and Free Men* was published, was Chairman of the Department of Defense Research and Development Board (RDB).

The RDB was formally empowered to advise the Secretary of Defense as to the status of scientific research relating to the nation's security. It was composed of a civilian chairman appointed by the President and two representatives each from the Army, Navy, and Air Force. The RDB had been authorized by the 1947 National Security Act to replace the Joint Research and Development Board, an agency of the Secretary of War and Secretary of the Navy.

Before the establishment of the Joint Research and Development Board (JRDB), guided missiles coordination had been accomplished through a guided missile committee of the Joint Committee on New Weapons and Equipment under the Joint Chiefs of Staff. In August 1946 the research and development functions of the JCS were turned over to the newly formed JRDB, chaired by Dr. Bush.[56] Bush had been Chairman of the wartime Office of Scientific Research and Development. He had succeeded to the chairmanship of the JRDB, and then to the RDB. These positions gave him a great deal of influence and no doubt contributed to the lack of interest in long-range missiles at the highest civilian levels of the government.[57]

[55]*Hearings, Inquiry into Satellite and Missile Programs*, p. 823. Dr. Bush was also in favor of cancelling the air-breathing Snark and Navaho long-range missiles at this time. See testimony of Dr. J. Sterling Livingston, *ibid.*, p. 824. Referring to Bush, Dr. Livingston observed that in these hearings "you will find . . . that there are people who are highly creative at certain periods of time and then at other times conclude that creative things can't be done." *Ibid.*, p. 823. For Bush's defense see his testimony, *ibid.*, pp. 57–89.

[56]Memo written by General LeMay to Information Division, Office of the Director of Information, April 11, 1947. Air Force Archives, Maxwell Air Force Base, file 168.64–47.

[57]An Air Force history of weapons acquisition policy has stated that the Research and Development Board in the late 1940s was "inherently hostile to the military and openly skeptical of the Arnold viewpoint" (DeHaven, *Aerospace*, p. 13). Unfortunately, in an otherwise well documented study, this description is not attributed or otherwise supported. If the board were "openly

As early as 1947, then, funds limitations had placed long-range surface-to-surface missiles in competition with manned bombers. That competition was resolved by deciding that development of the long-range missiles would not be feasible in the foreseeable future. Thus resources should go to improving bomber capabilities.[58]

The policy of strongly maintaining forces in being and of continuously improving the capabilities of these forces through weapons improvements was given strong support during the latter half of 1947. At this time the final reports of the Joint Congressional Aviation Policy Board and the President's Air Policy Commission were issued. In September of 1947, when the Army Air Forces finally became the independent United States Air Force, these two reports were adopted as basic policies.

The President's Air Policy Commission (the Finletter Commission, after its head, Thomas Finletter) endorsed the Air Force goal of 70 combat groups as "the minimum forces neces-

skeptical of the Arnold viewpoint" regarding long-range missiles, that would have been one thing. So too were a lot of people. If the board were also "inherently hostile to the military," that would have been a different matter—and an interesting one in terms of efficient military operation and coordination. Regrettably, it has proved difficult to determine the truth of this contention.

It is known, however, that the Research and Development Board during the Bush period actively limited funds for military research and development. Only projects for which a positive military requirement could be demonstrated were to be maintained. (Interview with Dr. Donald M. McVeigh, Command Historian in Air Force Systems Command.) Unfortunately for the missile proponents within the Air Force, manned bombers appeared to be much more positive military requirements than did futuristic long-range rockets.

[58]It is well to note at this point that the funds shortage also had the effect of putting some manned bombers in competition with others, and particularly of putting future aircraft in competition with forces in being. The Air Force wished to make model improvements continuously in the B-36 while also developing at a steady and rapid pace the B-52 designed to replace it. To continue to implement model improvement of aircraft in being or already in production, however, implied an increasingly expensive production base. At the same time the B-52, an advanced heavy jet bomber, could be expected to experience substantially higher development costs than had been previously encountered. This created a direct strain which was only partially solved by charging model improvement costs to production funds. DeHaven, *Aerospace,* pp. 9–11.

sary at the present time.''[59] Under the heading ''The Requirements of the Air Establishment—Recommendations of the
Commission,'' the study observed,

The Air Force as presently composed is inadequate. It is inadequate
not only at the present time when we are relatively free of the dangers
of sustained attack on our homeland, but is hopelessly wanting in respect of the future . . . when a serious danger of atomic attack will
exist.[60]

The 70 groups called for were to be supplemented by 27 National Guard groups and 34 Air Reserve groups. Excepting the
Air Reserve, all groups were to be fully equipped, trained, and
ready for immediate action. Furthermore, the force was to be
kept modernized with the ''very best planes and equipment
available.'' Immediate readiness was vital because, in the event
of war, industry would be incapable of expanding quickly
enough to make up losses through the first year of hostilities.
The answer therefore was obvious. ''A reserve of aircraft in
storage must always be maintained.'' It was recognized that an
Air Force of these proportions (the 70 groups were expected to
include 6,869 front-line aircraft and an ''adequate'' reserve
would raise the total to 8,100 aircraft) ''would involve a substantial increase in expenditures.''[61]

[59]*Survival in the Air Age: A Report by the President's Air Commission*
(Washington, D.C.: GPO, 1948), p. 25. The Air Force Goal of 70 groups had
emerged early in 1945, before the close of World War II and before the realiza-
tion of the atomic bomb. During the next five years the 70-group goal was to
become sanctified in Air Force circles. (Huntington, *The Common Defense*, p.
373.) For an enlightening history of the evolution of the 70-group objective in an
atmosphere compounded of ignorance of the atomic bomb and assumptions of a
friendly Soviet Union, see Perry McCoy Smith, *The Air Force Plans for Peace*
(Baltimore: The Johns Hopkins Press, 1970), esp. chapter 5.
   To be fair, however, it must be noted that the principal goals of all three
services—Universal Military Training for the Army and the Navy's flush deck
supercarrier as well as the 70-group Air Force—had all been determined before
the close of World War II. As Huntington has observed, ''Whatever relevance
they had to the needs of the Cold War was fortuitous.'' *The Common Defense*,
p. 45.
   [60]*Survival in the Air Age*, p. 24. The origins of the 70-group Air Force, as well
as the role of the Finletter Commission, are also discussed in Walter Millis,
H. Mansfield, and H. Stein, *Arms and the State* (New York: Twentieth Century
Fund, 1958), pp. 147–48, 203–8.

Toward long-range guided missiles the report was respectful but cautious. The development of useful missiles for extremely long ranges was viewed as "still a tremendous problem." "The most intensive application of our best research talent, coupled with the expenditure of very large amounts of money" would be required before "we can hope to produce a pilot-less weapon of either class [subsonic or supersonic] that will have a reasonable chance of hitting a distant selected target." Nevertheless, it was recommended that research in these areas be given the highest priority, and not handicapped by lack of funds. Indeed, "what may appear to be over-generosity in appropriations now may easily prove most economical in the long run."[62]

Despite these latter suggestions, however, the tone of the report was quite clear. Manned airplanes, and lots of them, were extremely vital to the nation's security. They should be built, placed in service, and stockpiled as rapidly as possible. Innovations should be constantly encouraged and incorporated into the design. Guided missiles, despite the admonitions noted above, were clearly not so important. Their effectiveness, indeed their feasibility, as very-long-range bombardment weapons was not certain. Their expense, on the other hand, was very obvious and provided quite adequate reason for a slow, cautious approach.

From the evidence submitted, it appears that there may be some danger of over-running our basic knowledge in an effort to develop production articles too soon in order to justify the optimistic predictions of the "push-button warfare" protagonists. We must first be certain that we are on the right track and not permit ourselves to be led up blind alleys by too great impatience for results. There is a case where making haste slowly will certainly pay.[63]

The contradiction between the earlier note that overgenerosity at present might be best and the later call for making haste slowly was never formally resolved. Implicitly, the recommendations were clear. The language concerning missiles was obviously not of the same enthusiasm as the calls for the immediate

[61]*Survival in the Air Age*, pp. 26 and 25.
[62]*Ibid.*, pp. 82–83.
[63]*Ibid.*, p. 84.

construction of thousands of airplanes. A further indication of
the commission's cautious approach toward long-range missiles
lies in its relative assessment of the subsonic versus the supersonic efforts. The report stated that data supplied to the commission indicated a trend toward abandonment of the slower,
more vulnerable subsonic weapons. Noting this, the report observed that subsonic missiles "offer the most practical means of
testing and developing the intricate guidance mechanism for the
supersonic types," and suggested that "the technique be fully
exploited before funds for subsonic research are entirely eliminated." In other words, research should be continued, but in a
cautious, one-step-at-a-time manner. "Time and money will be
wasted unless a reasonable balance can be maintained between
research progress and development demand."[64]

The tone and substance of the Finletter Commission Report
was quite pleasing to the newly independent Air Force.[65] The
policy it advocated, building up forces in being while simultaneously developing follow-on weapons, was attractive. That policy
required funds, however. The Air Power Commission predicted
that implementation of its recommendations would increase the
overall military budget from the existing $10,090 million in 1947
to $11,590 million in 1948, and to $13,200 million in 1949. A step
was taken in this direction when Congress passed supplemental
appropriation funds for 1948 which exceeded the President's
budget. These additional funds were intended for purchases of
new aircraft toward the 70-group level.[66]

The immediate impetus for the supplemental appropriation
was the news in late February of the Communist coup in
Czechoslovakia. This event was followed by a cable from General Lucius Clay in Berlin warning that war might come with
"dramatic suddenness," and the continuing bad news from

[64]*Ibid.*, pp. 83, 84.

[65]The opening section of the report stated, "In our opinion the [United
States] Military Establishment must be built around the air arm. . . . Our
military security must be based on air power." *Ibid.*, p. 8.

[66]For a review of the political process behind the 1948 budget action see
Warner R. Schilling, "The Politics of National Defense: Fiscal 1950," in Warner
R. Schilling, Paul Y. Hammond, and Glenn H. Snyder, *Strategy, Politics and
Defense Budgets* (New York: Columbia University Press, 1962), pp. 40–47.

China. In the spring of 1948, however, President Truman announced a budget policy for FY 1949 which set the Air Force at 59 groups and promised stringent funding in subsequent years.[67] Under the combination of a restrictive budget policy and increasing international tension, the conflict between forces in being and long-range development projects for new weapons came to a head. And in this atmosphere the research and development function again suffered disproportionately.

The timing of the forces-in-being–forces-for-the-future budget squeeze was particularly unfortunate for the Air Force guided missiles programs. Research and development projects are by nature apt to begin at low levels of funding. In the initial stages of basic research and analysis, large expenditures are not necessary. If a project looks successful, funding requirements begin to reflect the demand for acquisition of hardware and testing facilities. This was exactly the position at which some of the missile research and development projects had arrived. In July 1948 the missiles personnel within the Air Materiel Command protested the repeated reductions in missile development funds:

It is quite obvious that even a minimum program of research and development in the field of guided missiles is extremely expensive. It is also quite obvious that this program has been increasing in level of expenditures over the past three years as we have proceeded from study, research and design into the fabrication phase where extensive testing is necessary. If the Air Materiel Command is to continue at a sound, economical rate of development on the present guided missile program, the level of expenditures beginning in calendar year 1950 for end item guided missile projects, component developments, and the operation and procurement of the necessary technical facilities to carry on these developments must be maintained at approximately $70 million per year. This will represent approximately 20 percent of Air Force research and development funds based on the present five-year research and development program. It must be recognized that the guided missile research and development program must be superimposed on the research and development program for aircraft, ground equipment and associate items. It represents a completely new job.[68]

[67]*Ibid*, pp. 46–47.

[68]Letter from Commanding General, AMC, to Chief of Staff, USAF, dated July 21, 1948. Subject, "AF R&D Program on Guided Missiles." DeHaven Document Collection.

By this time, funding for Air Force guided missiles research and development had fallen to a planned $11 million for FY 1949. General McNarney, the AMC Commander, requested that funding be increased to at least $21 million for FY 1949. If this were not possible, McNarney warned, it might become necessary to cancel the MX–775 Northrop subsonic 5,000-mile surface-to-surface missile and other projects.[69] The plea was to no avail. No immediate help was forthcoming.

In the situation of the late 1940s, a strong, prepared force in being was considered paramount by the Air Force. Other matters, including various long-lead-time weapons, were secondary. As Air Secretary James Douglas was to observe at a later date, "In 1947 and again in 1949, long-range ballistic missile projects were cancelled when the necessity for maintaining the deterrent bomber force dictated the use of all available resources for the purpose."[70] The Air Force emphasis was supported by Secretary of Defense James Forrestal, who embarked on a one-week trip to Europe in November 1948, to meet with allied leaders and American military personnel. On his way back to Washington, Forrestal composed a series of "Points for the President." These can be found in his diary. Among them was:

. . . the atomic bomb—its potency as a weapon should not be depreciated. Both Clay and Huebner [Lieutenant General Clarence B. Huebner, Commander, United States Army Headquarters at Heidelberg] believe the Russians do not want their people to know what it can do. Churchill has the same feeling. Clay says the Russians are constantly putting fear into Western Europe by talking about the tremendous power of the Red army, and we have a weapon far more terrifying which we are apt to underestimate.[71]

In his diary, the secretary expanded upon these points:

Throughout my recent trip in Europe I was increasingly impressed by the fact that the only balance that we have against the overwhelming manpower of the Russians, and therefore the chief deterrent to war, is the threat of the immediate retaliation with the atomic bomb. I have

[69]*Ibid.*

[70]*Hearings, Organization and Management of Missile Programs,* p. 5.

[71]Walter Millis, ed., *The Forrestal Diaries* (New York: Viking Press, 1959), pp. 537–38.

substantial misgivings that reduction in the potential of the Air Force in the long-range bombing field might be misunderstood both by the world at large and particularly by our only enemy. The Air Force will have the heavy bombers necessary for carrying the atomic bomb, but these atomic carriers will need support by conventional bomb groups.[72]

In December 1948, Forrestal developed two fiscal plans which he thought should provide an extra $700 million for military appropriations without breaking the ceiling imposed by the President. Operating from the views noted above, Forrestal proposed to spend the bulk of these new funds on six more long-range bomber groups. The logic of this proposal was that since the President's budget ceiling had greatly weakened the "balanced" forces which Forrestal advocated, the country was going to be forced to rely increasingly upon the atomic bomb. Thus it was all the more necessary to ensure the effectiveness of the strategic bomber force.[73]

Forrestal's views were transmitted to the Air Force and received favorably by the Senior Officers Board. The result was that in planning forces in being, this board increased both the number of long-range strategic bomber units and the number of heavy, long-range bombers in each squadron.

The Air Force had by this time modified a number of B–29s to carry atomic bombs. The Soviet Union was in possession of several B–29s, which had been impounded during World War II after their crews had taken refuge in Soviet Siberia. This fact gave added weight to support of the B–36 intercontinental bomber. This plane became the center of an intensive interservice controversy which came to a head in an extensive Congressional investigation in the spring of 1949. The situation arose from the Navy's strong disapproval of the cancellation of the first flush-deck "supercarrier." In defense of the supercarrier the Navy attacked the capability of the B–36, claiming the Air Force was not honest in its performance predictions.[74]

[72]*Ibid.*, p. 538.
[73]*Ibid.*, p. 330.
[74]See Paul Y. Hammond, "Supercarriers and B–36 Bombers," in Harold Stein, ed., *American Civil-Military Decisions* (Tuscaloosa: University of Alabama Press, 1963).

The result of the investigation was to clear the Air Force's name and provide increased support for the B–36. This was formalized in July of 1949 when the National Security Council recommended to the President that highest national priority be given to atomic bomb production and second highest priority to the B–36. Nothing was said of long-range missiles.[75]

[75] Harry S. Truman, *Memoirs,* II, p. 304.

3

The Interim Years, Part 1. Budget Cuts and Continuing Rivalry

THE YEAR 1949 had been a particularly hard one for military research and development projects. In March, Louis Johnson had succeeded James Forrestal as Secretary of Defense. Johnson soon came to be the foremost advocate of a Defense budget ceiling of $13.5 billion. As one commentator has noted, "By the summer of 1949 Johnson had become so fully committed in public to a far-reaching economy program in the Military Establishment that it was identified with him, rather than with the administration itself."[1] The original budget re-

[1] Paul Y. Hammond, "NSC–68: Prologue to Rearmament," in Schilling, Hammond and Snyder, *Strategy, Politics and Defense Budgets,* p. 292.

quest for fiscal year 1950 which Johnson came to support so strongly included funds adequate only to support an Air Force of 48 groups. This action would necessitate retrenchment, since by December of 1948 the Air Force had reached a total of 59 groups. Air Force research and development programs suffered more than their share of the cut. In an interview, Dr. Donald McVeigh talked of a cut of around $75 million from a budget of approximately $180 million.

For the next two years, until early 1951, the only long-range surface-to-surface missile projects within the Air Force were of the air-breathing, cruise type. These were the Snark, the Navaho, and the 500-mile Matador.

Furthermore, the priority ordering accomplished in June 1947, which had placed long-range surface-to-surface missiles in fourth place in a five-item list, was not noticeably altered. In late February 1949, a meeting at Air Force headquarters—which included members of the technical evaluation group of the Guided Missiles Committee, RDB, and Brigadier General William Richardson, chairman of the guided missiles group within the office of the Deputy Chief of Staff (Operations)—elicited the following view:

General Richardson brought out here that we do not expect long-range surface-to-surface missiles to be available or to be required at this time, but that air-to-surface missiles are desirable for enhancement of the long-range bomber in carrying out the strategic mission of the AF. DCS/O does not expect a serious interference in the carrying out of this mission from anti-aircraft guns or from interceptor fighters. They are, however, concerned about the possibility of an operational Wasserfall [surface-to-air, anti-aircraft missile] defense in the next five year period, and it is for this purpose that the requirement exists for the air-to-surface missile.[2]

At this meeting, General Richardson outlined current Air Force priorities. They were, first, guided missiles which enhance the capability of manned aircraft to carry out the strategic

[2]Memorandum for Record by Major James R. Dempsey, February 28, 1949. Subject: "Meeting of technical evaluation group with Brigadier General Richardson." File "Committee on Guided Missiles, RDB–1949." Box "Guided Missiles Committee." HQ USAF, DCS/D, GM Branch, National Archives.

mission of the Air Force. This included both air-to-surface bombardment missiles and a bomber-launched air-to-air missile. Second priority went to guided missiles to be used to implement the Air Defense mission of the Air Force. This category included surface-to-air missiles and fighter-launched air-to-air missiles. Third and last priority went to long-range surface-to-surface missiles. General Richardson made the point that terminal guidance was the primary limitation on all-weather operations, and that this was true for both piloted and pilotless aircraft. A member of the visiting technical evaluation group then asked if the development of long-range missiles should not be put off, since "we could do nothing with them that we could not do with manned bombers." General Richardson agreed that "the procurement of long-range missiles should be deferred." He did add the common qualification, however, that research and development of these weapons should be strongly supported so that the missiles would be available "when bombers could no longer do the job."[3]

The three-item priority listing offered by General Richardson in 1949 differed little from the ordering determined two years earlier. There were elements within the Air Force who were not pleased with this emphasis. They were, however, found generally within the middle grades of the Research and Development agencies, not at the Air Staff level.[4] Research and development personnel differed sharply in two ways from the analysis of General Richardson. First, they thought that manned bombers, and particularly subsonic ones, were apt to be significantly more vulnerable and at an earlier time than Richardson implied. Second, they saw the potential of supersonic (including ballistic) missiles in a much more optimistic light. The cancellation in 1949 of the Convair MX–774 ballistic missile project as even a high-altitude test vehicle was recounted above. Before that event some effort was put forth by Air Force personnel to garner support for the MX–774 among the Joint Chiefs of Staff.

[3]*Ibid.*

[4]Interview with General John Sessums. *Hearings, Inquiry into Satellite and Missile Programs,* p. 1877.

In late January 1949, the Guided Missiles Branch of the Directorate of Research and Development within the office of the Deputy Chief of Staff (Materiel) put on a formal presentation replete with intelligence summaries of enemy capabilities and films of Air Force Programs to a special committee of the JCS. The presentation opened with a clear statement of the central issue:

The keynote of the guided missile program is "Expense." . . . this will cost the Government, for the entire National Guided Missile Program, between one and two billion dollars. We can buy our missiles in ten years or twenty years—depending on what rate we wish to pay for them. There is enough technical competence in this country to solve our longest term problem before 1960 if we are willing to provide the dollars.[5]

The presentation then moved to the threat. A surface-to-air wasserfall missile was seen as an effective counter to the U. S. strategic bomber force beginning in 1952. It was projected that by 1954 the threat would have assumed serious proportions. The conclusion drawn from this evaluation was that "the surest way to penetrate enemy defenses is by the supersonic surface-to-surface missile." It was recognized, however, that "to have even a one thousand mile supersonic atomic carrier ready by 1954 would require an effort somewhat comparable to the Manhattan Project."[6]

The potential vulnerability of the manned bomber force had been long recognized within the Air Force. Indeed, first priority in the June 1947 ranking of guided missiles had been for bomber-launched air-to-surface missiles. As early as 1946 Army Air Forces guided missiles personnel had stated their opinion that "a successful anti-aircraft guided missile of 35-miles range is feasible and will be undergoing service test by 1949." They continued,

[5]"Guided Missiles Presentation to Special *ad hoc* Committee of JCS," by Col. M. C. Young, Chief, Guided Missiles Branch, Jan. 25, 1949. Box "Guided Missiles, Pilotless Aircraft." HQ USAF DCS/D, GM Branch, National Archives.

[6]*Ibid.*

It is necessary to assume that potential enemies of this country are at least as capable as ourselves; therefore it must be concluded that they will also have a successful anti-aircraft missile developed by that date. The conclusion to be drawn from such an assumption is that possibly as early as 1949 the delivery of a bomb load to a defended target by conventional subsonic bomber type aircraft will have become highly problematical.

This report discussed surface-to-surface missile alternatives and stated that recent advances in automatic navigation systems indicate "that within two years knowhow may possibly be available to build an automatic stellar navigation system accurate to within one (1) mile in five thousand (5,000) miles."[7]

Although this expectation may have proved optimistic, as were many other predictions in 1945–1946, the threat remained. First priority for supersonic air-to-surface missiles had not changed by early 1949, as noted above in discussion of the meeting between General Richardson and the technical evaluation group. Such missiles continued to be deemed vital in order to allow the manned bombers to stand off outside the range of enemy defensive missiles.

The Guided Missiles Branch presentation to the JCS accordingly proceeded to an evaluation of air-to-surface attack missiles. "Although it might be necessary to build a special airplane in which to carry it," the Guided Missiles Branch concluded that "a supersonic air-to-surface missile carrying the atom bomb could successfully penetrate enemy defenses if it had enough range." Furthermore, "by an all-out effort we could probably produce one by 1954 or 1955. Its range would be in the order of seventy-five miles."[8]

However, the Guided Missiles Branch continued, "the relatively short range makes the project look somewhat indetermi-

[7]"Prepared briefing for General Aurand." Dated only 1946, it was found in a March 1946 file. General Aurand was Chief of Research, War Department General Staff. The briefing is unsigned but includes the following identifying comment: "It is the considered opinion of the technical staff in the Army Air Forces Guided Missile field that . . . " Box "A–7 Catapults." HQ USAF, DCS/D, GM Branch, National Archives.

[8]"Guided Missile Presentation to Special *ad hoc* Committe of JCS."

nate in the matter of military worth." The idea was at that time undergoing "extensive evaluation" at the Air Materiel Command, and was to receive further consideration at Air Force headquarters by the Directorate of Research and Development. If the relatively short range undermined the project's military worth, the solution seemingly would have been to increase it. The presentation proceeded to discuss this alternative, but reached some unusual conclusions. "Longer-range supersonic air-to-surface missiles will take as long to develop as the long-range supersonic surface-to-surface missiles and so emphasis in this category might best be placed on the latter."

Then, the branch made an interesting comment on current Air Force projects: "Some of the studies of long-range surface-to-surface missiles look like special applications of air-to-surface missiles with mother aircraft designed for the particular purpose."[9]

In summary, the Guided Missiles Branch observed that the gist of the problem facing the United States was to produce a long-range supersonic missile for use as an atomic bomb carrier by 1960 or before, and also to be able to defend American territory against such missiles within the same period. It was estimated that this would require an average expenditure of about $64 million a year—a spending rate that looked quite high at that time, particularly in light of the restricted budgetary allowances then available and projected. The Guided Missiles Branch argued, however, that the cost was relatively economical compared to various aircraft programs, Navy aircraft carrier programs, submarines, armored division equipment, and the costs of such cold war operations as airlift operations and aid to foreign governments. Given these programs, and the potential security value of the proposed missiles, the cost estimates seemed rather small and the expenditure highly worthwhile.

Other studies of the relative merits of missiles and present and projected manned bombers were underway during this period. At this time the B–52 was under development as a follow-on strategic bomber to the current B–36. In late March 1949 a

[9]*Ibid.*

memo comparing the B–52 with a long-range missile was sent by the Guided Missiles Section, Engineering Division, Air Materiel Command, to the guided missiles division within the office of the Deputy Chief of Staff for Operations. The memo incorporated the findings of a study undertaken by the Guided Missiles Section to review the place that long-range missiles would take in National Defense. The review had been prompted by the approaching delivery dates, between 1949 and 1952, of several long-range missiles. The first missile expected was the Northrop Snark, a subsonic cruise weapon whose original project completion date was January 1, 1949. The Guided Missiles Section had decided to make a comparison between the B–52 manned bomber and the Snark in terms of relative costs to deliver equivalent bomb loads.

Before describing the results of this study, some background on the Snark should be provided. By 1949 the Snark had had an interesting if somewhat tortuous history. Northrop had been one of the seventeen contractors invited in late 1945 to bid on one-year study and research contracts "leading to the practical designs of ground-to-ground pilotless aircraft." In December 1945 Northrop submitted proposals for both subsonic and supersonic 5,000-mile models. In March 1946, a letter contract was issued to Northrop and work was begun on both the supersonic and subsonic vehicles. As related in chapter 1, in December of 1946, the recently started and relatively broad Air Force missiles program had been sharply curtailed. Projects were reduced from 26 to 17. Six more eliminations were made in the spring of 1947, and by the summer of 1948 the Air Force missiles program had been cut again to eight projects.[10]

The Snark survived, but not without changes. In December 1946, Northrop was told that because of the general reduction in R&D funds, it was necessary to curtail the scope of their project. To permit continuance of some part of the program, the AMC proposed that Northrop concentrate on the supersonic missile and delete the subsonic model. John Northrop, President

[10]Memo to Chief of Staff, USAF, from Joseph T. McNarney, AMC, July 21, 1948. In document collection appended to J. Allen Neal, *The Development of the Navaho Guided Missile, 1945–1953* (WADC, ARDC, 1956).

of Northrop Aircraft, was not pleased with the proposed cancellation of the subsonic portion of his contract. In early 1947, he visited Air Force Headquarters several times to argue for reinstatement of the subsonic missile. Northrop's arguments were that subsonic missiles could be produced much more cheaply and more quickly than supersonic weapons of the same range; that although the subsonic weapon would likely be much more vulnerable than the supersonic model, at least some of them would get through any defense; and that our having large numbers of the subsonic missiles would thereby deter another country from attacking the United States. Northrop's appeals were at first rejected by Air Force Headquarters, but his continuing representations appear to have prompted doubts about the wisdom of concentrating exclusively on supersonic missiles. The result was that headquarters requested the Air Materiel Command to conduct a review of the entire question of subsonic versus supersonic strategic missiles. The verdict was that the advantages of the subsonic vehicle in terms of cost and availability were not sufficient to place it ahead of the supersonic model, particularly as the subsonic weapon would have a limited tactical worth that would disappear completely once an enemy acquired air defense guided missiles, which were expected shortly.[11]

This evaluation was accepted at Headquarters and incorporated in the June 1947 priority ordering, which stated that there was no operational requirement for subsonic, surface-to-surface bombardment missiles. Northrop, however, continued to press his case in visits to Washington in late June and again in July. These finally bore fruit. In August, the Air Materiel Command was notified that the Northrop subsonic project had been included in the fiscal year 1948 budget presented to Congress and that money was available to continue the program. The reversal was formalized on October 18 by the Headquarters of the newly independent Air Force. Northrop was authorized to continue

[11] The discussion of Northrop's appeals is based on Perry, *Development of the Snark*, pp. 6–10, and from a memo from Major General Grandison Gardner, Deputy Assistant Chief of Air Staff to Commanding General, AMC. May 19, 1947. Found in the document collection appended to Perry.

the supersonic project at a slower rate while proceeding "at full capacity with the design, development and production of service test items of the subsonic long-range missile."[12]

There is no firm evidence available to explain this about-face. Perhaps John Northrop's arguments about the lag between the availability of the subsonic missile and its supersonic follow-on proved compelling. At any rate, the result was that Air Force Headquarters overruled the judgment of its technical staff that the Northrop subsonic missile would prove unnecessary and highly vulnerable while supersonic versions should be pursued. The Air Staff decided instead to pursue the more conservative subsonic missile and delay the supersonic developments.[13]

In comparing the B–52 and the Snark, the Guided Missiles Section of the Air Materiel Command employed several different standards. The bomber was considered to have a better chance against fighter interception after detection had taken place because it would be armed. This advantage was expected to disappear, however, as soon as the chief defensive weapon changed from conventional fighters to surface-to-air missiles or air-to-air missiles launched from radar-directed fighters. The authors of the review predicted that these defensive weapons would probably make their service debut in 1954. Furthermore, the memo noted that "intelligence reports indicate that the Russians may have an effective surface-to-air missile even sooner."[14]

The review then moved to cost considerations. At that time (late March 1949) each B–52 was expected to cost about $3

[12]Letter, Major General E. M. Powers, Asst. DCS/M, USAF, to Commanding General, AMC, October 18, 1947. Quoted in Perry, *Development of the Snark*, pp. 11–12.

[13]Robert L. Perry is unable to explain the Air Staff reversal on the project. He assumes that John Northrop ultimately sold his case at the highest levels of the Defense Department. Interview.

[14]Memo from Chief, Guided Missile Section, Engineering Division, Air Materiel Command, to Chief of Staff, USAF, Attention DCS/D, Guided Missiles Group, March 23, 1949. Subject, "Relative Costs of Bombers versus Missiles for Accomplishing the Long-Range Bombardment Mission." File "P–180—General." Box 111. HQ USAF, DCS/O, Assistant for GM, National Archives.

million. Including unit overhead it was expected that each Snark would cost about $150,000. Costs for training and equipping all crews lost in bombers, insurance and family gratuities for lost crewmen, air fields, service aircraft and facilities for bombers ("which decidedly exceed those for missiles"), maintenance and repair of aircraft, fighter escorts, and all attendant costs for training, facilities, and maintenance were not included in the analysis.

Using these figures, an analysis was made of the cost of delivering equivalent, large bomb loads by each weapon at different attrition rates. The range of attrition was set at from 3 percent to 13 percent, which seemed reasonable under expected conditions. The cost advantage lay with the bomber only at the lowest rates of attrition. Very early in the comparison the cost advantage shifted to the missile and then rose dramatically as the attrition rates approached the chosen upper limit of 13 percent. Since the condition of low rates of attrition "will not prevail if development of defense systems proceeds at the presently anticipated rate," the conclusion was obvious.[15]

No particular note was made of this study at Air Force Headquarters. Snark continued to be funded, but at a relatively slow rate. The MX–774 presentation to the ad hoc committee of the Joint Chiefs of Staff described above was also to little avail, as has been noted.

Another review, in April of 1949, discussed the merits of glide rockets versus the Navaho Ramjet program in the light of the Convair MX–774 rocket cancellation.

For ranges of over 3,000 miles, North American's studies indicate that the glide rocket is promising and worthy of future development and investigation. All authorities in the guided missile field agree that the rocket will be the solution to the satellite problem. If an ultimate goal is a 4,000 mile missile and the primary mission of the Air Force is bombardment from that range, and North American and Rand agree that the rocket is the best at that range, why does the Air Force spend time and money on the intervening ram-jet rocket combination?"

Three reasons or problem areas were offered: the required aerodynamics were not available, skin temperatures were too

[15]*Ibid.*

high, and guidance and control were difficult. The review continued,

The Convair proposal would attempt to solve these problems, which we must solve eventually anyway. . . . The guidance and control problem may not necessarily be as difficult as predicted. The flight time, and therefore time for errors, of a glide rocket will be only one-third that of the MX–770 rocket ramjet. The altitude will be only slightly higher. The higher speed of mach 8 will only require faster response rates of the control equipment for a glide rocket. The present inertial guidance systems under development can be applied to this glide rocket.

The large ram jet selected for cruise propulsion of the USAF interim long-range missile is a long way from a reality and further away than a large rocket motor to do the same job.

Ram jet development facilities are far more costly than liquid rocket motor development facilities.

There are rocket motors available today, which when combined in multiple units, would give a propulsion unit suitable for missiles of over 1,000 mile range. This cannot be accomplished by ram jets for some time to come.

The MX–770 will slow down to mach 1.1 in its terminal dive, making counter-measures more easily effected than against the glide rocket with its higher speed. . . .

Many authorities in the field agree, including North American, that the glide path rocket or ballistic rocket is our ultimate goal. No one yet has been able to disprove that the glide type rocket might be more efficient than the MX 770 rocket-ram jet combination. It is possible that the glide rocket for this range would be available as soon or sooner than the MX 770 vehicle.[16]

Later in 1949 another challenge to current Air Force missile development policies appeared. The RAND Corporation, throughout the summer of 1949, had been conducting review studies of its own in the guided missiles field. On September 19, 1949, a briefing was given by RAND at the Air Materiel Command on the comparative usefulness of long-range guided missiles powered by ramjets and by rockets. The ramjet missile then funded by the Air Force was the North American Navaho,

[16]Inter-office memo to D. L. Putt, Dir. of R&D, DCS/M, from Major Cole, April 14, 1949. Subject "Proposed Extension of MX–774 by Convair." File "MX–774." Box "MX–774." HQ USAF, DCS/D, GM Branch, National Archives.

the second of the two long-range projects in the Air Force program.

The Navaho (MX–770) was also a result of a successful proposal initiated in response to the Air Force invitation in late 1945. North American's original design had been for a missile with a range between 175 and 500 miles. In 1947, after the cancellation of the Convair rocket project, the Air Force decided to fund a 5,000-mile project at North American. This missile was to have lowest priority, after the 500- and 1,500-mile North American designs then under contract. North American had originally considered a rocket approach for the 175-mile missile, but by the beginning of 1948 the Air Force had begun to doubt the value of this rocket in light of an expected development cost of $58 million. The Air Materiel Command undertook a study to determine if a longer-range weapon could be accomplished for the "tremendous amount of money involved." The AMC determined that rockets "were not practical for guidance and structural reasons at range in excess of about 500 miles." Therefore, a ramjet missile "in the atmosphere" was chosen.[17]

By February 1948, the Navaho was a three-phase program, with all three phases pursued concurrently. The first version was a 1,000-mile air-launched (from a B–36) missile; the second was to be an improved version of the first, with a range of 1,700 miles; the third was to be a surface-launched missile with a range of 5,500 nautical miles. It was hoped that service testing of the first missile could be completed by 1956 so that procurement could then commence; the phase II missile was to be ready in 1958, and the phase III version in 1962.[18]

In the RAND evaluation of long-range ramjet and rocket missile types, comparison was made on the basis of performance, reliability, vulnerability and accuracy. The results, as summarized by an AMC engineer, were:

For all characteristics, the relative value of two-stage rockets was superior at ranges in excess of 5,000 miles, and when the four charac-

[17]Neal, *The Development of the Navaho Guided Missile*, pp. 6–7.

[18]*Ibid.*, p. 10. These completion dates had not changed by January 1950. Memo to Commanding General, AMC, January 30, 1950. In Document collection appended to *ibid.*

teristics were combined into a single graph, having the effect of multiplying the individual factors, the superiority was very marked.[19]

RAND personnel made a similar presentation, outlining in addition the general results of their several years of studies in the field of long-range surface-to-surface guided missiles, at USAF headquarters on September 26, 1949. These series of briefings "precipitated quite considerable discussion" in Washington about the value of the Navaho.[20]

The RAND conclusions were those that had been offered at AMC. The ramjet had a small superiority over rockets for only "a moderate spread of intermediate ranges where heavy, inexpensive payloads are carried. *For all other conditions*—short ranges, very long ranges, *small* or *costly* payloads, the glide rocket has superiority."[21]

After the RAND presentation at Air Force Headquarters, the Guided Missiles Branch within the office of the Deputy Chief of Air Staff for Development (DCAS/D) recommended that the North American Navaho project be continued at the currently planned rate. This was in keeping with RAND's conclusions which stated in part, "RAND does not recommend development of rocket missiles to the exclusion of ramjets or any drastic change in emphasis from ramjets to rockets."[22]

However, the Guided Missiles Branch also recommended that, "in view of apparent advantages of long-range rocket-propelled vehicles over ramjet-propelled vehicles," a glide rocket research program should be initiated at the rate of at least $1 million per year for its first year. It was further recommended that the Convair MX–774 project be reinstated to fulfill this program. Only test vehicles were to be built.

[19]Memo for record. Subject, "RAND briefing September 19, 1949." Written by V. S. Roddy, Guided Missile Engineer. File "RAND Douglas 1949." Box "Defense Systems." HQ USAF, DCS/D, GM Branch, National Archives.

[20]Office memo dated February 17, 1950. Written by Colonel H. H. Sands, Assistant for Guided Missiles, Aircraft and Guided Missiles Section, Engineering Division, AMC. DeHaven Document Collection.

[21]Memo to General Putt, from Majors Cole and Carey, Guided Missiles Branch. October 2, 1949. File "Boosters—1949, 1950." Box "Binac Computer." HQ USAF, DCS/D, GM Branch, National Archives.

[22]*Ibid.*

The Air Materiel Command personnel in charge of building the Navaho were not pleased with the implications of the RAND briefings. They considered the step-wise development of long-range missiles through the subsonic turbojet Snark and the low supersonic ramjet Navaho to be the most sensible approach. Ballistic rockets were still considered to be far in the future. Accordingly, within the Engineering Division of the Air Materiel Command, it was "believed desirable for us to defend our MX–770 program and the reason behind our work in the ramjet field." Early in December a presentation was made at the AMC headquarters and then in Washington, outlining the Navaho program and "the reasons for us not being actively engaged in the long-range rocket hardware development." During the Navaho presentation, in the words of the Assistant for Guided Missiles within the Air Materiel Command,

We agreed that ultimately, and by ultimately is meant the period after 1960, we might have enough knowledge of very high number aerodynamics, and control data at these speeds, to intelligently enter into a long-range rocket program. We do not have this knowledge now and feel that the ramjet range of speeds is about as far as we can go in the next ten years. This philosophy was accepted as far as I know by HQ USAF, and although I have no written approval of this thinking and our program, I feel that HQ USAF accepted the present plan.[23]

AMC engineers conducting the presentation also spoke informally with RAND personnel and decided that the RAND review "was primarily geared to that period after 1960" and that RAND "did not believe our present program should be reoriented."[24]

Having apparently gotten the above concession from RAND, the Engineering Division at AMC emerged from the presentation and counterpresentation convinced that the current ramjet program was satisfactory and that "both RAND and HQ USAF consider the matter concluded."[25]

As was noted above, RAND had not recommended devel-

[23]Office Memo, February 17, 1950. Col. H. H. Sands, Engineering Division, AMC. DeHaven Document Collection.
[24]Ibid.
[25]Ibid.

oping rockets to the "exclusion" of ramjets, nor had it suggested a "drastic" change in emphasis from ramjets to rockets.
Nevertheless, RAND did put on a formal presentation at both
AMC and USAF headquarters designed to demonstrate the
merits of rockets, which suggests that it did indeed favor some
reorientation of the Air Force program. Ramjets were not to be
excluded and the change was not to be drastic; but a change, if
only a moderate one, was obviously intended.

Despite the RAND presentation, however, no realignment
in the missile field was undertaken. The AMC Assistant for
Guided Missiles quoted above was correct in deciding that Air
Force headquarters had accepted the present AMC-sponsored
approach and that the matter was indeed again "concluded."
The Air Force continued throughout 1949 and 1950 to support,
in the field of long-range surface-to-surface missiles, only the
turbojet Snark and the ramjet Navaho.

On another level, however, the Air Force was quite interested
in long-range strategic missiles of any construction. It will be
recalled that during and immediately after the war, a number of
conflicts developed between the services over control of the
strategic bombardment mission. Much of the Air Force's opposition to the supercarriers planned by the Navy after the
war—and much of the Navy's interest in those vessels
—concerned their long-range-bombardment capabilities. This
same competition was reflected in the area of missile development. Some accommodation was made within the War Department before the passage of the National Security Act of 1947.
After the creation of an independent Air Force, the division of
labor and authority then in force was in many ways abrogated.

The Army Air Forces had generally held responsibility for the
research and development activities associated with guided missiles, but it was specifically construed as not controlling the
assignment of operational responsibilities for the missiles
developed. With the creation of an independent Air Force, this
arrangement was no longer satisfactory to the Army. The directive remained in force, however, until July 19, 1948, despite
intensive representations by Army personnel and lengthy nego-

tiations. On that date the Air Force was formally relieved of responsibility for the guided missiles research and development program of the Army, which service again assumed that function.[26]

The Navy had throughout this period continued to undertake missile projects according to its own interests, as evidenced by the competition between the Viking and the MX–774. That the Navy recognized the political nature of many of the missile decisions is also evident. Discussing tests of the Navy surface-to-air Terrier missile in the summer of 1949, the Navy test station reported to its superiors that "these missiles are being fired primarily for advertising and budget purposes. Newsreel coverage on these missiles is to be extensive."[27]

Various joint agreements aimed at coordination in the missile field had been worked out among the three services after unification. By late 1948 the Air Force had several agreements with the Army. According to them the Air Force would handle all air-launched missiles, surface-to-surface missiles used for strategic bombardment, surface-to-air missiles used in close support of ground combat operations, and surface-to-air missiles used to defend ground troops on the battlefield. It was known within the Air Force, however, that "the joint agreements are not completely satisfactory to some people, and an effort may be made to have them changed."[28] For example, one Air Force memo from late 1948 notes that the Army Ground Forces want the range division between strategic and tactical to be raised to 500 miles. The memo concludes, "It is considered that the army field forces have responsibility only for the destruction of targets which have a direct effect on current ground operations, and

[26]Self, *History,* p. 15.

[27]Memo from U.S. Naval ORD Test Station, Inyokern Calif., to Head, Aviation and Test Dept., July 6, 1949. File "Missiles Bu-ord 1949–50." Box "Missiles, Navy." HQ USAF, DCS/D, GM Branch, National Archives.

[28]Letter from General McKee, DCS/O to Captain Arnold at Pt. Magu, November 5, 1948. Box labeled "000 General." Files of HQ USAF, DCS/O, Assistant for G.M., National Archives. This latter comment specifically refers to an Army Field manual which apparently contradicts these agreements.

that such targets will not be found further than 150 miles from the ground front lines."[29]

As the Truman Administration continued to attempt to hold the military budgets at a stable level, and to the military quite a low one, there were several calls for greater coordination by the three services in the missile field, in order to effect savings. This led to a series of negotiations between the services, usually conducted, at least in the early stages, through the machinery of the Committee on Guided Missiles of the Research and Development Board. In the spring of 1949 several subcommittees of the Committee on Guided Missiles were appointed to review aspects of the guided missiles program.[30]

One subcommittee was appointed in January 1949 to review the national guided missiles program and, among other things, to "eliminate duplication and decide necessary shifts of emphasis" in research and development. The subcommittee consisted of two voting members from each service. The purpose, within the services, was to agree on mutual cancellations so that other or greater cancellations would not be imposed from above.[31] Previous meetings of the three services occasioned by lowered budget ceilings had resulted in the elimination of eight projects from the Air Force program.[32]

Guided missiles personnel from the three services met on January 14, 1949, and again on February 4. The Air Force examined all major guided missile items and decided to offer for cancellation the Boeing "GAPA," a surface-to-air, antiaircraft

[29]Memo for Record, written by John Brown, Chief, Guided Missiles Division, Guided Missiles Group. File "GM Policy 1946–48." Box "GM Policy from Higher Authority." HQ USAF, DCS/D, GM Branch, National Archives.

[30]It was one of these subcommittees which evaluated missile requirements for upper atmosphere research and chose to support the Navy Viking over the Air Force MX–774.

[31]Interoffice memo, March 7, 1949, Colonel Terhune, Directorate of Research and Development, to General Putt. File "Committee on Guided Missiles, RDB–1949." Box "Guided Missiles Committee." HQ USAF, DCS/D, GM Branch, National Archives.

[32]"Presentation to Special *ad hoc* committee of JCS," by Col. Young, January 25, 1949.

weapon, and the Martin "Matador," a 500-mile surface-to-surface missile.

In exchange, the Army agreed that its requirement for a long-range surface-to-surface missile would be met by the Air Forces' contract for the Navaho. The Navy cancelled a 2,000-mile missile project which before the meetings had not formally existed.[33]

To the Air Force, the importance of these coordinated actions was that it would retain control of the strategic bombardment mission. While the missile projects within the Air Force were not receiving particular emphasis, when compared to the expenditures for the development of new aircraft and modernization of existing aircraft, long-range missile programs in the hands of the other services might threaten the Air Force's primary function. They were to be taken over by the Air Force or eliminated if at all possible. If it was necessary to demonstrate superior Air Force missile projects, then the Air Force weapons were to be strongly supported. Thus the Air Force approach to long-range guided missiles had a dual nature—missiles were downplayed within the Air Force, while they were urged over competing projects of the other services.[34]

Despite this agreement, the Air Force continued to worry about those missile developments by the other services which might possibly intrude into the long-range strategic function. For example, an August 1949 Air Force memo charged that "The department of the army is making an all-out bid for control of a disproportionate share of the guided missile program."[35] Another memo in September observes that, "receipt of the navy's letter does not indicate acceptance by the USAF of the

[33] Interoffice memo, March 7, 1949. From Terhune to Putt.

[34] *Ibid.* In longhand at the bottom of this memo is a note to General P. (Putt) from J. S. (John Sessums), saying, "The important thing here is: USAF gets cognizance of the 'strategic' missile for the NME (National Military Establishment). Against this we lose GAPA-Boeing after substantial expenditures and progress." The interpretation offered above is supported by an interview with General Sessums.

[35] Memo, from Gen. Putt, Dir. of R&D, to DCS/M. August 23, 1949. File "Holloman AFB 1949–50." Box "Holloman Air Force Base." HQ USAF, DCS/D, GM Branch, National Archives.

idea that the navy will be permitted to develop ssm's of 'strategic' range, i.e., over approximately 500 miles."[36]

The Air Force reacted to these threats in kind.

An additional benefit accruing from programming the proposed guided missile units is the possibility of establishing more firmly the air force requirements for operational responsibility and control of such units. The value of this particular point cannot be underestimated in view of the current discussion regarding this matter. Since the air force feels that guided missiles are necessary for performance of air force functions, guided missiles should be incorporated in air force programming at the earliest practicable time.[37]

Actions aimed at coordinating service efforts, or in many cases mere discussions among the three services, remained centered in the Guided Missiles Committee of the RDB. Pressure toward budget tightening and elimination of unnecessary or duplicating projects persisted throughout 1949 and into the spring of 1950. Air Force judgments of one duplicative effort are revealing.

The navy is developing a 2,000 mile surface to surface missile, the Triton, for an overall research and development cost of at least $197,208,000, as compared with the $190,190,000 the air force contemplates spending on development of the 5,000 mile sur to sur navaho a–6. These comparative costs are interesting, of course, in the light of the navy's contention that the long range missile is not of prime importance.[38]

The Navy's response to Air Force criticism of the Triton was, "The Navy Dept. does not recognize the validity of the Air Force's objections to this missile on the grounds that it is not within the Navy's operational responsibilities. No such determination has been made by higher authority."[39]

[36]Memo from Deputy Chief GM Branch to Dir. of R&D, DCS/M. Sept. 9, 1949. File "Policy from Higher Authority." Box "Plans." HQ USAF, DCS/D, GM Branch, National Archives.

[37]Memo from Assistant for Guided Missiles, DCS/O, to Chief War Plans Division, DCS/O. Sept 26, 1949. File "Plans 1949–50." Box "Plans." HQ USAF, DCS/D, GM Branch, National Archives.

[38]Memo from Thomas Lanphier, Jr., Spec. Asst. to Secy, to Air Secretary Symington. Feb. 23, 1950. File "National Guided Missiles Program." Box "MX–1011." HQ USAF DCS/D, GM Branch, National Archives.

[39]Report of Special Inter-Departmental Guided Missiles Board. Feb. 3, 1950. File "Special inter-Departmental Guided Missiles Board." Box "Hurricane." HQ USAF, DCS/D, GM Branch, National Archives.

Despite the agreements reached in the spring of 1949, by early 1950 pressures had again mounted, both among the services and from Defense Secretary Louis Johnson. In response to the pressure for action, the Joint Chiefs of Staff on March 15, 1950, issued another set of guidelines. The new assignments were approved by Johnson on March 21. The most important result of this action, in the words of an assistant to the Air Secretary, was that

The Air Force now has formal and exclusive responsibility for strategic guided missiles. The Air Force retains responsibility for tactical guided missiles. The Army remains in the tactical guided missile field at the tolerance of the Air Force.[40]

At this point the Air Force had as continuing weapons development the Falcon (air-to-air), Rascal (air-to-ground), and Navaho. The Secretary of Defense had approved a JCS recommendation eliminating the Snark from the list of approved developments. The project was, however, to be continued, using existing and programmed missiles as guidance test vehicles.[41] The JCS directive also established an interservice group to serve in coordinating and expediting guided missile requirements. The group was ordered to "formulate and recommend to the Joint Chiefs of Staff a requirements program for guided missiles research and development, and for production of operational guided missiles," by September 1950. In a memo to the secretary of the Air Force, the Air Force assistant quoted above notes that this directive was

in effect, a dictate from the JCS to itself to arrive at a realistic priority listing for the research and development of guided missiles, and to do so soon. A subsequent verbal directive by Secretary Johnson that he wants the guided missiles program reviewed every ninety days tends to supplement the urgency of this directive.

[40]Memo, March 22, 1950. From Thomas G. Lanphier, Jr., Spec. Asst. to the Secy., to Stuart Symington, Secretary of the Air Force. Subject: "Analysis of JCS 1620/17 on guided missiles." File "GM Policy within USAF." Box "Guided Missiles, Pilotless Aircraft." HQ USAF, DCS/D, GM Branch, National Archives.
[41]Perry, *The Development of the Snark*, p. 16.

Again, the Air Force had retained responsibility for the strategic bombardment function. The matter was not permanently settled, however, and Air Force fears regarding the intentions of the other services continued, as the memo makes clear.

. . . It is worth noting that the recommended re-orientation of guided missiles projects leaves both the Army and the Navy in the design and study phase of development of missiles which could become competitors with the Navaho in the strategic field. These are the Hermes B-1 and Hermes II, test vehicles for the Army, and the Triton for the Navy.

In this regard, the reduction of a guided missile weapon project to the status of a test or study vehicle does not eliminate from nor necessarily reduce its cost to the research and development program. For instance, the Navy could go ahead with the Triton program under only slightly reduced steam—as could the Air Force with the Snark program—and come up at some future time with a missile developed close on to the status of a weapon.

It is important to remember that in the guided missile business the service that develops a missile tends to have a sound argument based on experience and technical know-how, for using that missile as a weapon—whether the missile falls within that service's operational responsibility or not. In summation, the air force position in the field of guided missiles is considerably improved by the JCS action. Improved, that is, to the extent that the air force now has a legitimate basis upon which to act in the extension, with guided missiles, of all its assigned responsibilities and functions. Needless to say, the license to act is footless without continuing exercise of that license in a highly competitive and critical field of research and development.[42]

More evidence of the same fears can be seen in the reaction of the Director of Research and Development to a 1950 proposal to limit the Navaho to component development only. In a memo to the Deputy Chief of Staff, Development, General Donald Putt stated,

Although I realize that you do not agree with the thinking presented below, I am compelled to forward this information because I am convinced that a grave error and mistake is being made with regard to the Navaho project. The program that you propose to follow with regard to

[42] Memo, March 22, 1950, Lanphier to Symington.

Navaho will play into the hands of those who would gladly see the future Air Force relegated to the position of a transport service.

Irrespective of the urgent requirements of the Korean situation or the Air Force buildup in 1950, the fact still remains that the Air Force and the United States need a long-range, strategic guided missile at the earliest possible date. To slow up the achievement of this objective to any rate less than that which the state of the art will allow is suicide to this project. . . .

Although the other services are now limited to ranges below those of our interest, in pursuing them they will have achieved completed missiles which, with relatively minor modifications and improvements, can be made into long-range missiles. By limiting Navaho to component development only, we will find ourselves in the position of having a bird in the bush, whereas the Army and the Navy have one in the hand, and any impartial judge will state that it is perfectly obvious that to obtain a long-range missile, it should be done by modification or improvement of one already in existence.[43]

One potential threat appeared in July 1950 when the Army Ordnance Department initiated formal development of a short-range ballistic rocket. This project eventually became the Redstone. The original goal of the authors of the project, and the von Braun group working for the Army at the Redstone arsenal, was a 500-mile weapon. The Army authorities decided—against the wishes of the Redstone group—to pursue an evolutionary program starting from the Hermes C-1, which was simply an improved model of the V-2. The goal of the Redstone arsenal therefore became a 200-mile missile, viewed as an extension of artillery. It is interesting to note that in this cautious, evolutionary approach, the Army planners acted much like their counterparts in the Air Force.[44]

[43]Memorandum for General Saville from General Putt, Director of R&D, Office of DCS/D, August 4, 1950. Subject: "Navaho." Tab U to *History of the Directorate of Research and Development*, Office of the Deputy Chief of Staff, Development, USAF. File K140.01, July–Dec. 1950, vol. 2. Historical Archives, Maxwell Air Force Base. Another Air Force memo of the time mentions, "a political move on the part of the Navy to discredit, if possible, the falcon project." (Memo from Putt to DCS/D, April 26, 1950. File "Missiles, Budget 1949–50." Box "Missiles Navy." HQ USAF, DCS/D, GM Branch, National Archives.)

[44]See Robert L. Perry, "The Ballistic Missile Decisions," paper prepared for the fourth Annual AIAA meeting, Anaheim, California, October 23–27, 1967, p. 8. Also Wernher von Braun, "The Redstone, Jupiter and Juno," in Eugene M. Emme, ed., *The History of Rocket Technology*, pp. 108–9.

There is little that differs in the Air Force analysis in 1950 from its position in 1946–1947. The strategic bombardment function was still the most important within the Air Force. The chosen means to accomplish the mission remained the manned bomber fleet and would continue to be so with the future deployment of the B–52. Long-range surface-to-surface missiles were not important within the relevant future of the Air Force. It was important, however, that other services not develop such weapons which would then compete with the Air Force responsibility and the chosen Air Force vehicles. Air Force distribution-of-responsibility agreements with the other services were designed to prevent such competition. By June 1950, the Air Force missile program was down to four projects from an immediate postwar high of twenty-six, and there was every indication that the program might be reduced further if budgetary restrictions continued to be imposed. It was in this environment that the North Koreans on June 24 launched an invasion of South Korea.

4

A Revealing Sidelight: Creation of the Air Research and Development Command

MOST OF the Air Force's research and development took place at or under the direction of the Air Materiel Command from the mid-1940s until 1950. At the Air Staff level, a directorate of Research and Development had been established within the office of the Deputy Chief of Staff, Materiel, on October 10, 1947. Other staff agencies with an interest in research and development, and sometimes an explicit responsibility for such work in their particular fields, included the Director of Armament (DCS/M), the Special Assistant for Guided Missiles (DCS/O), the Comptroller, and the Surgeon General.[1]

[1] Among areas assigned to the directorate of Research and Development was the Uniform Clothing Branch, which was transferred in the fall of 1949 from the directorate of Maintenance, Supply, and Services, DCS/M. Its assignment was to develop a distinctive uniform for the male and female military personnel of the Air Force.

As Air Force budget allocations shrank, one reaction within the service was to cut R&D funds sharply in order to maintain current forces in being and current procurement. Another result was an attempt to remodel and improve weapons in hand at the expense of development of future items. This procedure was not without its critics—particularly in the Engineering Division of the Air Materiel Command and in the directorate of Research and Development at Air Force headquarters.

General George C. Kenney summed up some of these feelings in a comment to General Vandenberg during an Air Force Review of its R&D procedures:

For some time I have been gravely concerned about the unsatisfactory state of Air Force Research and Development. There has been evidence from many sources that the Air Force is seriously deficient in providing for its own future strength.[2]

General Kenney's comment was included in a letter sent with the final report of the Air University Committee on Research and Development. He saw the serious deficiency in Air Force R&D as a result of three complementary factors: the recent heavy pressures of war, which caused a strong emphasis on immediate forces; the vast strides of science in recent years, which had made it necessary to know a great many different sciences, thus tending to make the old Air Force R&D structure obsolete; the need to maintain technical superiority in weapons, which required pioneer basic research in many fields that formerly had been the province of commercial or academic organizations.[3] Kenney therefore felt that the Air Force must change its outlook and reorganize its efforts in the R&D field.

The several civilian scientific advisory bodies to the Air Force also made complaints. Their criticisms had some noticeable results in the spring and summer of 1949. At the April 1949 meeting of the Air Force Scientific Advisory Board, the Air Force Vice Chief of Staff, General M. S. Fairchild, presented a state-

[2]Letter from General George C. Kenney, Commander, Air University, to General Vandenberg, November 19, 1949. File K 201–82, vol. 2, December 1954. Historical Archives, Maxwell Air Force Base.
[3]Ibid.

ment from General Vandenberg asking the Scientific Advisory Board to undertake a study of the research and development function in the Air Force and to make recommendations on how to improve the current situation. The Scientific Advisory Board responded by appointing a special committee under the chairmanship of Dr. Louis N. Ridenour, which looked into Air Force research and development programs throughout the summer of 1949. Its report, intensely critical of current Air Force practices, was presented to General Vandenberg on September 21, 1949.

The report was forwarded to General Vandenberg by Dr. Theodore von Karman, Chairman of the Scientific Advisory Board. Dr. von Karman's covering letter summarized several of the report's most salient points:

The committee found that the existing organizations, personnel policies, and budgetary practices do not allow the Air Force to secure the full and effective use of the scientific and technical resources of the nation. Neither do they allow the use of AF civilian and military technical personnel to full advantage, nor do they permit deriving the benefit that the AF should. . . . only USAF-wide understanding of the serious nature of these problems and concerted action on the part of the entire organization can ever rescue Air Force research and development from the progressive deterioration it is now undergoing. . . .

The Air Force presently has far too few officers with technical qualifications, despite the highly technical nature of the Air Force mission. Even the present inadequate number of technically qualified officers are not used now in the most effective way. Both of these difficulties can be traced to the belief, general among officers, that career advancement cannot be secured by excellence in technical work, that there is no sound Air Force policy to utilize highly-trained officers in technical jobs and that opportunities for promotion in and for technical work are far from equal to those offered in other Air Force duty. . . .

Proper organizatory measures and a definite reform in personnel policy must go hand in hand, and only both together can secure the expected results. . . .

Research and Development activities cannot be brought to full effectiveness without making corresponding sacrifices elsewhere in the Air Force. A decision to correct some of the deficiencies in the present research and development situation will be valueless, unless it is im-

plemented in terms of competent men, money, and effort; and such
men, money, and effort must come from a fixed, possibly even a declin-
ing, total Air Force allocation.[4]

This position was in opposition to the funds allocations recommended by Dr. Vannevar Bush. It was Bush's view that the
military services should engage only in research directly applicable to immediate or quickly expected military operations, while
basic research was conducted by such nonmilitary agencies as
the National Advisory Committee for Aeronautics and the National Science Foundation, which was then being created.[5]

The implications of the Ridenour Report, if not its outright
recommendations, struck hard at established Air Force doctrine
and practice. One of the most touchy of the report's suggestions
was certainly that research and development activites could not
be promoted "without making corresponding sacrifices elsewhere in the Air Force." This situation was outlined at greater
length in the full Report:

The most important single factor in securing effective Air Force research and development is continuity of support, both policy support
from the top command and budgetary support from year to year. Such
support, though well worth giving, can be given only at the expense of
other Air Force activities. . . .

[4]Letter, Dr. Theodore von Karman, Chairman, Air Force Scientific Advisory
Board, to General Hoyt S. Vandenberg, Air Force Chief of Staff, 21 September
1949. Letter was a cover to Report of a Special Committee of the Scientific
Advisory Board to the COS, USAF, "Research and Development in the
USAF" (hereafter referred to as the Ridenour Report). Contained in *History of
Separation of Research and Development from the AMC,* Vol. 2, Historical
Research Division, Maxwell Air Force Base, Montgomery, Alabama. File K
201–82, vol. 2, December 1954. Maxwell Archives.

[5]The first director of the National Science Foundation was finally appointed in
March 1951. The foundation had been conceived in late 1944. In June 1949, the
commander of the Air Materiel Command canvassed the directorate of Research
and Development for opinions on the idea of the National Science Foundation.
During this survey, approval of the legislation incorporating the NSF was expressed by Air Force Secretary Symington, and the Air Force members of the
Research and Development Board. Secretary Symington stated: ". . . to fill the
gap, the military establishment must for the present pursue basic research on a
broader scale. However, this should be an interim measure, and upon establishment of the foundation, which is expected in the near future, the agency should
undertake the major responsibility for basic research which has as its goal the
pursuit of knowledge for its own sake." Quoted in DeHaven, *Aerospace,* p. 27.

The Air Force should increase allotments of technical personnel for research and development. This can only be done by reducing the force-in-being to enhance the effectiveness of the Air Force of the future; but in the opinion of the Committee such a sacrifice is necessary and fully justified.[6]

It was obvious to the authors of the Ridenour Report that this kind of recommendation was likely to encounter widespread resistance, particularly from any agencies nominated for cutbacks. Therefore, the committee attempted to explain and defend its reasoning:

A reduced appropriation for the Air Force expresses the opinion of the Congress that war is not immediately likely. . . . If war is not imminent, then the Air Force of the future is far more important than the force-in-being and should, if necessary, be supported at its expense. When war seems imminent, the reverse will be true; but at such a time funds will almost certainly cease to be the limitation on programs, being replaced in this role by manpower.[7]

Having called for greatly increased support for technical personnel (including more personnel) and research and development directed toward future Air Force requirements and away from forces-in-being, the report turned to a series of recommendations. One was equal promotion rates for technical personnel and regular flying airmen. To this, General Benjamin W. Chidlaw, Commander of the Air Materiel Command, observed in a marginal note on his copy of the Report, ''Very doubtful point. I am perhaps a pessimist but I'll never live to see equal recognition.''[8]

Another of General Chidlaw's marginal notes is equally revealing of the Air Force's temper. Early in the report the observation is made that, ''Presumably, the present committee would not have been appointed if there had not been a considered

[6]Ridenour Report, Section 1.

[7]*Ibid.,* p. IV–3.

[8]The copy of the Ridenour Report which the author read at the Air Force Archives at Maxwell Air Force Base, Montgomery, Alabama, was received in 1954 by the Historical Office of the AMC from the office of the Commanding General. An AMC historian's note at the time states that the marginal notes were probably made by the Commanding General. On this authority they have so been attributed.

opinion that the research and development accomplishment of the Air Force could be improved." To this the AMC Commander observed, "Many people have given lip-service to the magic phrase 'Research and Development.' Very few of us have really fought for it—and made sacrifices for it."[9]

The primary recommendations of the Ridenour Report were for the creation of a deputy chief of staff for research and development, and a new air command for research and development. It may be recalled that in December of 1945 such an office had been created and General Curtis E. LeMay was appointed to the post. At that time the rationale for creation of the new post was that research and development was fragmented, disorganized, and underemphasized. The reader may therefore wonder what happened to that old office. The answer is that despite the high-level support given to formation of the first office in late 1945 and the appointment of a well known and respected officer to fill the position, General LeMay's office never became a homogeneous staff organization at the deputy level. Rather, "it was a special office or carbuncle."[10]

General LeMay's office had been staffed with only a very few officers and thus never handled the broad functions appropriate to a deputy chief of staff. For example, General LeMay's office never had concentrated under it the research and development staff activities of the Army Air Forces and later the USAF. In December 1947, the office was eliminated. In its place was created a directorate of Research and Development, within the office of the Deputy Chief of Staff, Materiel. There matters had remained until 1949.

As noted above, the recommendations of the Ridenour Report and the reasoning behind them were quite revolutionary. Those within the Air Force who were favorably disposed to the suggestions had some fear that the report might be easily dismissed as the impractical or uninformed visions of a group of long-haired civilian scientists. Therefore, it was decided to have

[9]Ridenour Report, Maxwell AFB, copy 1, Section 1.
[10]Air University Study, "Research and Development in the United States Air Force." File K 201–82, vol. 2, December 1954. Maxwell Archives.

a respected, high-level military group conduct a similar review.[11] One of the strong supporters of the Ridenour Report's conclusions was Major General Donald L. Putt, who was at this time Director of Research and Development in the office of the Deputy Chief of Staff, Materiel. Putt had previously been Deputy Chief of the Engineering Division, Air Materiel Command. This lengthy experience in the research and development arms of the Air Force had led him to several conclusions about the significant deficiencies in the Air Force programs in this area.[12]

On the other side there was strong opposition to the idea of a fully empowered DCS/Development from the Air Materiel Command (as indeed there had been opposition earlier in 1945 to the idea of a less-than-fully empowered DCS/R&D). General Chidlaw felt that with proper Air Staff stimulus the Air Materiel Command could perform effectively in this area without the supervision of a DCS/D. He believed that creation of such a new office might simply clutter the field even more and further dilute authority and responsibility.[13] In general, AMC personnel (apart from the Engineering Division) felt simply that research and development was an integral part of production and could not efficiently be separated from procurement. Putt and others like him concluded, on the other hand, that the immediate (and almost always apparently pressing) requirements of the Air Force-in-being tended to monopolize almost all the attention of the top staff of the AMC, and consequently almost all the available funds.[14]

General Putt took an active role in formulating and obtaining final acceptance of the Ridenour Report. He also supported the idea of a parallel effort by a top-level military group to promote broader respect for whatever findings resulted. This action was undertaken when General Vandenberg ordered that a committee

[11] Interview, Dr. Donald McVeigh, Historian, Air Force Systems Command. It is not clear why this original office never prospered. It is possible to speculate that a man of LeMay's temperament was not particularly happy in a research and development desk job.

[12] Letter to author from General Putt. February 16, 1972.

[13] Marginal notes on Maxwell AFB copy of Ridenour Report.

[14] Letter to author from Gen. Putt; interview, Gen. John Sessums.

under the auspices of the Air University be appointed to study the whole area of Air Force Research and Development. A committee was duly formed, consisting of General O. A. Anderson of the Air University as chairman, General Putt, and a representative each from the Air Materiel Command and the Air Proving Ground.[15]

The Anderson Committee conducted extensive interviews with appropriate Air Force personnel and spent several months in preparation of its report, which was completed November 18, 1949. The intention of those who initiated the committee, and who had gained the support of General Vandenberg, was to produce a document that would support the Ridenour conclusions. The committee member from the Air Materiel Command provided some opposition to certain of the Ridenour recommendations, as well as to the report's implied strong criticism of Air Materiel Command procedures in the areas under study. This was hardly unusual, and, as will be seen below, the language of the Anderson Report reflected the Air Materiel Command opinions at several points. Nevertheless, the general results of the Anderson Committee Review were as expected. The new report strongly endorsed the conclusions of the Ridenour study:

The United States Air Force is now dangerously deficient in its capacity to insure the long-term development and superiority of American power. . . .

We are not providing an adequate foundation within the USAF for the productive operation and healthy growth of the Research and Development structure. . . .

No positive working system is provided within the Air Force which assures the maximum interaction between strategy and technology. . . .

Research and Development functions are submerged and diffused in a logistics structure, resulting in the subordination of Research and Development to day-to-day operations. . . .

. . . Current emphasis upon day-to-day operational and materiel problems has been so great as to radically and adversely affect the long-term development of the Air Force.[16]

[15] Air University Study, "Research and Development in the United States Air Force" (hereafter referred to as the Anderson Report). File K 201–82, vol. 2, December 1954. Maxwell Archives.
[16] Anderson Report, Maxwell Archives.

The Anderson Report warned that the Army and the Navy might readily "take over responsibilities abdicated by the USAF." This was usually an effective ploy in arguments within each of the services. The Anderson Report discussed the results of such abdication and consequent role reorganization in terms of the general damage it would cause to the nation's security. The explicit damage it would do to the future of the Air Force was made quite evident, and intentionally so. The report dealt with the question of the numerous roles and missions agreements which had been worked out between the three services. Since the strategic mission had been in most cases reserved to the Air Force, opponents of the proposed new reorganization and reemphasis were expected to cite these agreements as forestalling any loss of responsibility to the other services. This argument was met directly:

Evolutionary processes and logic will ultimately dictate that the service possessing the combination of technical competence and strategic understanding within a particular field will be the service which controls and operates within that field. In other words, the current fencing for protective agreements will not solve the problem, regardless of the substance of any such inter-service agreements entered into.[17]

To meet the various problem areas facing the Air Force in this whole field, the Anderson Report recommended (indeed, said it was "imperative") that "drastic action [be] taken which will insure continuous impetus behind the Research and Development function." First, the matter of reordering current priorities and consequently current funding was discussed, with some sacrifices in current projects and in current operational strength envisioned. Second, the report strongly recommended the "immediate" establishment of a Deputy Chief of Staff, Development, under which all Air Staff Research and Development activity would come to be consolidated, as well as a Research and Development Command.

The existence of AMC and Air Staff opposition to these moves and the desire to placate such resistance can be seen in the following qualification:

[17]Ibid.

It must be emphasized that the conclusions [as above] . . . must be implemented on a carefully time-phased plan of an evolutionary rather than revolutionary nature, with the particular purpose in mind of not disrupting or putting undue burden on the existing structure and program, especially at the Air Materiel Command and in the Air Staff.[18]

Despite this stated recognition of the value of an evolutionary approach, the gist of the Anderson Committee Report and of the parallel Ridenour Committee effort was obvious. The research and development function in the Air Force was seriously deficient; personnel and funding practices should be significantly changed. To further these purposes, a new DCS/Development and a new R&D Command should be immediately established. The two reports were given a significant push on September 3, when a radioactive cloud was detected in the North Pacific and tracked to the British Isles. Analysis of samples of the cloud determined that an atomic explosion had taken place on mainland Asia in late August. This fact was confirmed publicly by President Truman on September 23, 1949.[19]

Action was not long in coming. General Order No. 9, dated January 23, 1950, from Hq. USAF, established the Office of the Deputy Chief of Staff, Development, and transferred the Directorate of Research and Development from the jurisdiction of the DCS/Materiel to the new office. At the same time, a new Air Research and Development Command was created.[20] Major General Gordon P. Saville was named the first DCS/D in January 1950. Major General D. M. Schlatter was shifted from his previous post as Assistant Deputy Chief of Staff, Operations (for guided missiles) to the new position of Commanding General, Air Research and Development Command.

Steps were soon underway to effect a general transfer of authority and responsibilities to accord with the new organizational arrangements. A memo was sent to the Directorate of Research and Development from General Saville saying that a procedure would have to be set up for the gradual transfer of

[18]*Ibid.*

[19]*New York Times,* Sept. 24, 1949, p. 1.

[20]History of the Directorate of Research and Development, DCS/D, Hq., USAF, July 1949–June 1950. File K 140.01, vol. 1, p. 10. Maxwell Archives.

that office's functions and responsibilities from the office of the DCS/Materiel and other functions from the DCS/Operations to the DCS/D. However, in keeping with the evolutionary conception of the changeover, the directorates of requirements and of Research and Development were to continue to attend the regular staff meetings of the DCS/O and the DCS/M as they had before. Furthermore, they were to continue to perform all services requested by these supervising offices as they had before reorganization.[21]

The idea of a smoothly operating, phased takeover of all Air Force Research and Development activities by the DCS/D and ARDC did not work out exactly as planned. Progress was slow. First, as noted, the realignment was intended to be "evolutionary," not "revolutionary," and this approach was originally widely accepted. Second, General M. S. Fairchild, Air Force Vice Chief of Staff, who had been charged with directing the procedure, died suddenly. A third very real constraint was the outbreak of the Korean war and the consequent focusing of attention on the immediate needs of the forces in the field. Furthermore, the Korean crisis heightened speculation about the chance of a general war, which also directed interest toward immediate forces in hand and short-term prospects. Beyond these causes, however, other factors were also operating to slow, and indeed hinder, the reorganization.

Considerable opposition seems to have arisen in some areas of the Air Force, particularly from the Air Materiel Command, whose large Engineering Division was to be transferred in its entirety to the new ARDC. The Air Materiel Command appears to have been in no hurry to effect the changeover. Rather, they seem to have envisioned the slow, careful process of evolution as taking place over a period of several years, during which time the Air Materiel Command would continue to exercise the vast majority of its previous responsibilities.

To the new Commander of the ARDC, General Schlatter, the phased transfer as implemented by the Air Materiel Command was no transfer at all—at least in the most important areas of

[21]*Ibid.*, p. 11.

his command. Personnel within the new command were understandably eager to assume their responsibilities and to begin business. The conflicting viewpoints became increasingly evident through the summer and early fall of 1950. Apparently believing that an evolutionary takeover would not prove satisfactory to the purposes of his command and the intent of the reorganization, General Schlatter asked the Air Staff to approve a rapid, all-at-once changeover. This view was disputed by the Air Materiel Command.[22]

The two opposing attitudes were considered by the Air Staff in the fall of 1950. A decision came on October 12, 1950, in the form of a memo from the Vice Chief of Staff to the Assistant Vice Chief of Staff and the Deputy Chiefs of Staff for Personnel, Comptroller, Operations, Materiel, and Development. Titled "Organization for Research and Development in the Air Force," the memo read in part:

Hqs. ARDC will be moved to Wright-Patterson AFB and assigned to the Air Materiel Command. Authority will be granted to permit the retention in the Washington area of an echelon of ARDC headquarters for planning liaison with appropriate air staff agencies pending move of the headquarters to its permanent location.

The Commanding General, Air Materiel Command, will be charged with the responsibility for supervising the organization and manning of the ARDC and phased assignments to it of all research and development activities and responsibilities now under its cognizance. . . .

The CG AMC will insure that by 15 May 1951 the ARDC will be capable of performing all administration and contractual functions required in the accomplishment of its mission, so that it can be transferred on that date to the status of an independent major command.[23]

This was not so immediate a change as General Schlatter had preferred. It did, however, set a terminal date of May 15, 1951, for completion of the reorganization. The friction between the Air Materiel Command and the infant Air Research and De-

[22]The above story has been pieced together from a number of sources. Interviews with General John Sessums, Col. Ray Soper, Dr. Donald McVeigh, and letter to author from Harry Jordan.

[23]Tab B, attached to *History of the Directorate of Research and Development,* DCS/D, Hq. USAF, 1 Jan. 1951–30 June 1951. File K 140.01, Jan.–June 1951, vol. 2. Maxwell Archives.

velopment Command continued, however, despite the Air Staff
directive. Differing approaches, mutual suspicions, and charges
of bad faith marked the relations between the two commands.
General Schlatter felt forced to complain again to the highest
levels of the Air Staff through the late fall of 1950 and into the
following spring.[24]

Partly in response to these approaches, in early February a
new directive was issued from the Air Staff specifically delineating the division of responsibilities and functions between the two
commands.[25] A further action aimed at alleviating the tensions
surrounding the changeover occurred when General Vandenberg appointed Lieutenant General J. H. ("Jimmy") Doolittle
(ret.) as his special assistant to oversee the AMC/ARDC reorganization. After visiting Air Material Command Headquarters
and reviewing the "gradual transition" process, Doolittle came
down strongly in favor of the ARDC approach of immediate
separation. He reported to Vandenberg that the new command
was doing well and could, if properly supported, handle the
responsibilities assigned to it. Accordingly, in late March 1951
Vandenberg issued an order stating that effective April 1, the
ARDC would no longer be assigned to AMC, as had been ordered the previous October, but would rather proceed to report
directly to Hq. USAF. In addition, all personnel, equipment,
responsibilities, and assignments currently under the control of
the Air Materiel Command's directorate for Research and Development were transferred to the ARDC.[26]

Thus, by April 1951, and despite the resistance encountered,
the new Air Research and Development Command was an autonomous, functioning unit. The effect of the reorganization was
basically to divide the weapons acquisition process into two
parts, with the point of separation occurring between completion

[24]Interview, General Sessums.
[25]Memo to CG, AMC, and CG, ARDC, February 2, 1951, from General
Nathan F. Twining, Vice Chief of Staff. Tab C, *History of the Directorate of
Research and Development*, DCS/D, Hq. USAF, 1 Jan. 1951–30 June 1951.
File K 140.01, Vol. 2, Maxwell Archives.
[26]Interviews with Col. Soper, General Sessums, Robert Piper (Historian,
SAMSO), and letters from Harry Jordan and General Putt. Alfred Goldberg,
ed., *A History of the United States Air Force*, p. 197.

of development and start of production. That exact point, however, was not always easy to define. What occurred was the evolution of a system of joint project offices for major weapon systems which had the effect of again bringing together the development engineers and the weapon producers. This procedure had been preceded by the team concepts earlier worked out by the Engineering Division and the Procurement and Production Division of the Air Materiel Command. After transfer of the Engineering Division to the new Research and Development Command, the team approach was continued and in fact expanded.

Despite this apparent continuation of past procedures, the creation of the new command did have its intended purpose. As an Air Force historian has stated,

Separation of research and development from procurement and production had the effect of alleviating the unbalance of emphasis between the related but distinct functions. Even though vast portions of the "development" process continued to be dependent on "production" funds, the creation of a new major command and of a key air staff element with specific responsibilities for fostering research and development tended to enhance both the prestige and the effectiveness of that function. Additionally, the custodians of the newly autonomous functions took their assignments very seriously, fiercely defending the integrity of research and development and actively promoting the creation of an effective field organization.[27]

During this same period, some organizational restructuring also took place at the Department of Defense level. General Putt, who had participated in both the Ridenour and the Anderson study projects for the Air Force, was a strong supporter of missile programs. The apparent neglect of some of the missile projects and of missile thinking in general by much of the Air Force had helped to convince him of the need for a reorganization of the entire research and development function. At the Department of Defense level, however, an organizational innovation was to be implemented directed specifically at the missile programs of the American military.

Reports of Soviet activity in the field of guided missiles had

[27] De Haven, *Aerospace,* p. 18.

been received regularly at Air Force Headquarters since the close of the Second World War.[28] Much of the American military was slow to admit to Soviet progress in the long-range missile field. In October 1948 an article in the *New York Times* stated that a long-range Joint Chiefs of Staff plan had estimated 1977 as the date that the Soviet Union would have intercontinental rockets utilizing atomic warheads.[29] This judgment may have resulted from a serious scrutiny of the intelligence reports. It may also have reflected a tendency to assume the Russians were acting as the United States was, but less competently. It may even have been a conscious or unconscious attempt to justify one's own policy choices by attributing similar choices to the enemy.[30]

[28] Interview with General Sessums.

[29] Cited in Warner R. Schilling, "The Politics of National Defense: Fiscal 1950," in Schilling, Hammond, and Snyder, *Strategy, Politics, and Defense Budgets,* p. 38.

[30] There is evidence that the Soviet Union began a serious effort toward long-range ballistic missiles as early as 1947, which had the approval of no less an authority than Joseph Stalin. At the March 15, 1947 meeting of the Council of Ministers of the USSR, Stalin ordered a commission to be formed to study the problems of long-range rockets. By September two designs had been submitted. Also by this date a Russian version of the V–2 was in production and an improved model was entering testing. By the summer of 1947 the Soviet Union had authorized a formal, although gradual, development program leading to a long-range ballistic missile. (G.A. Tokaty, "Soviet Rocket Technology," in Eugene M. Emme, ed., *The History of Rocket Technology.)* The Soviet ballistic rocket program continued from 1947 on, which was not the fortune of the Convair MX–774.

One could speculate that the "bomber gap" of the mid-1950s may have been at least partly the result of Air Force planners assuming the Soviets would build as many heavy bombers as they could, just as the Air Force was doing. It is interesting to note that even after Premier Khrushchev publicly stated that he saw missiles replacing manned aircraft, General Thomas White, Chief of Staff of the Air Force, claimed that "the Soviet manned bomber force constituted the greatest potential threat to the United States at that time [summer 1958] and would continue to do so for some time." (Khrushchev interview with James Reston, reported in the *New York Times,* October 8, 1957, p. 1. White quoted in Moulton, "American Strategic Power," p. 212.) It may also be interesting to recall that Khrushchev later partially retracted his statement, saying instead that missiles lessen the importance of manned aircraft, but do not make them obsolete. *(New York Times,* March 22, 1958.) In this case Premier Khrushchev may have rationally come to a different strategic evaluation, or he may have suffered enough pressure from officers of his own air force to have decided it was wiser to back down.

Reports of Soviet missile activity also surfaced in the public press. Such reports, and the comment they engendered, particularly when critical of the American efforts, doubtless had an effect in prodding the Defense Department to action. Early in 1950, prior to the outbreak of the Korean war, Senator Lyndon Johnson, a member of the Senate Armed Services Committee, issued an urgent call for a revision of the United States guided missiles program. Senator Johnson claimed that the Russians, and possibly other nations, were two or more years ahead of the United States in this area. Much of the prospective usefulness of the hydrogen bomb had been "nullified" by the country's tardy pace in developing guided missiles to deliver that weapon.

Our guided missile program is a minor, almost obscure, item in the defense budget. "Each of the three services has a guided missile program of its own—but, as yet, no really worthwhile guided missile. Publicity about some of our rocket research has created a largely false impression that we have missiles which would be used in the defense of this country. As for now, we have none."[31]

Similar sentiments were expressed a few months later by Hanson Baldwin, the military analyst for the *New York Times* and a man known to have excellent contacts in the Defense Department:

It is rather clear that Dr. Vannevar Bush was wrong when he wrote in his recent book that long-range intercontinental guided missiles would be prohibitively expensive. It is true that the finished guided missile of great accuracy and an almost human brain is still in the future, and long-range missiles of supersonic speeds offer major problems. But it is clear that those problems are being licked. Russia's progress in the guided missiles field is an unknown quantity in this country, but it seems probable that she is ahead of us in the development of missiles—particularly rockets for ground-to-ground (field artillery) use—and she has continued with German assistance work on longer-range missiles like the V–1 and V–2.[32]

This column may have been partially inspired by a news item a few days earlier quoting a refugee from a concentration camp in the Soviet Union to the effect that the USSR had already

[31]Lyndon B. Johnson, quoted in the *New York Times*, February 14, 1950, p. 16.

[32]*New York Times*, May 7, 1950, Section 4, p. 5.

constructed rocket installations in the Arctic and Baltic regions of the Soviet Union.[33]

In a later article, Baldwin discussed a number of errors of omission and commission operating to slow or limit the missile programs in the United States. These included interservice rivalries, excessive parochial possessiveness in terms of proving grounds and other facilities, competition for scientists and technicians, security restrictions, and—in the words of one of his sources—a plague of experts and boards and committees. Nevertheless, Baldwin noted that,

Some observers feel that the long-range guided missile—capable of at least bursts of supersonic speeds and of transoceanic range—has been developed already to a point where it is possible to say that the missile of tomorrow can deliver a ton of explosive on an area target in another continent far cheaper than can a piloted plane.[34]

Another *New York Times* article, this one written by Cabell Phillips, expanded upon some of the problem areas cited by Baldwin. After observing that the U. S. Government had worked intensively, but "at times confusedly," on guided missiles work, Phillips proceeded to describe the current situation:

Each service has at the Assistant Chief of Staff level a branch devoted to guided-missile work. They are free within limits to set up their own facilities and to devise their own developmental programs. However, acting as a sort of traffic cop over the whole business is the Guided Missiles committee of the Research and Development Board, the chairman of which is Dr. Clark Millikan, director of the Guggenheim Aeronautical Laboratory of the California Institute of Technology. The civilian and military personnel of this committee is [sic] supposed to minimize duplication and wasteful competition between the various services, and, at the same time, see to it that no important gaps develop in the research program. In actuality, the guided missile program, up to quite recently, at least, has been marked by a great deal of duplication. One of the difficulties has been the so far insoluble problem of allocating the various types of guided missile warfare among the respective services.[35]

This kind of publicity was not pleasing to either the military or the civilian high command. In order to answer the growing

[33]*New York Times,* May 2, 1950, p. 21.
[34]Hanson Baldwin, *New York Times,* June 15, 1950, p. 2.
[35]*New York Times Magazine* July 16, 1950, pp. 13 and 20.

charges of confusion, inefficiency, and lack of foresight, Secretary of Defense Marshall appointed K. T. Keller, President of the Chrysler Corporation, as a special adviser charged with coordinating all military activities connected with research, development, and production of guided missiles. It was announced to the press that

Creation of the new post was recommended recently by the Secretaries of the Army, Navy, and Air Force, and by the Joint Chiefs of Staff as a means of dove-tailing the separate programs of the various services and preventing waste and duplication.[36]

Mr. Keller was expected to "keep in close touch" with the Armed Forces Research and Development Board and the Munitions Board, responsible respectively for perfecting and producing new weapons.

Years later, during the period immediately following the launch of the first Soviet Sputnik, President Truman was to rely heavily on his appointment of Mr. Keller, and the latter's accomplishments in coordinating the missiles program, in defending his administration from charges of laxness in guided missiles development. Referring to the Keller appointment, Mr. Truman stated,

During my Administration . . . as soon as I saw the program lagging, due to inter-service rivalry, I called in a top industrial engineer, put him in full charge of the missiles program, responsible only to the President, and with instructions to knock heads together whenever it was necessary to break through bottlenecks [and] assured him I would back him to the hilt. . . . I told him to get them together, and if they didn't get together, I'd help him knock their heads together.[37]

The appointment, however, may have been as much a public

[36]*New York Times,* October 26, 1950, p. 1. As will be seen in a later chapter, appointment of a special assistant to oversee the entire U. S. guided missile effort was a common response to public criticism in this area.

[37]Article by Arthur Krock, *New York Times,* Nov. 1, 1957, p. 26. Also see *New York Times,* Nov. 14, 1957, p. 5. Truman stated in 1957 that Keller resigned early in the Eisenhower Administration because "they gave him so much trouble he had to quit." Keller, however, confirmed in 1957 that he left the Government at his own request, apparently because he thought the guided missiles programs were adequate and progressing well. *New York Times,* Nov. 14, 1957, p. 5; *New York Times,* Nov. 13, 1957, p. 4.

relations effort as a sincere and aggressive attempt at reorganizing and firmly coordinating the various guided missiles programs of the Armed Forces. This judgment is based on the fact that Keller served in a part-time capacity only and retained his job as Chrysler President.[38]

On the other hand, Arthur Krock has stated that President Truman first offered Keller more authority than the latter finally accepted:

The first powerful impetus for a concentrated guided-missiles program was given by two memoranda submitted to Secretary of the Air Force Finletter, in August 1950, by John A. McCone, then Under Secretary. . . . The main recommendation was for a "Manhattan-type" missile project under a chief with absolute authority and responsible only to the President. These memoranda and related documents were discussed with President Truman by Secretary of Defense Johnson. One document was a complaint by Stuart Symington, now Senator from Missouri (then, before and since disturbed over the missile program), that five different groups were working on one type of missile. The President and Johnson agreed on K. T. Keller of the Chrysler Corporation as the industrial engineer to take charge. . . .

President Truman made the offer to Keller . . . [as] recommended by McCone. Keller was to institute a Manhattan-type project, and, in the President's words, was to have power "over every building in the capital, the Pentagon included." Keller replied that first he wanted to analyze the problem, which he did for six weeks. He found 4,000 service and 11,000 civil workers engaged on the program. He decided that a Manhattan-type project would require a year to institute, at that much loss of time; also that his best contribution would be made by serving as an "appraiser" of the program instead of as its administrative "czar." On that self-limited basis Keller went to work with a staff that never totaled more than nine or ten.[39]

[38]The Harry S. Truman Library in Independence, Missouri, has only a few items relating to the Keller appointment. Two notations are, however, of interest. In a letter to President Truman on December 8, 1952, Keller expressed his regret that Truman was leaving Washington and undertook a brief summary of guided missiles progress with the comment, "You will recall you told me to produce something to knock the enemy airplanes out of the skies, and this was our first concentration." Keller was appointed in August 1950. On July 10, 1951, Keller requested a meeting with Truman, saying, "he had been on the job for eleven months and had not as yet reported to the President." "Requests to see the President," Official File, Harry S. Truman Library.

[39]*New York Times,* Nov. 1, 1957, p. 26.

The McCone memoranda were summarized in 1957 in a series of articles by Arthur Krock during the height of the initial shock from the Sputnik launching. The above quotation came in a first article. In a second article Krock outlined the specific memos. The first McCone memo was written August 10, 1950. In it McCone made the following points: all existing defense plans against the delivery of the atomic bombs recently demonstrated by the Soviet Union are "relatively ineffective." Therefore, the United States must "maintain in being at all times a powerful counter-offensive capacity, first, as a deterrent, second, to deal with the enemy who dares to attack us." Present U. S. defensive systems will not prevent a "devastating attack."

The solution to the problem described "rests in the development, perfection, and production of supersonic ground-to-air guided missiles for which a crash program should immediately be initiated." McCone felt that the program should also concern itself with the entire field of guided missiles. In his view American progress in the missile field to date had not met "the urgent need" for these weapons, and the "manner of organization . . . within the three services . . . and the very serious lack of funds" were primarily responsible for that situation. In this line, McCone observed that the Nazis had spent the equivalent of $1.5 billion in developing the V–2 rocket and had fired 1,500 tests. McCone then noted simply that when perfected, the ground-to-air guided missile would be a very effective "if not an absolute means" of defending the continental United States against an atomic attack, and that the long-range missile would be "an invaluable offensive and strategic . . . weapon." Finally, McCone concluded that

There should be created, with the "highest priority," a Project "under the most capable man who can be drafted . . . with absolute power over the entire effort," supplied with all the technical and other resources of the Armed Forces and those available among civilians. As a "link" between this Project, the Department of Defense, Congress and the White House, there should be a Pentagon Board of Directors. And the minimum initial spending on the Project should be "in the order of $2 or $3 billion."[40]

[40]*New York Times,* Nov. 5, 1957, p. 30.

McCone sent a second memo dealing with these issues to Secretary Finletter on August 15, 1950, outlining more fully the kind of organizational changes he envisioned. In the new setup,

All current and future funds for the purpose [guided missiles] now given to the armed services should be turned over to the Project Director and Board; also all existing contracts for research and development, for administration by the Director. He should be authorized to enter into any new contracts he deems necessary.[41]

Procurement of finished missiles was to be left to the service which required that missile in its particular mission. This suggestion was undoubtedly included in order to allay some of the fears of members of the Armed Services that personnel in the proposed project would control the roles and missions of the services. In McCone's view this new program would "be more like the Manhattan Project." McCone also appears to have been the one to suggest K. T. Keller for the head position. Truman then may have made the offer much along the lines McCone had envisioned. Whatever his options, Keller chose instead the much more limited role of analyst and coordinator, thus giving up both administrative and budgetary control.

The statement that President Truman "may have made the offer" as McCone had suggested is intentional. It would only have been natural that the service secretaries and the armed forces might have opposed creation of a new organization "like the Manhattan Project" outside of their control and designed to take over certain of their functions and responsibilities. Furthermore, when Keller apparently turned down the job of missiles "czar" (if indeed it was offered in that form) and accepted no budgetary control and only a part-time position as an advisor, he was granted the position on his terms. No other equally competent man was found to take the job with the full powers envisioned by McCone. Since budgetary control is often vital to effective policy control, and since budgetary allocations were jealously guarded and fought over by all three services during this period, there is at least room for doubt whether that control was ever actually offered to Keller. At any rate, the outcome of

[41]*Ibid.*

the McCone memoranda was quite consistent with a suspicion that there was considerable opposition within the civilian and military offices of the defense establishment. Thus, instead of a powerful, independent, budget-controlling office for guided missiles, which could dictate policy to the military services, there was created only an office for a part-time analyst and advisor without budgetary or administrative control. An attendant result was retention by the individual services, as well as the Defense Secretary, of almost all their previous authority in the guided missiles field.

In mid-1950, the guided missiles programs in general began to benefit from the budgetary loosening occasioned by the Korean war. Keller's appointment was also at least partially inspired by the greater interest in military preparedness after the outbreak of hostilities. Keller saw his job as leading to less missiles duplication and greater coordination, but he also recognized that he was expected to promote guided missiles. Among other acts, Keller approved production of the 500-mile surface-to-surface Matador and recommended acceleration of the Snark, Falcon, and Bomarc.[42] In the spring of 1951, an intercontinental ballistic missile program was again initiated by the Air Force with Keller's blessing. Despite these actions, the subsequent history of the ICBM demonstrates that Keller's appointment had little effect in substantially altering Air Force thinking in this area. Although virtually all of Keller's recommendations became official orders, this conclusion remains.[43]

[42] AMC Operations Report, Feb. 21–23, 1951. Document 252 in Appendix C to Self.

[43] New York Times, Nov. 1, 1957, p. 26. On Keller's impact, Dr. Wernher von Braun did testify in late 1957 that the Redstone program had begun to move after Keller was brought into the Pentagon. New York Times, Dec. 15, 1957, p. 42.

5

The Interim Years, Part 2. Technological Change and Organizational Rigidity

THE OUTBREAK of the Korean War caused an increase in defense spending. Although the immediate task was to provide forces and materiel for the operation in Korea, some of the new revenues filtered down to the research and development programs. The increase came soon after the creation of the new Air Research and Development Command. The new command had specific responsibilities for research and development, as distinct from production. This factor alone tended to promote research and development at a greater rate as the new organization began to exercise and promote its responsibilities.

The guided missiles program was assigned to the Research and Development Command. Early in February 1950 (probably to some extent as a result of RAND studies, made available to Air Force planners in late 1949, detailing the advantages of long-range rocket propelled missiles) Air Force headquarters had revised requirements for all elements of the long-range missile program.

North American's Navaho effort received the bulk of the emphasis, since it was the only currently funded program involving possible supersonic intercontinental bombardment missiles. The crux of the February decision was that North American should immediately renew efforts to develop a 5,500 nautical-mile missile with consideration of a variety of options: ramjet, rocket, and "other" propulsion modes; both surface and air launching; glide, ballistic, and aerodynamic cruise techniques; and all feasible means of solving the guidance problem.[1]

During the same period the decision was made to eliminate the Snark except for the use of existing and programmed vehicles for guidance testing. Faced with this action, the Northrop Company had developed plans for a "Super Snark," which would provide much improved performance characteristics. Soon after the North Korean invasion, the Engineering Division of AMC recommended that Snark be reinstated, incorporating the new plans. On October 16, Air Force Headquarters issued revised military characteristics which included most of the expected performance goals of the "Super Snark."[2]

International events in 1950 had a clear influence on this decision and on Air Force planning overall. After the outbreak of the Korean War, Congress authorized a 70-group Air Force. By the end of 1950, nearly $25 billion had been appropriated for defense, which was nearly double the original Administration request of $14.4 billion.[3] Supplemental appropriations requested by the President for fiscal 1951 totalled another $17.85 billion.[4]

Faced with the prospect of loosened budget strings, the Air Force in the summer of 1950 also began to consider reinstitution

[1] De Haven, *Aerospace,* p. 19.
[2] Perry, *The Development of the Snark, pp. 16, 19.*
[3] Warner Schilling, in Schilling, Hammond, and Snyder, *Strategy, Politics, and Defense Budgets,* p. 52.
[4] Paul Y. Hammond, in *ibid.,* p. 356.

of contracts in the long-range rocket field with Convair. Since the spring of 1949 Convair had had no such contracts. The original MX–774 had been cancelled in 1947, after less than a year of operation. A later authority to continue to build fifteen test vehicles had been voided in April 1949. Funding for Project MX–774 was continued during 1949 and 1950 by Convair itself, to the amount of approximately $3 million by the end of 1950.[5] During this period contacts were maintained between Convair and the Air Force in the field of long-range missiles, but these contacts were initiated unilaterally by Convair and consisted primarily of technical presentations ("sales pitches" in the words of Karel Bossart, Chief MX–774 engineer).[6]

Having been given indication of new Air Force interest, Convair, in October of 1950, made a presentation at Air Materiel Command headquarters which described a series of missiles that the company proposed to develop under Air Force contract. The program included missiles of varying ranges. Ironically, a ramjet engine was to be employed in the ultimate 5,500-mile missile. Convair had apparently decided that the Air Force was committed to the ramjet and inflexibly opposed to development of rocket-propelled vehicles at that time. Therefore, the company chose to go with the flow of opinion (and dollars) and at least get some contract money for its missile work. Furthermore, some Convair personnel felt that a ramjet missile contract would improve access to the Air Force planners and might thus indirectly benefit the cause of rocket development as well as directly supporting it through complementary work in guidance, airframe, aerodynamics, etc.[7] The Air Force was, however, thinking once again about rockets, a field in which Convair possessed most of the expertise available. In December 1950, the Engineering Division (soon to become formally a part of the new Air Research and Development Command) ordered a study that would determine the optimal means of developing a long-range surface-to-surface rocket. Plans were further made for the

[5] *Time,* January 20, 1958, p. 79. Interview with William Patterson, ex-Convair rocket engineer.
[6] Letter from Karel Bossart to author.
[7] Self, *History,* p. 94. Also interview with William A. Patterson.

initiation of a development program after the study had been completed.

This project was approved at Air Force Headquarters by the Deputy Chief of Staff, Development. That office directed the Engineering Division to award the study contract to Convair, in view of its unique previous experience and evident interest in the rocket missile field. A contract was determined upon, and appropriate technical instructions were issued to Convair in January of 1951. The project was labeled MX–1593. Initial funds were authorized in the amount of $500,000.[8]

Before this final decision was made to resurrect the rocket, some informal assistance had been forthcoming. In late 1950, Richard Swanson, Convair's Washington representative, visited General Putt, the Director of Research and Development, with a final appeal for funds in the rocket program. General Putt made available some funds for the project and then strongly supported the creation of the MX–1593 rocket research contract and urged that it be awarded to Convair. This was in the way of subterfuge, since an earlier approach to Assistant Secretary Arthur Barrows had been refused, but was legitimized after the assignment of the formal MX–1593 contract in January 1951.[9]

The contract, as formulated by the Air Force, was "a study and test program leading to the design of a long-range surface-to-surface tactical rocket-propelled missile with a primary use as a strategic bombardment weapon."[10] The Air Force had two alternative approaches in mind. There was still considerable skepticism about the possibility of developing a "pure" ballistic missile. Convair was therefore asked to study not only that approach but also the seemingly less difficult "glide" type, a semi-ballistic missile which is fired into an elliptic arc through the outer atmosphere but which glides to its target by the use of wings after reentry.

The glide approach was more favorably viewed within the Air Force for several reasons. Accurate guidance was still considered a major problem. A pure ballistic missile had to be fully

[8]Chapman, *Atlas,* p. 61.
[9]Letter to author from General Putt.
[10]Chapman, *Atlas,* p. 63.

aimed within minutes after launch. A glide missile, it was thought, could be controlled from the ground long after its engines had burned out. Therefore, it did not need to be targeted finally until the last stages of flight and it could be steered from almost any direction.[11] An equally great problem afflicting ballistic missiles was reentry. It was widely believed that a ballistic missile would simply burn up when it plunged back into the atmosphere and that protection for the nose cone would prove extremely difficult.[12] The glide rocket would avoid some of this difficulty because it would traverse the denser portions of the atmosphere at considerably reduced speed. The glide rocket would also be smaller, which would allow use of more common propellants. For all these reasons, it was expected that the glide rocket could be developed more rapidly.

Convair immediately began work on the two-part rocket study, and by late summer of 1951, its engineers had chosen the pure ballistic-type rocket. There were several reasons for this decision. Of primary importance was the belief that the slower glide missile would be too easy to intercept in light of expected developments in both ground- and fighter-launched antiaircraft rockets. This reasoning, of course, closely resembled the thinking of many Air Force research and development planners, who had long been predicting the emergence of very effective defensive weapons—particularly against subsonic or low-supersonic targets. The ballistic missile, on the other hand, was still considered unstoppable by any current or projected means. Other reasons for choosing the pure ballistic rocket involved technical design matters. To develop the glide rocket would require that the entire vehicle be designed to withstand the rigors of atmos-

---

[11] Two types of guidance were contemplated, mid-course and terminal. It never proved feasible to provide remote guidance to a glide missile. The exchange of data between either aircraft or ground stations and a guided missile is feasible only on a line-of-sight basis unless some relay station is provided. Given that the only feasible relay station would be a satellite and that this discussion occurred in a period when satellites were unthinkable, the best explanation here is that either gross optimism or significant planning blind spots were operating.

[12] Interview with General Sessums, who stated that as late as 1950, members of the Air Force Scientific Advisory Board told him that in his advocacy of ballistic rockets, he was promoting a comet that would burn up upon atmospheric entry.

pheric reentry, since the last stage of the vehicle's flight would be the wing-supported glide. This problem was significantly lessened with the pure ballistic rocket, since only the warhead would need to survive reentry. After separation, the remainder of the missile body could be allowed to burn up. For the same reason, the ballistic missile body could be designed for much shorter lifetimes—in effect, just long enough to adequately power the warhead, which could then be separated. The entire vehicle would require less smoothness of line, since it would spend only a very short time in the atmosphere.[13]

Convair's review was presented at Air Force headquarters on September 12, 1951. The main point of the presentation was the feasibility, at that time, of development of a long-range rocket missile. The Director of Development within the Air Research and Development Command observed, "The problems involved in attaining the end objective are enormous, but not insuperable, in the opinion of the Contractor and of this command."[14]

The Air Research and Development Command predicted that this ballistic missile would be available two or three years after the Navaho III ramjet vehicle then under development. That weapon was already experiencing delays. It appears that ARDC was at this point projecting an operational Atlas by the early 1960s. It was expected that the Atlas would be "far more invulerable" than the Navaho "because of its speed and outside atmosphere trajectory." It was therefore "strongly recommended" by the ARDC

that the program of study and development leading to an operational long-range rocket missile be adopted by the Air Force at this time and that a directive be issued by your Headquarters [DCS/D] together with the necessary Military Characteristics, putting the program into effect. . . .

It is estimated that approximately $4.5 million FY '52 funds will be needed to continue the program until September 1952, in addition to the $500,000 already allocated.[15]

[13]The Convair review of the two rocket approaches is discussed in Chapman, *Atlas*, p. 64.

[14]Letter from Brigadier General J. S. Sessums, D/Dev., ARDC, to Dr. of Research & Development, DCS/D, HQ, USAF, September 25, 1951. Subject: "Approval of long-range rocket missile program Atlas (MX–1593)." DeHaven Document Collection.

[15]*Ibid.*

In accordance with this judgment by the ARDC, the glide rocket study was cancelled.

A second letter was sent from ARDC Headquarters to the Director of Research and Development, DCS/D, on October 25, 1951, outlining the merits of the Convair ballistic rocket program and again emphasizing the need for additional funds for the project. This recommendation was not accepted. On November 16, 1951, a reply was forwarded from the Research and Development Directorate to the Air Research and Development Command, specifically denying the increased funds request and ordering a slowdown of the proposed Convair development program.

This headquarters does not concur with using any additional FY '52 funds on this project.

This headquarters does not agree with the rate of development outlined by Convair in their recent presentation. The proposed Atlas program should be revised and the funding recalculated to provide the completion of the preliminary test program in about five years.[16]

This directive stated that continuation of the Atlas program beyond the test stage would be contingent on demonstration during the test period program of success in such areas as the feasibility of adequate throttling of the rocket motors, accurate control of velocity, and the entire guidance and control system. Beyond this, the directive recommended that Convair employ a smaller test vehicle than that planned. Development of a missile which might have interim tactical use was discouraged. "It is believed that this smaller vehicle would more economically provide the answers which will be needed before more emphasis is placed on the program."[17]

One effect of the stringent restrictions on funds allocations to the Atlas program was that early solution of the problems mentioned by Air Force headquarters was made more unlikely. The Convair proposal was not particularly grandiose in terms of weapons development costs at the time. The $500,000 allocated

[16]Letter to Commanding General, ARDC, from Director of Research and Development, Deputy Chief of Staff, Development, HQ, USAF. November 16, 1951. Subject: "Program Guidance for Long Range Strategic Rocket—Atlas (MX–1593)." DeHaven Document Collection.

[17]*Ibid.*

to the project was barely enough to continue basic research studies and could provide almost no support for hardware development. The Convair personnel engaged on the project were convinced by this time that they were already far enough into the program to see that the Atlas was clearly practical and not an unproven risk. This view was supported by the Air Research and Development Command, the agency of the Air Force most familiar with the program. The view was not, however, generally accepted elsewhere in the Air Force and, most importantly, not at the Air Staff level. A further problem was that the ARDC was the newest command within the Air Force and, perhaps for that reason, one of the weakest in the Air Force inner councils. As late as May of 1953, an ARDC spokesman was to note the separate interests of certain Air Force commands and to complain about the relative imbalance in funding and authority between these commands.

Under the present administrative and budget conditions which prevail within the Air Force, it can be stated that, in the large, piloted bomber developments are supported by the Air Materiel Command with its large budget program, while pilotless bomber developments are being financed by this Command under a greatly restricted budget program.[18]

The situation described was even more apparent in the earliest period of ARDC operations. Nevertheless, the Convair personnel continued to make representations in behalf of their program at Air Force Headquarters in late 1951 and early 1952.

An eight-volume interim summary report on the Atlas project had been prepared by Convair in July of 1951 before the Air Staff denial of additional FY '52 funding. The final "Project Atlas Summary Report" was furnished to the Air Force in the first days of January, 1952. In addition, a verbal summary of the report was presented at Air Force headquarters on January 31, 1952. The gist of the report was once again that development of the Atlas ballistic missile was practical at that time, but that increased funding was required. If the funding were made avail-

[18]Letter from HQ, Air Research and Development Command, to Director of Research and Development, DCS/D, HQ, USAF, May 13, 1953. Subject: "Realistic Evaluation of the Snark, Navaho, and Atlas Programs." DeHaven Document Collection.

able, the Atlas should be able to proceed at a steady and efficient pace. The balloon type of body was deemed practical and very useful. The guidance system was adequate and improving. The gimballed motors were quite effective.

The Air Research and Development Command supported this presentation. In a letter to his old office of Research and Development (DCS/D), General Putt, who had become Commanding General of the ARDC, noted the "preponderance of advantage of ballistic over glide" rocket types. Furthermore, the ballistic rocket was eminently feasible within existing and safely expected technology. "With proper application of funds and priorities, it would be possible to have this missile in operational form by 1960." The ARDC Commander then clearly set forth his position.

It is the opinion of this Command that this project should be approved now as a strategic weapons system because of its complete invulnerability to all presently known countermeasures and because of the relative simplicity of the entire weapons system. The basic features of the vehicle have already been successfully demonstrated; namely, the Azuza guidance system, high thrust rocket motors, guidance control by means of gimballed motors alone, and the feasibility of the type of structure proposed for this pilotless aircraft.[19]

Proceeding to the question of the limited amount of R&D funding available, he pointed out that the Snark surface-to-surface subsonic cruise missile was absorbing at that time a large part of the R&D funds available for developing strategic missile systems. The Snark, however, was expected to become operational within the next few years and would not then require additional R&D funding. At that point the Atlas program could "be supported more heavily than is practicable now."

It was recognized that "the other strategic pilotless bomber," the Navaho, "has already provided additional capability to the Air Force and Army, in rocket power plants and guidance systems . . . and this capability will be enlarged in the ensuing

[19]Letter to Director of Research and Development, DCS/D, HQ, USAF. From Commanding General, ARDC, March 20, 1952. Subject: "Long Range Rocket Pilotless Aircraft Program, Atlas (MX–1593)." DeHaven Document Collection.

years." The Navaho was also demanding a large portion of the R&D funding available. Despite the apparent success of the Navaho program, however,

the Atlas program appears so promising that it is believed highly desirable to undertake its development in addition to Navaho. Atlas will use the power plants developed in the Navaho program. It is noted in this regard that the Air Force is undertaking the development of high and low altitude piloted bombers simultaneously, so there seems to be no reason why Atlas should not be undertaken because Navaho is a present requirement.[20]

The letter then turned to a discussion of current intelligence estimates of Soviet activities. It was noted that Air Force intelligence sources had reported that a 120-metric-ton (284,000 lb.)-thrust rocket engine employing a mixture of liquid oxygen and kerosene as fuel had been under development in the Soviet Union since 1947. In addition there were reports that a 250-metric-ton-thrust rocket engine had been under study since May 1951. Since the end of the Second World War, the Peenemunde complex had been under the control of the Soviet Union. In the spring of 1952, it was reported to be the scene of intense activity, and "very great precautions" were being taken to guard the installation.

In view of this activity, it is believed quite possible that the Soviets may be engaged in developing an inter-continental rocket missile, and if we delay our Atlas program, we may be running grave risks of being subjected to an intense bombardment to which we may not be able to retaliate.

The letter then closed with a very specific recommendation:

It is considered extremely vital that General Operational Requirements for a Strategic Ballistic Rocket Weapon of the general Atlas type be established immediately.[21]

It should be recalled that in November 1951, the Air Staff R&D office ordered a slowed-down test program that would have provided completion of preliminary testing in five years. Grave doubts were voiced about the adequacy of the rocket

[20]*Ibid.*
[21]*Ibid.*

engines and the entire guidance system. Four months later the ARDC Commander reported that most of these issues were already proven and that the entire vehicle was feasible. In addition he noted the "relative simplicity" of the whole weapons system. This last understanding was almost unknown at Air Staff Headquarters, where the prevailing view—despite the representations of the development engineers—was that the missile was incredibly complex and probably impossible.

From the ARDC letter the two thrusts of the pro-ICBM argument are clearly evident. First, the weapon is feasible and practical and, once built, will be very nearly invulnerable. Second, the Soviet Union appears to be very interested in the weapon and actively pursuing its development. This raised the possibility of a future devastating Soviet attack which could not be answered.

This most recent call from the Air Research and Development Command for establishment of a general operational requirement for a long-range ballistic rocket was referred to the Guided Missiles Committee of the Research and Development Board. There was evident skepticism within this body over both Convair's development proposals themselves and the planned rate of the development. In the late spring of 1952 the RDB approved a continuation of studies and component developments, but not a whole weapons system. Rather, the RDB proposed a cautious, phased approach to the problem, stressing basic studies and individual component testing. The board specifically directed that funds above the level they were thereby authorizing (apparently around $2 or $2.5 million) were not to be granted the project without prior approval by the board. The contractor was thus warned to proceed with caution and not exceed his budget for the fiscal year.[22]

The Air Research and Development Command personnel associated with the Atlas project were not pleased with this response. Nevertheless, they proceeded to do the most with what

[22]Letter, DCS/D, Director of R&D, HQ, USAF, to CG, ARDC, June 18, 1952. DeHaven Document Collection. Letter to author from Harry Jordan, SAMSO Historian.

they had. Basically they established a series of component development programs. By October of 1952, the outlook at ARDC for the development of an Atlas-type ballistic missile envisioned flight tests starting late in 1955. A first prototype of an operational missile could be available in 1957. Under this schedule, service tests of operational missiles could start in 1961. This was the most optimistic outlook available under the then current development program.[23]

It was increasingly evident that there existed two quite distinct schools of thought within the Air Force regarding the feasibility and usefulness of long-range ballistic missiles. One of the issues central to the argument over ballistic rocket feasibility was the whole question of the weight of the vehicle. Many of the missile's opponents said that to get a missile moving as fast as planned would take an enormous amount of fuel and consequently an enormous vehicle to carry it. Others said that the missile might go fast enough by itself but that the weight problem would become insurmountable when a warhead was added.

Warhead weight had been used as an argument against the ballistic missile since the earliest contracted studies.[24] Indeed, the most common explanation of the failure to begin a serious intercontinental ballistic missile program prior to 1954 is that the warhead weight precluded success before that date. It was claimed that high warhead weight and low yield would necessitate an enormous vehicle (to lift the warhead) and impractical accuracy. A very concise statement of this view was provided retrospectively by Air Force Secretary James Douglas in 1957.

In the late 1940s jet bombers were the weapons of tomorrow and ballistic missiles the weapons of day after tomorrow. At that time rocket development was not promising because of the great weight of the atomic warhead; then, when a scientific breakthrough produced a relatively small thermonuclear warhead, we were able to press forward with ballistic missile development.[25]

At another point, Secretary Douglas identified this "thermonu-

---

[23] De Haven, *Aerospace*, p. 20.
[24] Interview with William Patterson. Letter to author from Karel Bossart.
[25] Hearings, Inquiry into Satellite and Missile Programs, p. 841.

clear breakthrough'' as having occurred in 1953.[26] Air Force General Bernard A. Schriever, who was to become famous as the head of the Air Force crash ICBM development program initiated in 1954, has supported this summary in public testimony.[27]

Warhead weight was in many ways a false issue, however. The imminent arrival of ''light'' thermonuclear weapons did not eliminate Air Staff resistance to the ICBM, but simply caused a retreat to other arguments. The issue's falseness is shown by the plans, existing since 1948–1949, to develop nuclear warheads for the Snark and Navaho cruise missiles. This is clear evidence that warhead weight and effectiveness were considered adequate for long-range missiles.[28]

Operation Sandstone in April and May 1948 had demonstrated that new types of warheads were practical and that the doctrine of scarcity could be discarded. These findings were followed in April 1949 by a report from the Atomic Energy Commission that warheads had grown appreciably lighter.[29] Dr. Louis Dunn has stated that in 1949, while he was Director of the Jet Propulsion Laboratory at Cal Tech, ''it became obvious that one could develop an atomic warhead small enough to carry in a guided missile.''[30] In fact, President Truman noted that atomic warheads for guided missiles and atomic cannons for use by ground forces were available or nearly available as early as 1950.[31]

The arguments that atomic warheads were too heavy to be delivered by long-range ballistic missiles and too scarce to be trusted to such an unreliable carrier even if the warhead could be lifted, should have ended here. Atomic weapons were light

---

[26]*Hearings, Organization and Management of Missile Programs,* p. 5.

[27]*Hearings, Study of Airpower,* p. 1156.

[28]Interview with Robert L. Perry, the RAND Corporation, Santa Monica, California. See also Robert Perry, ''The Ballistic Missile Decisions,'' paper prepared for the 4th Annual AIAA Meeting, Anaheim, California, October 23–27, 1967, p. 7.

[29]Perry, *Development of the Snark,* p. 6.

[30]*Hearings, Organization and Management of Missile Programs,* p. 155.

[31]Harry S. Truman, *Memoirs,* vol. 2: *Years of Trial and Hope, 1946–52* (New York: Doubleday, 1956), p. 312.

enough and soon to be plentiful. But this was not to be. President Truman has also said that in February of 1950, "the military chiefs were going on the assumption that the test of the H-Bomb would be successful and that for this reason they recommended authorization to plan for full-scale production of facilities, equipment, and appropriate carriers."[32] ICBMs were apparently not considered "appropriate carriers."

Truman gave his approval to the development of an H-bomb in January 1950.[33] The Atomic Energy Commission concluded from tests conducted at Los Alamos in May 1951 that a thermonuclear warhead was feasible. This evidence plus the calculations of Edward Teller predicting light warheads should have given a boost to the ballistic missile and struck directly at the prime arguments of its detractors. A thermonuclear warhead would be lighter and much more destructive than its atomic predecessors. These qualities would make a ballistic missile more feasible, since it wouldn't have to lift so much weight, and the need for strict accuracy requirements would be lessened. The AEC apparently could not or would not predict a date when a thermonuclear warhead would be available. That it was coming, however, was little doubted. The "Mike" test explosion at Eniwetok in November 1952 proved the feasibility of thermonuclear technology.

The 1952 thermonuclear tests gave fresh support to the ballistic missile advocates who had said for years that such missiles were technically feasible and strategically vital even without thermonuclear warheads. Light, plentiful atomic weapons should have eliminated the need for exceedingly strict accuracy—particularly in light of the prevalent Air Force strategy of massive strategic bombing of the industrial heart of the enemy. The potential yield of thermonuclear warheads further voided the accuracy requirements.

New representations stressing the AEC results were accordingly made to the Air Staff by ARDC personnel. As a result, the Scientific Advisory Board was asked to undertake a review

---

[32]*Ibid.*, p. 310.

[33]The political and strategic dimensions of this decision are detailed in Warner R. Schilling, "The H-Bomb Decision: How to Decide without Actually Choosing," *Political Science Quarterly*, March 1961, pp. 24–46.

of the recent AEC tests in order to determine whether any changes ought to be undertaken in the Air Force missile programs. An ad hoc committee chaired by Dr. Clark Millikan was appointed to conduct the review. This committee met December 8–13, 1952. It did not recommend a basic acceleration of the entire program, as had been sought by the ARDC, but did suggest that the Air Force modify the current military characteristics for the Atlas project in light of present and anticipated increases in warhead yields, which would relax accuracy requirements and ease the problem of guidance development.

Prior to this point the c.e.p. (circular error probable—the radius of a circle within which 50 percent of the missiles aimed at its center are expected to land) had been 1,500 feet and required warhead weight varied up to 10,000 lbs.[34] The Millikan Committee now recommended that c.e.p. be relaxed to one mile and payload weight be specified at 3,000 lbs.[35] The committee saw no real urgency for the project, however, and disagreed with Convair's plan to build a very large test vehicle at once. Rather, the committee proposed that Convair (and consequently the Air Force) "pursue a three-step program leading first to a single-engine test vehicle, then to a three-engine vehicle, and finally to a five-engine operational prototype."[36] As the committee observed,

this step-wise program makes possible a review of the project at appropriate intervals. When sufficient basic information has been obtained, a re-evaluation should be made of the relative desirability of constructing the proposed Convair test vehicle or of proceeding directly with the prototype missile.[37]

[34] The original MX-774 project had included specification of a 10,000-lb. warhead. (Interview with William Patterson.) General Bernard Schriever has stated that the Atlas Component program in 1952 was designed around a 5,000-lb. warhead. (*Hearings, Study of Airpower*, p. 1156.) The 1,500-foot accuracy requirement was included in the specifications of the MX–1593 (Atlas) project let in January 1951. (Technical Instructions to Directorates of R&D, Procurement and Industrial Planning, and Supply and Maintenance, AMC. January 31, 1951. Document 251. In Appendix C of Self. Appendix C is File K 201–78, Historical Archives, Maxwell Air Force Base.)

[35] Report of the USAF Scientific Advisory Board's ad hoc Committee on Project Atlas. (Hereafter cited as SAB) DeHaven Document Collection.

[36] DeHaven, *Aerospace,* p. 21.

[37] Report of SAB meeting, December 8–13, 1950. DeHaven Document Collection.

The committee listed a number of continuing problem areas including structural weight of the vehicles and accurate control of the propellant–mixture ratio. This last was necessary to avoid masses of unused propellant. The committee concluded that a realistic estimate of the time required to attain a successful prototype military weapon could not yet be made. It noted the current Convair estimate of 1962 and observed that that was an optimistic date, based on "a high level of emphasis."[38]

The Air Research and Development Command took the recommendations of the Millikan Committee and drew up a revised program schedule for the Atlas project which would conform to the three-step approach. The new program was submitted to the directorate of Research and Development, at Air Force headquarters, in March 1953. The program outlined a ten-year effort. It was basically optimistic, foreseeing successful solutions to the admittedly difficult problems of guidance, propulsion, and reentry. A funding program was proposed for the ten-year cycle which was considerably greater than that being currently provided. This was, of course, necessary because the current level was meant only to support a basic research program with some component development, not whole vehicle construction. The differences between the Millikan group and the ARDC personnel actually involved with the Atlas project could not be more evident. The committttee believed that a slow, cautious program should be followed which might be speeded up only "when sufficient basic information has been obtained." ARDC, on the other hand, already considered the study phase an almost complete success and projected rising costs as actual test vehicle production was initiated. But ARDC had no reason to assume the funds would be forthcoming.

Indeed, at this time another event occurred which could only be expected to reinforce ARDC's plight. In November 1952 a new Republication Administration was elected. In January of 1953 it took office and immediately stopped expansion of Air Force forces-in-being and reduced the proposed Defense budget then before Congress. A new Joint Chiefs of Staff was ap-

[38]*Ibid.*

pointed and charged with conducting a major review of American military strategy and force requirements.[39] It was widely known that the review was expected to produce a rationale for reduced military spending. Waste, excess fat, duplication—any unnecessary costs—were to be searched out and eliminated. As in many such previous reviews, long-term research and development had cause to worry.

When the Eisenhower Administration entered office in 1953, Harold E. Talbott was appointed Secretary of the Air Force. As part of the economy drive, Talbott in turn appointed Trevor Gardner as his special assistant to look into research and development. Gardner was ultimately to have an enormous influence on the American ICBM program.[40]

One of Gardner's areas of responsibility was the Air Force missile program. The Millikan Committee report had been received differently by each of the various agencies of the Air Force. The slow, cautious pace it had advocated was approved by many members of the Air Materiel Command, Strategic Air Command, and Tactical Air Command, each of which might be expected to lose some of its resources and influence if long-range ballistic missiles were stressed. Elements closer to the research and development functions, and certain officers in the planning areas, were not pleased and indeed felt that further delay could prove dangerous to the nation.[41] Trevor Gardner came to agree with the second group.

After assuming office, Gardner had quickly begun to inspect the long-range missile program—particularly its assumptions and consequent military requirements specifications. The Millikan Committee had already recommended that the very strict accuracy and warhead weight requirements be relaxed significantly. Gardner felt that even greater changes should be implemented.

[39] Pressure from Republicans in Congress had helped to cause the changeover. The previous Chiefs were considered to be too closely identified with the Democrats. Glenn H. Snyder, "The 'New Look' of 1953," in Schilling, Hammond, and Snyder, *Strategy, Politics and Defense Budgets,* pp. 410–13.

[40] Gardner had been trained as an engineer. When tapped by Talbott, he was serving as President of the Hycon Manufacturing Company and Hycon Engineering Company.

[41] Interview with General Sessums.

Recent technological advances, particularly in the lowering of warhead weights, dictated more sensible specifications than the strict limits then in effect. "In the light of existing knowledge, the final performance specifications for the Atlas missile are open to serious question."[42]

In April 1953, Gardner requested a review of all the Air Force long-range missile programs, expressing concern about the most optimistic current estimate of ten years before the United States possessed a ballistic, atomic-armed missile with adequate guidance. The Air Research and Development Command was ordered to provide a response. It submitted a memo, entitled "Realistic Evaluation of the Snark, Navaho, and Atlas programs," to Air Force headquarters on May 13, 1953. ARDC determined that Snark, Navaho, and Atlas could and should all be continued. Snark, however, was considered most expendable. The ARDC concluded that because the estimated operational date of the Snark was 1958, "it is doubtful that it will possess much of a survival capability in its present configuration." ARDC did note that modifications might be made which would improve its effectiveness. If budget cuts became necessary, ARDC suggested discontinuing the reconnaissance model of the Snark. The Navaho was thought of more highly and deemed "essential to the operational capability of the Air Force." The Atlas ballistic rocket received even stronger praise.

The Atlas weapons system appears to be so promising because of its invulnerability that we believe its development should proceed as quickly as possible. There are many problems in connection with the guidance, structure and housing of the warhead, but our studies so far indicate that these problems can be solved. The ballistic rocket appears at present to be the ultimate means of delivering atomic bombs in the most effective fashion.[43]

Although the projected operational dates of the Atlas and Navaho were quite close, the ARDC believed that it was wrong to consider that Atlas duplicated Navaho since there was apt to be some slippage in completion dates.

[42]Trevor Gardner, April 1953, quoted in Schweibert, "USAF's Ballistic Missile," in *Air Force and Space Digest* (May 1964), p. 80.
[43]"Realistic Evaluation of the Snark, Navaho, and Atlas Programs."

The Snark was also recommended for continuation, despite hesitancy and skepticism. The ARDC evaluation may have reflected the pressures of sunk costs and the identification of certain ARDC personnel with each of these weapons. Further, Snark represented the only imminent long-range missile program that was expected to be "easily" completed. Snark demonstrated a potentially deployable long-range missile—and would perhaps quiet critics of Air Force foot-dragging. Another influence may have been the simple organizational reaction of not wanting to lose any current projects, and hence funds. If it was admitted that some current project was not necessary, funds intended for that project might simply be withdrawn instead of being freed for other use by the ARDC.[44]

The realistic evaluation did, however, make certain very telling points concerning the feasibility and likelihood of new weapons development and operational deployment.

The ARDC long-range missile development program is aimed at achieving maximum capability for the next 15 to 20 years. It is based on the general premise that during this period pilotless aircraft will probably replace piloted aircraft for most strategic purposes, so that both types must be developed until this premise has been clearly demonstrated. *It is evident that if the pilotless bomber developments are not supported, then, of course, they will not be available to replace manned bombers.* Under the present administration and budget conditions which prevail within the Air Force, it can be stated that, in the large, piloted bomber developments are supported by the Air Materiel Command with its large budget program, while pilotless bomber developments are being financed by this Command under a greatly restricted budget program.[45]

[44]The Snark was finally to become operational in 1958, only to be phased out a few years later. An interesting comment on the longevity of the Snark has been provided by Dr. Herbert York. "We realized, several years before Snark became operational, that it would become obsolete by the time it was finally deployed, and repeated recommendations for dropping the project were made. However, in this case as in so many others, the momentum of the project and the politics which surrounded it made it impossible to do so." [Herbert York, *Race to Oblivion* (New York: Simon and Schuster, 1970), p. 80.] Dr. York was a member of the von Neumann Committee, which will be discussed at length later in this study. He later served as Director of Department of Defense Research and Engineering. The "we" in the quoted passage refers to the von Neumann Committee. (Letter to author from Herbert York, December 1, 1971.)
[45]Memo, ARDC to Dir. R&D, May 13, 1953. DeHaven Document Collection. (Emphasis added.)

Here was precisely the crux of the long-range-missile–manned-bomber controversy. If the missile projects were not funded, then the missiles would not be built. This seems obvious, but it was an observation the ARDC nevertheless felt obliged to make again and again. There was a form of self-fulfilling prophecy operating in the statements of certain Air Force planners that long-range ballistic missiles were so unlikely as to be impossible or so hard to guide as to be useless, and that money should not therefore be wasted on them. If the money was not allocated to work on the problems associated with the new weapons, the problems would not be looked at, much less solved. If the continued existence of the problem was then employed as justification for not providing funding for the weapon, the circle was complete. What should have been an obvious lesson—that no basically new weapon system could be economically justified in the earliest stages of its development, that economic comparisons could and indeed must be made eventually, but that they could not be conducted adequately before technically perfected models were available for the comparison —was not widely accepted.

The second major point made by the ARDC, actually a subpoint to the issue discussed above, was simply that the AMC had a large budget with which it built piloted airplanes, while the ARDC, despite the good intentions surrounding its inception three years before, was still operating "under a greatly restricted budget program" in its attempts to develop pilotless systems.

This reasoning had little effect upon the Air Staff. The detailed program suggested by the ARDC in March and amplified by the "Realistic Evaluation" provided for Trevor Gardner's use was discussed at some length at Air Force Headquarters. The result was much the same as that encountered by previous ARDC calls for increased emphasis for the Atlas project. The reply sent to the ARDC from Major General Yates, Director of R&D (Deputy Chief of Staff, Development) approved the plan "in principle" for the purpose of "initiating the development program." The directed approach, however, was to be noticeably different from the ARDC proposal.

It is desired that your Headquarters submit a revised development plan which will incorporate a slowed down budgeting plan. It is extremely important that this expensive program be carried on at a relatively slow rate with increases planned only on the accomplishment of the several difficult phases of the program.

A considerably slower rate than previously contemplated must be established. It would be helpful if your development plan would indicate the amount of production support contemplated under the most conservative ground rules for the use of production funds in this connection. Your presentation to the Research and Development Board should reflect revised programming estimates and a longer period of time for development.[46]

General Yates noted that the ARDC proposal was an optimum for the next decade. He accordingly instructed that "Your initial program should not be aimed at a deadline of 1963, but more on a logical series of developments which may later permit augmentation to speed up the development."[47]

These instructions were a very clear directive for a significantly slowed-down long-range ballistic missile program. As such they were not happily received at ARDC. They were, nevertheless, clear orders. The ARDC sent a reply to Air Force headquarters on July 9 noting that some time and effort would be required to develop a reordered Atlas program to accord with the headquarters instructions.[48] Approximately two months later a revised development plan incorporating the slowdown directives was submitted and approved.

By the summer of 1953, then, the resurrected Convair long-range ballistic rocket project had existed for two and a half years but had made little real progress. The project had been marked through these years by a series of recalculations of funds and directed slowdowns and stretchouts. A conservative fiscal system of cautious, gradual component development and testing had governed the project. The contract with Convair had been initiated in January 1951 as a six-month study program. Convair

[46]Memo to Commander ARDC, from Major General D. N. Yates, Director, R&D, DCS/D. June 22, 1953. DeHaven Document Collection.
[47]*Ibid.*
[48]Memo, ARDC to Directorate of R&D, July 9, 1953. DeHaven Document Collection.

had submitted an interim report on schedule in July. This report, which described the feasibility and merits of the long-range ballistic rocket, was approved by the Air Research and Development Command at that time. The program remained at this stage, however, for a year while the ARDC attempted to convince Air Force headquarters of its validity. This period, and indeed the whole period 1950–1954, was characterized by ARDC attempts to obtain approval and, more importantly, adequate funding to support the program and by Air Staff resistance to such efforts.

A review of the various actions would probably be helpful here. ARDC made a formal request for authority in September 1951, including a request for additional funds for fiscal year 1952. This request was denied by Air Force headquarters, which office also opposed the proposed rate of development and certain aspects of the development program itself. The Directorate of Research and Development dictated a revision of the proposed program funding, and a stretchout of the project. It was suggested that ARDC plan that the preliminary test phases be completed in approximately five years.

New studies were undertaken by ARDC and a new program proposal was submitted in March 1952. This proposal was forwarded to the Research and Development Board, which approved the project in May 1952 as "a study and/or component development project." Stringent limitations were placed on the funding, however, and it was explicitly directed that no new funds were to be added to the project without approval by the board.

Later that fall the Millikan Committee of the Air Force Scientific Advisory Board approved a three-phase program that was to include a cautious review of prospects and costs at each stage. The ARDC then proceeded to submit another revised development program in March 1953, the funding requests of which were again disapproved by Air Force headquarters. Following this directive, the ARDC submitted yet another scaleddown, slowed-down, less costly proposal.

The last action by Air Force headquarters resulted in the

designation of the long-range ballistic project as a routine, nonurgent research program. At this point, no operational data for the missile was suggested or requested by Air Force head-quarters. No proposed target date was set. The result of this series of cutbacks and slowdowns, and particularly of the final action in May 1953, was to preclude the attainment of an opera-tional long-range ballistic missile in the foreseeable future. Air Staff interest in the project could best be described as indiffer-ent. Despite the long series of tests conducted by ARDC and the Convair Corporation and the very optimistic results ob-tained therefrom, skepticism generally prevailed. Urgency was entirely lacking (with the exception of the missile's advocates, who were consistently unsuccessful in selling their views).

The weapon was widely touted as the "ultimate" weapon of the future. That future, however, was left undefined, except that it was far beyond normal planning perspectives. The "ultimate" weapon was deemed impractical, or more often impossible, at the present time. Few funds were provided to try to change the prognosis.

6

The Process Is
Reversed:
Skirting the
Bureaucracy

THE PREVIOUS CHAPTER ended on much the
same note as had earlier chapters. The Air Force research and
development personnel and the Atlas contractor were highly
optimistic over the weapon's potential and were calling for
greatly increased funding. These calls were answered at Air
Force headquarters by instructions to continue this "expensive
program" only at a "relatively slow rate." Fund increases were
denied. Instead, the Air Research and Development Command
was told that "a considerably slower rate than previously contemplated must be established."

Trevor Gardner was not happy with the outlook for missiles

reflected in the ARDC's "Realistic Evaluation," and he was even less pleased with the Air Staff's reaction. Gardner believed that a number of factors were drawing together in such a way as to cast into grave doubt much of the Air Staff's reasoning about the long-range rockets. Most of these factors revolved about the nature and size of the prospective warheads. By early 1953 the United States had exploded a thermonuclear device. The Atomic Energy Commission was predicting that thermonuclear weapons could be much lighter than their atomic predecessors. The "Operation Castle" tests during the spring of 1953 gave further support to this expectation.[1]

The Air Staff, however, continued to deny effective funding to the Atlas project on the grounds that the weapon would never work or would become available so far in the future that funding now was unnecessary and even wasteful. Gardner found both these arguments less than convincing. The Air Force's reasoning had a kind of circular logic to it. First, and most important, if funds were denied the project, the problems involved in its development would not be solved and therefore the project would remain "impossible." Secondly, if operational specifications for the weapon were made exceedingly strict, the problems involved in building a vehicle to meet them would become correspondingly more difficult and thus the vehicle would again look more "impossible." As Joseph Alsop was to remark years later in discussing this period, "The specifications themselves effectively forbade a serious ICBM program" for they "would have required a weapon in the approximate size and configuration of the Empire State Building."[2]

Gardner was convinced that the Air Force's self-reinforcing negative approach to long-range ballistic missiles was both wrong and dangerous to the national security. He was also con-

---

[1] In a meeting of the Scientific Advisory Board of the Air Force held at Patrick Air Force Base in early 1953, Dr. Edward Teller and Dr. J. von Neumann stated that it would soon be possible to build a thermonuclear warhead weighing not over 1,500 pounds with a yield of one megaton. (Bernard A. Schriever, Speech to AIAA, Panel on Rocketry in the 1950s, Washington, D.C., October 28, 1971.)

[2] *Washington Post*, May 10, 1963.

vinced that the situation would continue unless some strong, external influence forced a change.[3] The newly appointed Joint Chiefs of Staff's review of the American military posture provided a possible means to create that external influence.

The ARDC personnel who had since early 1951 been vainly promoting the Atlas were ready allies of Gardner. So, too, was the contractor, Convair. Since January 1951, when the Air Force had again initiated a long-range ballistic missile project with Convair, that corporation had had a team of technical personnel who spent a considerable amount of time traveling about the country, and especially lobbying at the Pentagon, in favor of increased support for the Atlas (MX–1593) program. This team included Karel Bossart (overall engineer), William Patterson (project engineer), Charles Ames (design), James Crooks (guidance), William Radcliff (thermodynamics), and Lester Murray (marketing). At the end of June 1952, Patterson, Bossart, and Crooks happened to be in Washington, and Trevor Gardner requested a briefing.

The briefing, which lasted three to four hours, covered a wide range of subjects including various options for the United States, possible Soviet intentions and capabilities, design variations, guidance, payloads, and what could be done as a "crash" program. Gardner was impressed with the briefing and seemingly convinced of the Atlas's potential. He requested that the Convair personnel return to San Diego and prepare a detailed proposal outlining what could be done on a crash basis and without financial limitations.

Gardner was at this point apparently actively seeking estimates of Soviet capabilities and likely directions in the missile field from the various intelligence agencies in Washington. By the end of July 1953, the Convair engineers had returned to Washington and presented Gardner with an outline for a crash program, unfettered by considerations of budget or politics.

---

[3]Simon Ramo has stated that even after the thermonuclear advances there was strong refusal to "recognize certain of our basic assumptions which rested on the thermonuclear breakthrough" at Air Force HQ. (*Organization and Management Hearings*, p. 230.)

They projected the cost of the entire Atlas development program as $2.75 billion.[4]

Meanwhile, in June 1953 the Joint Chiefs, as part of their review, recommended to Charles E. Wilson, the new Secretary of Defense, that the missiles programs of the three services be reexamined, owing to changed technological factors and the possibility of unnecessary duplication.[5]

Since Gardner had already undertaken a limited version of this review, and since he was quite interested in looking into the missile field more closely, he eagerly supported the recommendation. Accordingly, the Secretary of the Air Force, with the approval of the Secretary of Defense, asked Gardner to conduct a review of the United States' missile programs. Secretary of Defense Wilson's intention was to effect greater economies in the programs. The purpose of the study, in his mind at least, was to eliminate wasteful duplication and, whenever practical, "to standardize on one missile for production and use by all military departments."[6]

Air Force Secretary Talbott assigned this task to Trevor Gardner, who decided that two committees should be organized, one for strategic missiles and the second for all other missile programs. The nonstrategic committee's activities need not concern us here. The committee set up to review the nation's strategic missiles is, on the other hand, of central importance. Gardner's decision that a full-time highly qualified group should be organized to undertake the strategic missiles review was opposed by elements of the Air Staff, who felt that the Air Force Scientific Advisory Board (SAB) should conduct the study. Gardner believed that the SAB, as a part-time group, could not perform the kind of review he wished to see.[7]

---

[4] Interview, William Patterson.

[5] Schweibert, "Ballistic Missile," p. 80. Indeed, Schweibert, an Air Force historian, has reported that Trevor Gardner's instructions "had been to eliminate some strategic missiles, *particularly the ICBM.*" *Ibid.*, p. 96 (emphasis added). Mr. Schweibert was able to interview Trevor Gardner before the latter's death and he may have thereby learned this information. I was warned several times, however, by persons close to the Air Force ballistic missile programs, to be careful when relying upon the Schweibert account.

[6] *Eleventh Report*, p. 13.

[7] *Eleventh Report*, p. 70.

By the late fall of 1953, Gardner had organized a particularly prestigious group, formally titled the Strategic Missiles Evaluation Committee (SMEC). The Committee, which held its first meeting on November 9, 1953, was chaired by Dr. John von Neumann of Princeton University. Other members of the Committee were Drs. Hendric Bode, Bell Telephone Laboratories; Louis G. Dunn, director of the Jet Propulsion Laboratory, California Institute of Technology; George B. Kistiakowsky, Harvard University; Charles C. Lauritsen, California Institute of Technology; Clark B. Millikan, President of the Guggenheim Institute, California Institute of Technology; Allen E. Puckett, Hughes Aircraft Corporation; Jerome B. Wiesner, Massachusetts Institute of Technology; and Lawrence A. Hyland, Bendix Aviation Corporation. Bode, Kistiakowsky, and Millikan had been members of the ad hoc committee, chaired by Millikan, which had met the previous fall to review much the same issues. Drs. Simon Ramo and Dean E. Wooldridge, who had recently left the Hughes Aircraft Company to form their own company (Ramo-Wooldridge Corp.) also participated in the deliberations with all the status of full members.[8]

It appears that very early in those deliberations, Trevor Gardner began thinking seriously about setting up some kind of ballistic missile development agency outside of the overall Air Force channels of operation. Drs. Ramo and Wooldridge were expected to play a central role in whatever procedure was finally decided upon.[9]

Trevor Gardner and Simon Ramo had known and liked each

[8]One indication of the potential direction of the committee was the fact that von Neumann had been, since early 1953, a consultant to Convair on the Atlas project. After Convair had submitted the "crash" Atlas program outline to Gardner in July 1953, Gardner had asked to borrow several of Convair's consultants, of whom von Neumann was the most important. Another indication of the expected direction of the committee investigations can be gleaned from the knowledge that since August 1953, William Patterson, Karel Bossart, and other Convair personnel had been actively briefing the personnel of the infant Ramo-Wooldridge Corporation on the progress and expectations of the Atlas program—and that this briefing had been initiated by Convair at Trevor Gardner's suggestion. Interview, William Patterson.

[9]Interviews with Reuben Mettler, President TRW Inc.; Thomas Lanphier, ex-Vice President, Convair; Ray Soper, Col., USAF (ret.), presently employed by Convair; Simon Ramo.

other since the time both had worked for General Electric.
Gardner had visited Hughes Aircraft in the summer of 1953.
While there, he had asked Ramo and Wooldridge, who had
developed a very high grade research and development organization at Hughes, to monitor the coming missiles committee
investigation and provide intimate technical expertise. The two
declined the offer on the grounds that they were much too heavily involved with Hughes at that time to undertake the other
effort. Soon after Ramo and Wooldridge left Hughes in September 1953 to form their own company, they were again approached by Gardner and again turned him down. This time
their reason was that they wanted to begin to produce hardware
items as soon as possible in order to start earning money.

Shortly after this exchange, Ramo and Wooldridge heard from
Roger Lewis, Assistant Secretary of the Air Force, that the new
company was not going to receive any more hardware contracts
from the Air Force after the three small contracts they presently
had. The reason was that the Hughes Aircraft Company had
complained about Ramo-Wooldridge at the highest levels of
the Defense Department. Hughes was worried that if Ramo-
Wooldridge were to grow rapidly, too many personnel would
leave Hughes for the new company. Since several important
Hughes employees had already done just that and several others
had indicated their desire to do so, this was probably a jus-
tifiable fear. As Hughes Aircraft was an important Defense contractor, which the military establishment did not wish to harm
unnecessarily, the Hughes wishes were respected. Trevor
Gardner then again contacted Ramo and Wooldridge. Con-
fronted by this situation, Ramo and Wooldridge reconsidered
their position and decided to accept a contract to "conduct research studies" in coordination with the von Neumann missiles
evaluation committee.[10]

[10]Interviews with Dean Wooldridge and Simon Ramo, Los Angeles, August
20, 1971. There is some indication that Gardner considered the RAND Corporation, and actually approached the California Institute of Technology and the
Massachusetts Institute of Technology to perform the technical support role to
the Strategic Missiles Evaluation Committee. RAND was ruled out as being too
closely involved with the Air Force, and both CIT and MIT declined. In light of
the friendship between Ramo and Gardner and Gardner's persistence in pursu-

Trevor Gardner was now actively attempting to instill a note of urgency into the strategic missiles program as a whole and particularly the von Neumann committee review. Gardner had developed the idea of creating the high level von Neumann group. He had then intentionally stacked it with long-range ballistic missile proponents.[11] Having received Secretarial-level approval for the von Neumann committee review, Gardner wasted no time in initiating its studies. At this time General Bernard A. Schriever was Assistant for Development Planning in the office of the Deputy Chief of Staff, Development. For some time, Schriever had been favorably impressed with the potential of strategic ballistic missiles. He had quickly come into contact with Trevor Gardner when the latter entered the Defense Department, and they had developed a close working relationship. A good indication of Gardner's methods of operation, and particularly the haste with which he was moving, can be found in a retrospective memo written in 1959 by a former member of Schriever's staff.

On the morning of 14 October 1953 I was informed that your office [General Schriever's] had received word that you should plan to come to the Office of the Assistant for R&D, Mr. Trevor Gardner, in the afternoon in connection with possible immediate employment of the services of Drs. Ramo and Wooldridge. . . . At the afternoon meeting in Mr. Gardner's suite, you and I were introduced to Doctors Ramo and Wooldridge, and were informed variously by Mr. Gardner, Lt. Colonel Ford, and Lt. Colonel Schenk of the Secretary's decision of that noon to proceed expeditiously with a group analysis to be monitored by Drs. Ramo and Wooldridge. Urgency was essential to procurement of an early analytical report to the Secretary.[12]

With Ramo and Wooldridge, then, as active participants in the process, the Strategic Missiles Evaluation Committee began

ing Ramo and Wooldridge, one might question how vigorously the other institutions were solicited. At any rate, Gardner eagerly offered the position to the Ramo-Wooldridge Corp. and pressured them to accept. See *Eleventh Report,* pp. 70–71.

[11]Interview with General Sessums. General Sessums was assigned to the Air Research and Development Command from its inception until September 1959.

[12]Letter from John C. Schroeter, Assistant for Plans, Directorate of Development Planning, DCS/D, to General Schriever. January 13, 1959. DeHaven Document Collection.

three months of intensive review. Their report was submitted on February 10,[1] 1954. The group's conclusions were noticeably more optimistic than the Millikan Committee recommendations had been a little over a year earlier. The SMEC believed that the Atlas could be built much more quickly than had been previously assumed—within six to eight years if its recommendations were adopted. The Millikan Committee Report of the previous year had spoken of 1962 as a very optimistic date for an operational Atlas. Since the committee suggested a slow rate of development, the 1962 date was probably discussed simply because it was ten years in the future, a round figure for planning purposes. During a later Senate inquiry, a Department of Defense memo filed to assist the inquiry reported that in 1953 Atlas availability was predicted as not earlier than 1965.

The SMEC was not confident that the Air Force structures as they then existed would accomplish that goal. Apart from the formal recommendation that Atlas development be vigorously pursued (which had hardly been the case heretofore), the SMEC stressed the urgent need that a new, separate, development-management agency be set up "to re-orient the program, supervise research, and exercise general technical and management control over all elements of the program."[13] The members of SMEC felt that an organization possessing the required prestige, technical expertise, and management competence did not then exist within the Air Force. Nor was Convair competent to handle the program on its own.

It is the conviction of the Committee that a radical reorganization of the IBMS project considerably transcending the Convair framework is required if a military [sic] useful vehicle is to be had within a reasonable span of time. Specifically, the Committee believes that the design must be based on a new and comprehensive weapons system study, together with a thorough-going exploration of alternative approaches to several critical phases of the problem adequately based on fundamental science. The new IBMS development group, which we proposed, would be given directive responsibility for the entire project.[14]

[13]*Hearings, Organization and Management of Missile Programs*, p. 5; *Eleventh Report*, p. 71; *Hearings, Inquiry into Satellite and Missile Programs*, p. 452.

[14]Von Neumann Report, quoted by General Schriever in *Hearings, Organization and Management of Missile Programs*, p. 11. See also p. 64. The ICBM was originally called simply IBM, but the designation was later changed for obvious reasons.

Furthermore, the committee observed that "the type of direc-
tional team needed is of the caliber and strength that may require the creation of a special group by a drafting operation
performed by the highest level government executives in university, industry, and government organizations."

The recommendation that Convair be superseded represented
a break from the findings of the earlier Millikan Committee,
which had been satisfied with the Convair operation. The proposed new development-management agency was considered by
the SMEC as the most urgent need in the ICBM program—more important than any of the technical problems such
as guidance, warhead weight, reentry, launch-time, or base
protection.[15]

The SMEC clearly felt that significant changes might be made
in the ICBM design. The proposed new agency was expected to
undertake an exhaustive study of the weapon, including all alternative approaches to the various problem areas. The agency
was then expected to update the military specifications for the
weapon, particularly in light of progress in atomic warhead
technology. After completion of the review the agency would
prepare, in detail, a redirected, accelerated ICBM program.
Until completion of this review, it was considered unwise to
commit large funds, freeze designs, or plan production. Accordingly, engineering and hardware production by Convair and
other contractors should be reduced or halted altogether. After
expansion and acceleration of the ICBM program was underway, the new agency was to continue to provide technical direction to the project by employing particularly competent scientists and engineers who could supervise research and completely
control the experimental and hardware production phases of
the program. In order to foster this procedure, SMEC recommended that the new agency be relieved of certain aspects of
normal governmental regulations.

At this same time another study was underway at the RAND
Corporation. It arrived at strikingly similar conclusions.
RAND, it will be recalled, had on several occasions in the past
prepared studies indicating the feasibility of intercontinental ballistic missiles. During the 1952–1953 period, RAND personnel

[15]*Eleventh Report*, pp. 71, 72.

had been well informed about the work on the H-bomb, and particularly the approaching certainty of very small, high-yield warheads. RAND was working closely at this time with Edward Teller at Berkeley. Frank Collbohm, Bruno Augenstein, Charles Hitch, and other RAND personnel, with Teller's assistance, prepared a study and briefing discussing the further merits of the ICBM in the light of the H-bomb developments, which was presented at Air Force headquarters and to the Defense Secretary. This study, which RAND had begun on its own rather than in response to an Air Force request, was undertaken during the summer and fall of 1953 and was formally issued to the Air Force on February 8, 1954. The report had been completed by late 1953, however, when the briefings at Air Force headquarters were undertaken. One of RAND's prime customers was the von Neumann Committee, whose members were briefed at several points.[16]

It is not surprising that the recommendations of SMEC and RAND were quite similar. In effect SMEC used the RAND Report and briefings by RAND personnel as source material for its own study. RAND also advocated a "drastic revision" of the Atlas program, a comprehensive study of the various approaches, a new Air Force agency to undertake the study and direct the resulting program, revision of the current performance requirements, and designation of high priority with appropriate funding. RAND also felt that an ICBM could be available by 1960–1962 if its suggestions were followed.[17]

The RAND Report concluded that the Air Force ballistic missile program as then constituted incorporated two serious defects. First, the effort being expended was clearly not adequate. Second, excessively stringent performance requirements were making the weapon appear nearly impossible and were forcing difficult and unnecessary research and development efforts in uncommon technological areas. These two factors greatly hindered the creation of an operational weapon and combined to produce a feeling of little or no urgency. This result was compounded by the complacent assumption that any poten-

[16]Interviews with Bruno Augenstein, Vice President, RAND Corporation, and Frank Collbohm.
[17]*Eleventh Report*, p. 73.

tial enemies would require the same performance standards and thus would encounter the same problems and the same delays. The RAND study concluded that by relaxing the present very severe performance requirements in ways that would not prevent successful fulfillment of the long-range ballistic missile's mission, the supposed enormous problems in guidance, propulsion, and reentry could be solved within the limits of present technology. RAND also noted "evidence of our enemies making progress in field" and called the long-range ballistic missile enterprise a "race against time."[18]

The nature of U. S. intelligence estimates in this period concerning Soviet capabilities in long-range rocketry is not entirely clear. News articles had appeared since the late 1940s calling attention to reported Soviet activities. The press reports may not have been accurate, however, and regardless of their accuracy it is not known precisely how they were interpreted by the Air Force. There were apparently a number of reports from 1947 on in the classified Air Intelligence Digest noting Soviet work on versions of the German V–2 and A–10 weapons, the last being a very long-range vehicle (5,000 miles or more). Other reports indicated construction of a number of missile test ranges on Soviet territory, some capable of handling long-range vehicles.[19]

In October 1952 a briefing was given at Dayton, Ohio, by the Air Technical Intelligence Center in which reports of repatriated German missile scientists captured by the Soviet Union after World War II were given wide distribution. The Dayton briefing seems to have resulted in the calm appraisal that the Soviets were following the same cautious, step-level approach through air-breathing missiles that the United States was. Apart from a few isolated dissidents, this view appears to have permeated the Air Staff.[20]

That the intelligence picture was still mixed by the spring of

[18]*Air Force Ballistic Missile Chronology, 1946–57* (Historical section, BMD, ARDC, Dec. 1957). Read at AFSC, Historian's office.

[19]Interviews with Ray Soper and John Sessums.

[20]The Dayton meeting is mentioned in Schweibert, "Ballistic Missile," p. 69. Dr. Walter Dornberger is reported by Schweibert to have dissented from the general interpretation. Other dissenting voices came from ARDC and RAND but were to little effect.

1954 can be seen from a memo Trevor Gardner sent to the
Assistant Secretary of Defense (Research and Development)
after the conclusion of the SMEC study.

I wish to call to your attention the general feeling of all members of the
Strategic Missile Evaluation Committee that the quality of the technical
intelligence concerning the Soviet capability is subject to substantial
improvement. During the time the guided missiles reports were in the
process of preparation, Mr. Garrison Morton devoted a large fraction
of his time to the exploration of the intelligence information available
and the interpretation of it. In the field of strategic missiles, he obtained
four separate intelligence estimates, each being substantially different
from each other. . . .

The lump impression gained from these estimates is that the Soviets
are significantly ahead of us in the strategic missile field.[21]

The conclusions of the von Neumann and RAND reports
were precisely what Gardner had desired. Even before the two
reports had been formally presented to the Air Force, Gardner
sent a memo to General Twining stating that the Air Force
ballistic missile specifications were too rigid, the program was
not aggressive enough, and not enough attention was being
given to it at the highest levels of the Air Force. He recommended abandonment of the present program, restudy by a
scientific, technical group, and centralization of authority for a
new program.

With the two reports formally in hand, Gardner organized a
meeting at Air Force Headquarters in late February which was
attended by personnel from Gardner's office, ARDC, DCS/
Operations and DCS/Development. At this meeting, Gardner
strongly advocated approval and immediate implementation of
the major recommendations advanced by RAND and SMEC.

The concept of a new Air Force agency designed to oversee
the long-range ballistic missile development program was not
widely appreciated. Despite the two reports many members of
the Air Staff continued to view the ballistic rocket as a "Buck
Rogers" idea. In addition, the creation of a wholly new agency
was deemed unnecessary and even counterproductive by those
who thought present Air Force organizations quite capable of

[21]Memo, February 16, 1954. DeHaven Document Collection.

handling the job. Even the ARDC, which had been in the fore-
front of the effort to promote long-range rockets, resisted the
idea of creating a separate agency to oversee their development.

This time, however, the effort to speed up development of an
ICBM was proving resilient. More important, Trevor Gardner
firmly believed in the urgency of the program, and Gardner had
the strong support of Air Secretary Talbott. Heretofore no
proponent of the ICBM effort had been given the authority to
force such a large, well supported program on a reluctant Air
Staff.

The previous seven years had been marked by a series of
civilian-imposed budget limitations the military had been told to
meet by whatever means it chose. In 1953 this process was
being reversed—not by the Air Force itself but by what was
basically an external influence. After the late February meeting,
and armed with the explicit language of the RAND and SMEC
reports, Gardner sent a memo to Secretary Talbott and General
Twining, openly stating that the present Air Force structure was
clearly inadequate to produce a long-range ballistic missile
quickly. Gardner further declared that the Convair Atlas program as then constituted was unsatisfactory. Needed was a
dramatic acceleration and reorientation of the program, which
could only be achieved by putting a high-ranking military officer
in charge of the ICBM program, and "giving him unusual channels of communication and strong authority."[22] Gardner stated
that an emergency capability could be attained by the period
1958–1960. He suggested funding the program initially from the
Defense Secretary's emergency budget.

By this date Gardner's case had been given another strong
and very visible push. Warhead technology was clearly outdis-
tancing delivery vehicle planning and the strategic thinking
reflected therein. The "Mike" test of November 1952 had
offered hard scientific evidence that small thermonuclear
warheads were likely to be available at an early date. During the
summer of 1953 further laboratory tests made the outcome even
more certain. These promises were confirmed with the

[22]*Eleventh Report,* p. 73. The Gardner memo was dated March 11, 1954.

166 Skirting the Bureaucracy

"shrimp" test of March 1, 1954, and later tests through April
and May in Operation Castle. After March 1, absolutely no
one could doubt whether an ICBM could lift an effective
warhead.[23]

A week after Gardner's memo, a memo was sent by Secretary
Talbott to General Twining with clear instructions.

As you are aware, my office has been conducting an evaluation of our
strategic missile programs. This evaluation has provided a technical
validation of the feasibility of accomplishing an intercontinental ballistic
missile operational system within approximately five years. At my direction, Mr. Trevor Gardner has developed a plan for accelerating our
efforts so as to achieve this capability. . . . It is imperative that the Air
Force immediately accelerate the intercontinental ballistic missile program. . . . we shall proceed with the first year's program at maximum
effort possible on the assumption that total funding required will ultimately be provided by Congress. . . . Requirements for FY 1955 funds
are estimated as high as $50 million.[24]

General Twining was directed to take the necessary steps to
implement the SMEC recommendations.

It is important to bring out certain factors at this time. First,
Trevor Gardner was by all reports an extremely bright and able
man, but not endowed with the most pleasing of personalities.
Gardner at one time or another has been described by men who
knew him personally as "sharp," "grating," "abrupt," "irasci-
ble," "cold," "unpleasant," and "a bastard"—in short, he was
not easy to get along with. Gardner was also a civilian, newly
installed in the Pentagon, who was suddenly giving orders to Air
Force general officers. Gardner not only gave orders on how to
run the Air Force, but they were also contrary to the way the
Air Force had been operating. This situation contained the potential for conflict. It developed.

One important underlying cause, apart from the personality
and civil-military irritations discussed above, seems to be a

[23]The reader is referred, however, to the argument in chapter 5 that the
supposed lack of an effective warhead had for some years been a basically false
issue. The importance of the thermonuclear warhead was that it finally eliminated any basis whatsoever for this argument.

[24]Memo for General Twining from H. E. Talbott. Subject: "Acceleration of
the Intercontinental Ballistic Missile Program." Dated March 19, 1954.
DeHaven Document Collection.

fear felt by Air Force officers that Gardner wanted to become
"czar" of a new missile empire similar to the Manhattan Project
or the AEC.[25] This was distasteful on two grounds. First, what
was seen as excessive personal ambition on the part of Gardner
was irritating on its own. Second, a new missile empire,
civilian-run and separated from the military, would remove what
was already a fairly large and could potentially be a very large
area of responsibility from the Air Force. Once again the dual
nature of the Air Force response to long-range missiles became
evident. On the one hand, the Air Force had consistently under-
rated their effectiveness and even their feasibility. Manned aircraft were continually promoted over the missile competitors on
grounds of cost, trustworthiness, efficiency, and capability. On
the other hand, missiles were generally admitted to be a potentially useful weapon for the future—but a future placed far
enough ahead to be meaningless.

Nevertheless, long-range missiles were considered to be an
Air Force weapon and an Air Force responsibility. This possessiveness had been demonstrated many times in territorial battles
with the Army and Navy. In each case the Air Force's responsibility for the strategic function in American defense planning
was stressed and with that functional responsibility came all
weapons capable of fulfilling it. Long-range missiles might not
be emphasized by the Air Force; but no one else was going to
build them either, if the Air Force could help it.

Several struggles with the other services over these weapons
have been noted. The perceived threat now appearing in the
form of Trevor Gardner's ambition to rule a missile empire was
regarded similarly by the Air Force. If missiles were ever to
replace manned bombers, or to be capable of doing so, it was
vital that the Air Force retain control of them. Otherwise it
might find itself significantly displaced by some sort of rocket
command. The language of the SMEC Report could be easily

[25] Interview with Ray Soper. Col. Soper was, at various times, Special Assis-
tant to General Brentnall (who was Special Assistant for Guided Missiles to the
Air Force Chief of Staff), chief of the Ballistic Missile Division within
Brentnall's office, and executive secretary to the Air Force Ballistic Missile
Committee.

interpreted to support such an action. It had been a "conviction" of the committee

that a radical reorganization of the ICBMs project considerably transcending the Convair framework is required if a militarily useful vehicle is to be had within a reasonable span of time. . . . the nature of the task for this new agency requires that overall technical direction be in the hands of an unusually competent group of scientists and engineers capable of making systems analyses, supervising the research phases, and completely controlling the experimental and hardware phases of the program.[26]

One Air Force comment at the time is particularly revealing. "In order to prevent the establishment of another Manhattan Project, the U.S. Air Force, in a letter signed by the Deputy Chief of Staff/Materiel, dated 21 June 1954, delegated to ARDC the responsibility of developing the entire weapon system and of recommending the logistics, operational and personnel concepts to be applied in supporting this weapon."[27]

Another important element was the demonstrated fact that Trevor Gardner had the strong support of Secretary Talbott. Therefore, if the Air Force strenuously opposed Gardner on all fronts, he might use such opposition to make a strong case that the Air Force was excessively rigid, dogmatic, and tradition-bound, and that a separate civilian agency was needed to meet the vital needs of the country.

It is not certain that the above logic was employed by the Air Staff, or what percentage of the Air Staff shared these views of Gardner's intentions. There is evidence that Gardner and the Air Staff were at odds during this period, and that some officers feared the entire long-range missile field would be lost to an outside agency. At any rate, a decision was made to cooperate with Gardner and to promote a new Air Force agency to oversee the ICBM program.

[26]SMEC Report of February 10, 1954. Quoted in "A Study of the Development Management Organization for the Atlas Program." August 18, 1954. DeHaven Document Collection.

[27]Memorandum for General Funk (Commander, Ballistic Missile Office, AMC), dated September 1955, from Assistant for Programming, Weapon System Division. DeHaven Document Collection.

Despite this acceptance, however, skepticism—and even opposition and resentment—remained within the Air Force. General Schriever later recalled that "when I went out to the west coast, to take over this job, the betting was fairly high that I wouldn't last more than six months."[28]

Following Secretary Talbott's message to General Twining directing that the Air Force program be reordered and that steps be taken to implement the SMEC recommendations, Twining asked the Air Force Council to examine the SMEC findings. The Air Council met on March 11 and 15 and reviewed proposals submitted by SMEC, the Aircraft and Weapons Board, and a program proposed by Trevor Gardner. The Council recommended that the Snark, Navaho, and Atlas all be continued and that CEP and payload requirements be broadened immediately and subsequently revised as appropriate in the light of latest projected warhead weights and yields. Regarding the Atlas program the council stated that "development and operation of such a system is a mission of the Air Force and must be under the control of the Air Force."[29]

This last comment was, of course, a clear reference to the proposals that Atlas be developed outside the control of the Air Force. To prevent this occurrence the Air Force Council recommended that field responsibility be assigned to ARDC and that ARDC be directed to establish a military-civilian group of the highest caliber to redirect, expand, and accelerate the program. These recommendations were approved by General Twining on March 23, 1954. Further evidence of a new interest in missiles at the Air Staff level came in April 1954, with the establishment of the office of Assistant Chief of Staff for Guided Missiles within Air Force headquarters. This office was designated the central point of contact for guided missile matters.

Following the approval by the Air Council and Chief of Staff for the Atlas program's acceleration and reorganization, Gardner continued to press for immediate implementation of the

[28]*Organization and Management Hearings*, p. 118.
[29]Memo of March 23, 1954, from General Thomas D. White, Chairman, Air Force Council, to Nathan F. Twining, Chief of Staff, USAF. DeHaven Document Collection.

changes. He directed that the program proceed at the maximum effort possible with no funding limitations.[30]

The Air Council recommendations General Twining had approved had directed the ARDC to establish a very competent military–civilian group which would be given a year in which to produce "in full detail a redirected, expanded, and accelerated program."[31] Trevor Gardner and Secretary Talbott had, by the spring of 1954, accepted the Air Force proposal for placing the new agency within the ARDC. Gardner had proposed that "the active direction of the IBMS program should be the sole responsibility of a major general with the position of ARDC Vice Commander, backed up by a brigadier general of unusual competence to work directly with the contractors in supply of top-level support and technical supervision."

To fill these positions, Gardner recommended Major General James McCormack, Vice Commander of ARDC, and Brigadier General Bernard A. Schriever, Assistant for Development Planning, DCS/D. When General McCormack retired because of illness, Schriever was promoted.[32] Schriever and Gardner had by this time become quite well acquainted through the von Neumann Committee, which had been administratively supported by Schriever's office. Gardner was quite impressed with Schriever, appears to have actively supported his promotion to Brigadier General in 1953, and advocated his assignment as head of the Western Development Division after General McCormack's retirement. General orders were published May 5 placing General Schriever in charge of the ICBM effort as of June 1, 1954.

In April 1954, General Putt shifted from command of ARDC to the position of Deputy Chief of Staff, Development. By this time a decision had been made to create an ARDC project office on the West Coast, which would have "sole responsibility for

[30]Memo, Gardner to Twining, April 14, 1954. Cited in *Air Force Ballistic Missile Chronology.*

[31]Air Council recommendations to General Twining, quoted in Schweibert, "Ballistic Missile," p. 87. See also p. 86.

[32]Various respondents cited air staff resistance to Schriever's elevation, but were unable to provide documentation.

the prosecution of research, development, test, and production leading to a successful intercontinental ballistic missile."[33]

On June 21, General Putt issued a basic Project Atlas directive to ARDC, officially authorizing establishment of a West Coast field office. Furthermore, ARDC was notified that the Atlas program had been given the highest priority in the Air Force.[34] All major commands had been directed to support the program accordingly. The West Coast office was to have authority to develop the complete weapon system including ground support, and operational, logistic, and personnel concepts.[35] By this directive direct communications between the West Coast office and the Air Staff were authorized.

In July, orders were issued by ARDC establishing the Western Development Division (WDD), with duty station at Inglewood, California. General Schriever assumed command of WDD on August 2, 1954. The Western Development Division was to be staffed by a military–civilian group of the highest technical competence. The group was then expected to conduct a year's study aimed at producing an accelerated, redirected program. On May 3, the Ramo-Wooldridge Corporation received a letter contract to undertake the study.

Ramo-Wooldridge had previously provided technical support to the Strategic Missile Evaluation Committee, which had nominally passed out of existence after completion of its report in February 1954. Gardner and others felt a continuing need for

[33]Memo from ARDC to AMC, April 21, 1954. Quoted in Schweibert, "Ballistic Missile," p. 89.

[34]On May 14, 1954, General White, the Vice Chief of Staff, had sent a memo to the four Deputy Chiefs of Staff announcing establishment of the Assistant Chief of Staff for Guided Missiles and stating that the Atlas program would be accelerated to the maximum extent technology would permit. It was to have the highest program priority in the Air Force. *Air Force Ballistic Missile Chronology, 1946–1957. Organization and Management Hearings*, p. 674.

[35]A memo was sent from Headquarters ARDC to all Deputy Commanders stating "all staff agencies of this headquarters are directed to support Project Atlas with a 1–A research and development priority which takes precedence over all other 1–A projects. Every possible assistance to General Schriever and his organization will be provided." Memo from General Power to Deputy Commanders and Executive Office. July 29, 1954. DeHaven Document Collection.

172 Skirting the Bureaucracy

such an authoritative scientific group, however, and so it was decided to continue the committee.[36]

In April the group was formally reconstituted as the Atlas Scientific Advisory Committee (at this time the entire ballistic missile program was known as "Atlas"), still under the chairmanship of Dr. von Neumann. The committee was expanded from eleven to seventeen, gaining, among others, Dr. Herbert York, Frank Collbohm (president of the RAND Corporation), and Charles A. Lindbergh. Ramo and Wooldridge left the committee, deeming it improper to remain a part while undertaking long-term contractual studies for the Air Force. The Corporation, however, continued as technical advisor to the ICBM Advisory Committee.[37]

The reconstituted von Neumann Committee met in July at the Los Angeles offices of the Ramo-Wooldridge Corporation. The meeting was specifically designed to hear General Schriever's plans for organization and management of the ICBM program. Discussion first centered on the question of whether Schriever had sufficient authority to control and direct the program. The committee was not certain that he had. The committee then heard a Convair proposal. The Convair Corporation wanted to be designated prime contractor for the Atlas with formal responsibility for the system. Convair thought the Ramo-Wooldridge Corporation an unnecessary appendage, which would only serve to slow and confuse the program. In their eyes, there was nothing RW could provide that Convair could not. Placing RW over Convair would simply be hiring two groups to do the same job, causing added expenses and delays.

The committee was not impressed with the Convair presentation. Convair continued to espouse its previous design configuration which, to the committee, took little cognizance of im-

---

[36]*Ibid.*, p. 74. *Organization and Management Hearings*, pp. 211, 215.

[37]*Eleventh Report*, p. 74. In fact, the Ramo-Wooldridge role in producing the original SMEC report which called for the employment of a highly qualified technical group to aid the Air Force ICBM program was later to be the cause of much investigation and some charges of impropriety after Ramo-Wooldridge became precisely that technical group. See *Organization and Management Hearings*, pp. 199–243 and elsewhere. *Eleventh Report*, pp. 72–73.

portant recent technological advances. Convair's proposal at
this time was to build a large five-engine missile. This was
somewhat smaller than the 1951 model, which called for seven
engines, but it was still much larger than the committee thought
necessary. "Generally the Committee expressed disappoint-
ment that the Convair stand was still so close to the one they
had held a few months before. . . . Discussion ensued then as to
whether or not Convair was strong enough for systems responsibility. There appeared to be unanimous feeling that Convair
was not strong enough for systems responsibility over the
project."[38]

The Advisory Committee also expressed concern about the
general organizational arrangements, which included the WDD
project office, the Ramo-Wooldridge Corporation as technical
staff, and various industrial organizations, including Convair.
The committee thought this structure "awkward" and likely to
delay the program; it urged "a strengthening of the organization
with a clear and single allocation of authority and responsibility
for system engineering."[39] The question was basically the extent to which responsibility would be held by WDD or assigned
to any single contractor.

On the second day of the meeting, Dr. Ramo made a presentation of his company's proposed relation to WDD and the industrial contractors. He proposed that RW provide a small but
highly qualified staff to assist Schriever with technical studies
and advice on program planning. Actual development work
would be undertaken by industrial contractors, including one
systems contractor that could be Convair or another company.
After their initial studies, which would set the basic approach to
the program, RW's role would be to support the contractors and
assist Schriever's office in evaluating the results.

General Schriever, who had earlier outlined it to the committee, favored this arrangement. The sometimes peripheral, sometimes authoritative position of RW confused the committee.

[38]Minutes of Scientific Advisory Committee Meeting, July 20 and 21, 1954.
DeHaven Document Collection.
[39]Ibid. Organization and Management Hearings, pp. 70–71, 459.

In particular, the evaluative role of RW—"keeping industry honest," in General Schriever's phrase—most disturbed the committee.

Donald Quarles, then Assistant Secretary of Defense (Research and Development), who was present at the meeting (technically as a guest), flatly stated that the organizational concept on which WDD was embarked would not work. He felt that either the so-called systems contractor (Convair) should be deemed competent, in which case RW was basically a part of the Air Force "customer" and could be kept small, or else RW must have clear responsibility, in which event its size should not be restricted but should be large enough to exercise strong technical direction in a line position over the other contractors.[40] The committee agreed with Quarles. Until a determination was made, the committee, in language clearly directed at the Convair Company, cautioned that care should be taken not to encourage any single corporation to assume it would be named systems contractor.

The committee's fears in some ways paralleled the Convair viewpoint. Neither was satisfied with the current Ramo-Wooldridge role. The proposed solutions were far apart, however. Convair wished to be assigned complete responsibility for the weapons system. The advisory committee, as noted above, considered the Convair management much too weak for such authority and felt the Air Force should organize a systems engineering group to manage the program centrally. A further recmmendation was that the industrial base of the project be expanded as rapidly as possible to ensure a maximum R&D effort.

The committee directed General Schriever to restudy the position of Ramo-Wooldridge and Convair. The General began the review immediately following the July meeting. At the same time, the ARDC commander, General Power, issued a directive to Schriever instructing the latter to exercise "complete control

[40]Memo for Major Franzel from General Schriever, August 4, 1954. De Haven Document Collection. *Organization and Management Hearings*, p. 71, *Eleventh Report*, p. 75.

and authority over all aspects of the [Atlas] program, including all engineering decisions."[41]

The result of Schriever's study, in the form of a staff paper titled "Development Management Organization for the Atlas Program," was submitted to General Power on August 18, 1954. It was clear to Schriever that the committee was nearly unanimous that systems engineering responsibility should be given to RW; they felt that no single organization, with the exception of Bell Labs, had the necessary scientific and technical competence.[42]

With this indicated direction, Schriever's choice was not difficult. He did find some opposition to RW from the professional military.

In discussing this matter with ranking military personnel, there appears to be unanimity in a view opposed to that of the scientific committee. They do not appear to take seriously the need for a draft on the scientific and technical competence of the country as a prerequisite to the success of the program.

Schriever felt it quite important to satisfy the civilian scientists on the advisory committee, however.

I strongly believe the program needs the continued support of the scientist; therefore, the organization cannot be an anathema to him. In a negative way, he would probably withdraw his active support; and, in a positive way, he might argue very convincingly at the highest levels the need for a special organization outside the military to carry out the program. If successful, such a move could permanently endanger the philosophy of military research and development.[43]

There is some evidence that Schriever considered several alternative approaches, including a single prime industrial contractor (as recommended by Convair), creation of a new large

---

[41]Quoted in Schweibert, "Ballistic Missile," p. 94.

[42]The exception was Frank Collbohm, who also opposed designation of Convair as system contractor. He felt another aircraft company, most notably North American, could do the job successfully. Far from clarifying responsibility, Collbohm thought that imposition of RW between the Air Force and the other contractors would further cloud the question. Interview with Frank Collbohm.

[43]Memo for Maj. Franzel from General Schriever, August 4, 1954. DeHaven Document Collection.

laboratory within a University, and the existing organization.[44]
In 1959 when the Government Operations Committee was criti-
cally investigating the Air Force–RW relationship with an eye to
the immense growth the corporation had enjoyed since 1954,
Schriever spent a good deal of time justifying the decision to
employ RW and outlining the detailed weighing of alternatives
he had undertaken. Given Schriever's close, and in some ways
dependent, relationship with the ICBM Scientific Advisory
Committee and that committee's clear preference for an expanded role by the RW Corporation, this post facto justification
should be taken with a grain of salt. Ramo and Wooldridge had
worked closely and effectively with the original von Neumann
Committee. That committee was intensely critical of Convair
and dissatisfied with the original arrangements. Schriever recognized their preference for a more responsible RW role. He then
chose that course and it is unlikely that he seriously considered
any other.[45]

Schriever's report was submitted August 18. Its conclusions,
specifically the recommended expanded role for RW, were dis-

[44]*Eleventh Report,* pp. 76–77. Another alternative which Schriever might have
considered would have been to call on the Army's Redstone missile group to
build the ICBM. As was later observed by an investigating congressional committee, "In mid-1954, when the ICBM management pattern was being developed, the Army team probably had more cumulative experience of a theoretical and practical sort in ballistic missiles than any other organization in the
country. A provision of law (10 U.S.C., Sec. 9532) gives the Secretary of the
Air Force the option of having needed supplies 'made in factories, arsenals, or
depots owned by the United States, so far as those factories, arsenals, or depots
can make those supplies on an economical basis.' But the possibility of using the
Army's missile-building resources was not seriously considered by General
Schriever." *Eleventh Report,* p. 78.

[45]It is interesting to note that industry, other than Convair, was also neutral or
opposed to the prime contractor approach. The reason seems to be that no company wanted another company to receive the enormous contracts involved in
being prime contractor for the ICBM program. In the absence of assurances that
they would be the chosen prime, each company seems to have been willing to
settle for a piece of the contractual pie rather than see a competitor get the lion's
share. This, at least, was the impression gained by Schriever in his review of the
situation. See "A Study of the Development Management Organization for the
Atlas Program," August 18, 1954, copy in DeHaven Document Collection. Sec-
tions of the Schriever Report are quoted in *Organization and Management
Hearings,* p. 65.

cussed at a meeting of the Scientific Advisory Committee on October 15, 1954. By this date, however, the matter was effectively settled. Schriever reported that Generals Power and Rawlings, of ARDC and AMC respectively, the Air Staff, Trevor Gardner, and Roger Lewis, Air Force Assistant Secretary for Materiel, had all concurred in the new management concept. The recommendations had been approved by the two commanders and presented on September 3 to Assistant Secretary Lewis. Formal approval and authority to proceed with the new organization was issued on September 8, when WDD was directed to implement the concept and amend the Ramo-Wooldridge contract accordingly.

The Schriever recommendations were favorably received by the committee and were endorsed by all members except Frank Collbohm. Mr. Collbohm, who was not present, sent a letter, which was read to the committee by Dr. von Neumann, in which he reiterated his belief that the proposed arrangement would separate responsibility and authority in the ICBM effort. Several contractors were capable of undertaking the program, while the RW Corporation had not demonstrated competence in the field. Much of Collbohm's concern seems to have sprung from a fear that industry would not like the idea and would refuse to participate in the ICBM program.[46] Later events

[46]*Organization and Management Hearings,* pp. 72, 227. Convair and other industrial concerns opposed imposition of another level of review between themselves and the Air Force, but they were also quite unhappy about providing access to their industrial secrets to what they considered to be a potential competitor. Ramo-Wooldridge was given a hardware exclusion in its contract with the Air Force which was designed to allay these fears by preventing RW from undertaking actual production of items for use in the ICBM programs. This was not entirely satisfactory to the aircraft companies involved, however, as they saw no safe distinctions between ICBM production and other future production competitions. Beyond the specific questions of industrial security, there was also general opposition to the idea of creating another large aerospace competitor, whether that competitor had access to its rivals' information or not. The issue was never resolved, and there remain to this day elements of irritation in the comments about TRW Inc. (the present form of the RW Corporation) voiced by its competition. In a frank comment, Edward Doll, TRW executive, noted that contractors withheld data and secrets because they feared RW would use them to compete someday, "which is exactly what some of us had in mind." Interview, Los Angeles, August 11, 1971.

proved these fears to be generally groundless. At the time the committee appointed a three-member panel, chaired by Charles A. Lindbergh, to study Collbohm's arguments. This panel decided against Collbohm and affirmed the expanded RW role, which position was then endorsed by the committee as a whole.[47]

The endorsement was little more than a formality since, as noted above, the concept had already been implemented by the Air Force. Thus, by the late fall of 1954 (and effectively since September 8), the ICBM organizational arrangement was set and the project had been designated the highest priority in the Air Force. The Western Development Division was established as a branch of Headquarters ARDC. General Bernard A. Schriever was both Commander, WDD, and Deputy Commander, ARDC, thus ensuring immediate coordination of WDD and the parent command. The Ramo-Wooldridge Company was assigned systems engineering and technical direction of the entire effort. RW and the WDD occupied the same headquarters building in Inglewood, California.[48]

[47] Interview with Frank Collbohm. Also, Memo for Major Franzel from General Schriever, August 4, 1954. De Haven Document Collection. Also, *Eleventh Report,* pp. 78–79. As has been noted above, Convair was particularly unhappy about the Ramo-Wooldridge situation and expressed themselves in no uncertain terms. After the elevated role of the RW Corporation was decided upon, noticeable strains persisted between RW and Convair. Since RW clearly had the favor of the Air Force customer, however, Convair was more or less forced to live with the decision. The RW–Convair conflict was attested to in interviews with Simon Ramo, Dean Wooldridge, Reuben Mettler, William Patterson, Thomas Lanphier, and others. Lester Murray, who had participated in the earliest Convair rocket projects, has stated that delays in the decision as to the rocket design were due to "the incompetency and empire building desires of the Ramo-Wooldridge combination." Letter to the author, December 29, 1971. On the other hand, Thomas Lanphier, former Vice President of Convair, has said that events proved that the selection of Ramo-Wooldridge was a good idea and that they significantly assisted the program by forcing Convair to continually defend its actions. Interview with Thomas Lanphier, Jr., San Diego, August 24, 1971.

[48] In the spring of 1954, when the RW corp. had been given its new (and later to be enlarged) duties, its directors had instituted a Guided Missiles Research Division to handle the Air Force ICBM contracts. This Division was subdivided into five groups: Guidance and Control, Aerodynamics and Structures, Propulsion, Flight Test and Instrumentation, and Weapons Systems Analysis. The Guided Missiles Research Division was made a subsidiary in November

This does not mean that there had been no difficulties in establishing the independent WDD. As has been related, the Air Staff had not been entirely pleased with the idea and had opposed the recommendations of the original SMEC and RAND reports. The concepts contained therein had been more or less forced upon an unwilling Air Staff by Gardner and Secretary Talbott. Joseph Alsop has stated that "the Air Staff response was bitterly all but unanimously negative."[49] This attitude was attested to by several persons interviewed for this study, although in perhaps not quite so striking language.[50]

The relations of the WDD and the Air Materiel Command are also illustrative. The history of the separation of the ARDC from the AMC and its attendant frictions has been related above. The succeeding years had tempered many of the bad feelings then engendered, but some remained. After his appointment as head of the WDD, General Schriever was interested in concentrating all management functions within his headquarters. This included not only planning, technical direction, and budgeting, but also contracting and procurement. These latter two areas infringed on the responsibilities of the AMC. The issuance of the basic vehicle contracts and related subsystems had been delegated to General Schriever's office. Procurement, however, was still controlled by the AMC. In April 1954, General Schriever visited General Rawlings, AMC

1957 and renamed Space Technology Laboratories (STL). The other non–Air Force work of RW was conducted by its General Electronics Group. The ICBM system engineering and technical direction contracts of RW included a hardware ban. The General Electronics Group actively sought contracts elsewhere, however, and was meant to be a profit-making division. Interviews with Simon Ramo, Dean Wooldridge, Reuben Mettler. *Eleventh Report,* pp. 83–84.

[49] Alsop also maintains that both Gardner and Talbott were later fired because of their missile efforts and related organizational changes. Joseph Alsop, "McNamara and the Chiefs," *Washington Post,* May 11, 1963. I am indebted for this citation to Claude J. Johns, Jr., "The United States Intercontinental Ballistic Missile Program, 1954–59." Ph.D. dissertation (University of North Carolina, 1964).

[50] Interviews with Charles H. Terhune, Jr., USAF (ret.), now Deputy Director of the Jet Propulsion Laboratories, General John Zoekler, USAF (ret.), General O. Ritland, USAF (ret.).

Commander, in an unsuccessful effort to have the procurement responsibility delegated to the WDD.

The remainder of the spring and early summer was marked by negotiations—sometimes acrimonious—between Schriever, the AMC, and the Air Staff. The WDD-ARDC personnel wanted AMC to redelegate a portion of its contractual authority pertaining to Atlas "in order to effectuate the desires of the Air Staff in accelerating the development of an intercontinental ballistic missile capability."[51]

This proposal was rejected ("unfavorably considered") by the AMC, who instead proposed an AMC Atlas project office on the West Coast.[52] The AMC was candid in its reasons for refusal. "This matter is of particular importance because there appears to be a trend toward establishing a number of separate organizational entities to solve particular problems which have the effect of cutting our regular organizational structure and of dissipating our already limited resources."[53]

This cutting of the regular organizational structure was, of course, precisely what the WDD was designed to accomplish and what SMEC and the Air Force Secretary had desired. The ARDC, as petitioner, took the issue to the Air Staff, where it was overruled. In late June, Lt. General B. L. Boatner, the Deputy Chief of Staff, Materiel, informed the ARDC Commander that "the contracting authority for Project Atlas will remain with the Air Materiel Command with such re-delegation to ARDC, consistent with current practices, as may be required."[54] At the same time Boatner instructed the AMC that "The Atlas program will be re-oriented and accelerated to the maximum extent that technological development will permit.

[51]Memo from Col. John Martin, ARDC, to Commander, AMC, April 21, 1954. DeHaven Document Collection.
[52]Memo from Col. H. Jones to Commander, ARDC, May 5, 1954. DeHaven Document Collection.
[53]Memo from General E. W. Rawlings, Commander, AMC, to General Power, Commander, ARDC, 11 June 1954. DeHaven Document Collection.
[54]Memo, June 21, 1954. Lt. General Boatner, DCS/M, to Commander, ARDC. DeHaven Document Collection.
[55]Memo from Gen. Boatner to Commander, AMC, June 21, 1954. DeHaven Document Collection.

. . . The Atlas will be given highest program priority in the Air Force. Processing of any aspect of this program will be given precedence over any others in the Air Force."[55]

Despite Boatner's good intentions, the attempted compromise was not satisfactory. Schriever continued to press for much wider "redelegation" of procurement authority than the AMC was willing to permit. Several meetings were held between personnel from Schriever's office and the AMC during July. The result was a treaty signed July 28 by General Power (ARDC) and General McKee (the new AMC commander) delineating procurement and contracting authority for Atlas. ARDC (WDD) was to initiate project requirements, prepare work statements and specifications, and make technical evaluation of contractors' proposals. The AMC would perform the contracting and procurement functions.[56]

The WDD was never pleased with the decision to establish the Special Aircraft Project Office of the AMC to perform the procurement and contracting functions for Project Atlas. By December 1954 the AMC Project office was complaining to General Schriever that his technical personnel were dealing with industrial contractors directly instead of through the AMC office and that the latter was not being kept informed of planning changes.[57] These strains between the WDD and its AMC counterpart were gradually eliminated, however, as the two offices came to identify with the health of the project and thus to see themselves as partners in a worthwhile undertaking. As partners, there was no reason to offend each other unnecessarily.[58]

Another matter that remained to be settled was the designation of the airframe contractor. As has been related above, the

---

[56]*Air Force Ballistic Missile Chronology.* The AMC duties were performed by a west coast "Special Aircraft Project Office" later designated the Ballistic Missile Office. This office continued in a tandem position with the W.D.D. throughout the development of Atlas, Titan, Thor, and Minuteman.

[57]Two memos to General Schriever from Col. Harold T. Morris, Chief, Special Aircraft Project Office, AMC. Both dated December 8, 1954. De Haven Document Collection.

[58]Interview with Col. R. K. Jacobsen, USAF (ret.) now with North American Aviation. The strains were further eliminated as Schriever gained more influence in the choice of the AMC office commander.

original von Neumann Committee recommendations had included the dictate that all production engineering should be halted—in effect, that the Convair hardware program should be stopped until further notice. The SMEC had been noticeably unimpressed with the Convair's original presentation, and particularly with the rigidity of its proposals. By early 1954 Convair had settled upon a large five-engine vehicle. Convair advocated freezing the Atlas design at its specifications and immediately undertaking production. The members of SMEC felt, on the other hand, that recent technological advances, particularly in limiting warhead size and weight, would permit construction of a much smaller vehicle. To SMEC, Convair seemed excessively inflexible and, ironically in light of Convair's long-unrewarded support for a rocket program, conservative. This attitude prompted SMEC's original call for a halt to Convair production plans and for the creation of a special technical group to review the entire program. The latter recommendation, of course, resulted in the WDD–Ramo-Wooldridge complex.

During the July review of progress to date, the reconstituted von Neumann Committee was again unimpressed with the rigid Convair support for what was to the committee members an outmoded design.[59] The first and second von Neumann Committees had explicitly recommended that until an Air Force contractor was selected, no corporation, including Convair, should be led to believe it would be chosen. Convair's hopes thus remained in limbo during the summer and fall of 1954 while awaiting an Air Force decision. Convair believed that its proposals were sound, well thought out, and based on a unique expertise that no other group in the country possessed. They were thus irritated by the negative response received from the Scientific Advisory Committee, whose members they considered ivory tower experts with no feel for the realities of the technical problems involved.[60]

[59]On January 3, 1955, the second von Neumann Committee, which had been in operation since the preceding spring, was formally chartered as the Intercontinental Ballistic Missile Scientific Advisory Committee to the Secretary of the Air Force. *Hearings, Organization and Management of Missile Programs,* p. 18.

[60]Letters to author from Karel Bossart and Lester K. Murray. Interview with

Discussion between Convair, other potential contractors, Schriever's office, and the Air Staff continued throughout the summer and fall. After what were sometimes heated exchanges, Schriever's office finally decided to stay with Convair. Dissatisfaction with Convair remained, nevertheless. "Effective the week of 25 October 1954, it was decided to recommend Convair as Air Force contractor in the ICBM program. . . . As with all other Air Force manufacturers, Convair has weaknesses in its organization and technical competence."[61]

Convair was judged weak in the areas of electronics and systems engineering, but competent as an airframe contractor. Convair also had the advantage of having long been engaged in rocket research. At the same time Schriever suggested a compromise with those who had opposed employment of Convair.

To introduce the element of competition with regard to Air Force contractors, it is believed wise to sponsor an alternative configuration and staging approach with a second source. In line with this thinking, it is presently believed that the second design should be oriented around a greater technical risk which might offer dramatic pay-offs.[62]

General Schriever presented his conclusions to Assistant Secretary Roger Lewis on October 29, 1954, at Air Force headquarters. Lewis retained some reservations about Convair's management and withheld approval at this meeting. He did, however, reassure Schriever about the Air Force management approach. He made it plain that he was not concerned about widespread criticism of the Ramo-Wooldridge setup. Indeed, he implied that he considered the comments entirely natural and that he was quite sympathetic to the RW position.[63]

Convair was finally accepted as Air Force contractor by Lewis after he had conducted further conversations with members of the Atlas Scientific Advisory Committee. By December 1954 the basic decision had been made to scale down the gross

William Patterson. All three men were involved in the Convair MX–774 and MX–1593 projects.

[61]Memo for the record, written by B. A. Schriever, October 25, 1954. DeHaven Document Collection.

[62]*Ibid.*

[63]Memo to General Sessums, ARDC, from General Schriever, October 29, 1954. DeHaven Document Collection.

weight of the missile and to lower the number of engines from five to three. These decisions were formally relayed to Convair on January 12, 1955.[64]

The reduction had been inevitable since the first von Neumann Committee review. The delay in its final implementation was due partly to the complexities of establishing the new West Coast agency and partly to the strong Convair opposition and the consequent need to marshal opposing technical arguments. Much of the latter work was conducted by Ramo-Wooldridge under the contracted review study.

To ensure that no single program element would prove faulty or unworkable and thereby paralyze the entire program, a decision was made to contract for alternatives to each of the major subsystems. When the refined Atlas design was proven sound, it became possible to employ the backup systems in a second ICBM. The decision to proceed with this weapon, which became the Titan, was made in May 1955. Titan differed from Atlas in airframe, engine, guidance system, and in being two-stage. The Atlas was "one and one-half stage," meaning everything was burning at liftoff. Convair favored this design because of the uncertainty of rocket ignition at very high altitudes. Titan was specifically planned for emplacement in underground, hardened silos. The original Atlas was to be above ground.[65]

By January 1955, then, the Air Force management organization had been determined, the airframe and other major contractors chosen, and the general vehicle design specified.[66] In early 1955, the Secretary of Defense stated that the development of

[64]*Air Force Ballistic Missile Chronology.* In fairness to Convair, it should be noted that Frank Collbohm, who dissented from the proposed role for the RW Corporation, also believes that it was a mistake to choose the small vehicle design that was ultimately settled upon. He thinks that it would have been wiser to build a bigger vehicle so that the margin for error would be greater and there would not have been such a strict need for all subsystems to work perfectly at their peak. Interview.

[65]Robert L. Perry, "The Atlas, Thor, Titan, and Minuteman," in Emme (ed.), *The History of Rocket Technology.* See also *Hearings, Study of Airpower,* p. 1162.

[66]The Atlas rocket engines were to be built by Rocketdyne Corp. and were outgrowths of the engine development work long undertaken by that company in connection with the Navaho program.

an ICBM was of "critical importance to the basic security of the United States and the free world."[67]

Problems remained, however, in the Atlas project's reception within the Air Staff. The original SMEC Committee had advocated placing the Atlas development program outside of normal Air Force channels, partly in order to protect it from hostile forces. WDD accomplished this to some extent, but reviews, budgetary battles, and, in some cases, noncooperation continued to mark the program. By June 1955, concern had developed at WDD that the Atlas program was abut to be jeopardized through delays in funding, interference from other interested major commands, and multiple review–approval levels required by Air Force regulations.[68] These fears were shared by Trevor Gardner. One major problem was the acquisition of facilities for design and static testing. The Air Force procedures then applicable in this area were felt to be bottlenecks. Similar problems existed in industrial facilities and military construction.[69]

These concerns led Schriever and Gardner to attempt to institute entirely new management and review processes for the Atlas program. The two realized that a procedure designed to bypass the established review and control points within the Air Force would face strong opposition from every group it sought to avoid. Roger Lewis supported the idea of a streamlined review process, but he and Secretary Talbott were unwilling to further offend the Air Staff over the ICBM program without higher support. Accordingly, Schriever and Gardner set about organizing such higher backing. It should be noted at this point that Schriever was a very effective advocate, and during his

[67]U.S. Dept. of Defense, *Semiannual Report of the Secretary of Defense and the Semiannual Reports of the Secretary of the Army, Secretary of the Navy and Secretary of the Air Force,* January 1 to June 30, 1954 (Washington: Government Printing Office, 1955), pp. 30–31.

[68]Letter to author from Harry Jordan, Command Historian, Space and Missile Systems Organization.

[69]Transcript of interview with Col. Ray E. Soper, Vice Comdr., BMD, November 29, 1966. Interview conducted and transcript provided by Harry Jordan, Command Historian, SAMSO. See also Schriever testimony, *Organization and Management Hearings,* p. 117.

tenure at WDD he enjoyed increasingly good relations with Congress. Schriever was a personable, intelligent, and patient man. He was very good at personal contact and he sought always to maintain and improve this ability. Schriever and Gardner decided to take their case to Capitol Hill, with the intent of employing Congress to prod the President to issue the appropriate directives.

Their task was made easier by a number of external events. Late in 1954 the Soviet Union displayed its first long-range turboprop bomber, the "Bear," which was considered capable of carrying out a nuclear strike against most targets in the United States and returning to Soviet territory. As one student of American defense policy during the period has stated, "For the first time American defense analysts began to doubt the significance of the nation's strategic and nuclear superiority."[70] Perhaps prodded by this event, the National Security Council undertook a comprehensive review of the *New Look* strategy in January 1955, which resulted in recognition of the possibility that the United States and the Soviet Union might be approaching mutual deterrence.

In May 1955, American observers were given a shock when ten to twelve four-engine jet strategic bombers (the "Bison," comparable to the B–52), participated in the annual May Day Flyby in Moscow. It appeared that the Soviet Union had caught up to the U. S. in strategic aircraft design. About the same time radar devices newly installed in Turkey revealed that the Soviets were testing large numbers of 800-mile-range ballistic missiles. This last revelation was given added import when the Eisenhower-appointed Killian Committee warned that unless the United States increased its effort, the Soviet Union would achieve a decisive lead in strategic missiles by 1960.[71]

[70] Harland B. Moulton, "American Strategic Power: Two Decades of Nuclear Strategy and Weapons Systems, 1945–65," (Ph.D. dissertation, University of Minnesota, 1969), p. 162.

[71] Samuel P. Huntington, *The Common Defense* (New York: Columbia University Press, 1961), p. 89. See also Moulton, pp. 162–163. The Killian Committee (formally titled the Technological Capabilities Panel) was created in the fall of 1954 by the National Security Council at the direction of the President. Its purpose was to reappraise the relative offensive and defensive capabilities of the

One immediate consequence of the new information on Soviet capabilities, and particularly of the May Day Airshow, was that the Air Force began a study of the feasibility of increasing the production of B–52s from twelve to seventeen a month. Secretary of Defense Wilson, during his January 1955 appearance before a House Appropriations Subcommittee, announced that the Air Force was scheduled to receive $14.5 billion in new obligational authority to continue the rapid buildup toward a 137-wing goal.

The Soviet advances in airplane design also prompted increased interest in the American strategic missile program, particularly in light of the evidence of strong Soviet interest in that field. Congress was therefore primed for just the pitch Gardner and Schriever contemplated. The two went to senators Clinton P. Anderson, Democrat of New Mexico, Chairman of the Joint Committee on Atomic Engery, and Henry M. Jackson, Democrat of Washington, Chairman of that Committee's Subcommittee on Military Applications. Anderson and Jackson were impressed by the presentation and especially by the evidence provided that the Soviet Union was actively interested in the ICBM and might at that time be considerably ahead of the United States.

During May and June, Committee members visited the WDD headquarters. The Military Applications subcommittee took extensive testimony from high civilian officials, military officers, and scientists, all of whom were associated with the ICBM program. Given the impetus of these hearings and the nature of the witnesses called, the findings were somewhat predetermined. Following the subcommittee hearings, Senators Anderson and Jackson sent a letter to President Eisenhower containing a list of findings and recommendations. First, the Senators expressed their concern with the present situation.

We fear that, despite our present accelerated program, the Soviet Union may now be ahead of us in the race for the ICBM. . . . We

Soviet Union and the United States in the context of the recent thermonuclear warhead advances. The committee's report was submitted to the National Security Council on February 14, 1955. Armacost, *The Politics of Weapons Innovation*, p. 50. *Study of Airpower Hearings*, p. 554.

believe the question of war or peace may depend upon who gets the ICBM first. This is truly the ultimate weapon. . . . If the Soviets win the race for the ICBM, and if they thereupon use it in a massive surprise attack against our cities and industries and the bases of the Strategic Air Command, effective retaliation may be impossible.[72]

After detailing the grave political consequences of a Soviet threat to Europe with even a medium-range ballistic missile, the Senators then offered comments upon the present U. S. program. Among these were that the ICBM, although designated as top priority in the Air Force, did not then have overriding priority within the entire defense program as they thought it should. The ICBM did not have a separate budget within the Air Force, which meant that "the time is nearing when the effort may seriously suffer because of budgetary conflicts with other Air Force programs of lesser importance."

Air Force and DoD planning on how to integrate the ICBM into the operational strike force was found to be lagging behind technological progress on the weapon. The Senators also included a telling aside on Air Force reactions to the program. "Although we fully understand the necessity for the detailed checks and rechecks which characterize Air Force procurement regulations, we believe that an overly rigid application of normal procurement policies to the ICBM is now slowing progress."

The Senators concluded by calling for a number of steps, including a special meeting of the National Security Council to receive a briefing by WDD personnel, issuance of a Presidential directive assigning the ICBM highest national priority, a separate budget for the ICBM, and relaxation of normal procurement regulations.

The nature of the problems facing WDD in its attempt to accelerate the ICBM program are concisely stated in a memo to General Schriever from one of his top staff:

Major operating commands are strongly oriented toward near-term programs and have a distinct reluctance for undertaking strong and specific action in connection with a program for 1960 and beyond. The

[72]Letter to President Eisenhower from Senators Anderson and Jackson. June 30, 1955. Copy received from J. K. Mansfield.

action levels in the Air Staff and in Commands will not (despite priorities and directives) be inclined to volunteer first attention to difficult problems of inter-command coordination.[73]

The Anderson-Jackson letter had precisely the effect desired by Gardner and Schriever. A meeting of the National Security Council was held on July 28, 1955, and was briefed by Schriever and others. Before any action at the Presidential level had been taken, a directive was sent throughout the Air Force "by order of the Secretary of the Air Force" and signed by General Twining, which included the following observations:

It is the responsibility of every Air Force activity to exert unrelenting efforts to insure the earliest possible integration of guided missile units into the weapons inventory where combat capability will be improved. . . . Guided missiles are weapons with special qualities. Plans for their use must be designed to exploit these features. Manned aircraft techniques have, of necessity, been the basis in the past for most of the development practices and planning for the use of missiles. Reluctance to depart from such development practices and planning procedures may prevent maximum progress.[74]

This action was, however, simply another "directive" without authoritative specifics. Those specifics began to appear on September 8, when the President stated that the ICBM had the highest priority in the nation and that this would be subject to change only by presidential action. The Secretary of Defense was directed to prosecute the program with maximum urgency.[75]

This was the action Gardner was waiting for. As noted, it had been his and Schriever's intention for some months to imple-

[73]July 18, 1955 memo to General Schriever from Col. William A. Sheppard, Deputy Commander, Plans. DeHaven Document Collection.

[74]Air Force Regulation No. 58–1. August 15, 1955. DeHaven Document Collection.

[75]*Organization and Management Hearings,* p. 26. Five days later, on September 13, Eisenhower approved a National Security Council recommendation for a 1,500-mile, nuclear-armed ballistic missile. This action had been recommended by the Killian Committee. Both land and sea basing were to be considered. This was the origin of the Air Force Thor and Army–Navy Jupiter, and ultimately of the Polaris. *Organization and Management Hearings,* p. 434. The reader is again referred to Armacost.

ment administrative control procedures for the ICBM program which would serve to bypass what he saw as obstructive Air Force review processes (and obstructive Air Force personnel directing the processes). On September 13, 1955, Gardner sent a memo to Hyde Gillette, Deputy for Budget and Program Management in the office of the Assistant Secretary of the Air Force for Financial Management, directing Gillette to serve as chairman of a working group to evaluate these matters. The Gillette Committee was to include General Schriever, officers from his staff, as well as members from the Secretary's office, the AMC, and the Air Staff.[76]

The Gillette Committee operated through a series of panels. On each, General Schriever or one of his key aides had a seat. The committee recommended sweeping revisions of Air Force and DOD procedures. To remove the intermediate layers of review in both the Air Force and DOD, the Committee suggested a much simplified administrative structure solely for the ballistic missile programs. A Ballistic Missiles Committee was to be established within the office of the Secretary of Defense, which would be chaired by the Deputy Secretary and would include the Assistant Secretaries and a member from the Budget Bureau. By this means the separate clearances by five assistant secretaries would be combined in one committee action, which would also accelerate Budget Bureau review. This committee would exercise final review and guidance on behalf of the Defense Secretary. Management responsibility would, however, be delegated to the Air Secretary, which responsibility would include facilities, procurement, and funding.

The Air Force Secretary was to have a counterpart ballistic missiles committee to coordinate Air Force review. The secretary would serve as Chairman. The Air Force and OSD Ballis-

[76]*Eleventh Report,* p. 22. The membership of the Gillette Committee is given in *Organization and Management Hearings,* p. 20. Schriever was later to be quite frank about his role in this matter. During a 1959 Congressional investigation, Herbert Roback of the staff of the House Government Operations Committee, said to Schriever, "Do I understand that you were a moving personality in setting up or getting the Gillette Committee created?," to which the General replied, "You are correct." *Organization and Management Hearings,* p. 117.

tic Missiles Committees were to be the sole reviewing authorities for the ICBM program. Furthermore, the Gillette Committee recommended that a yearly development plan be prepared for the ballistic missile programs so that instead of many separate processing and approval actions, the Ballistic Missiles Committees would review and approve the yearly plan in one action. ICBM appropriations were to be justified in a package separate from all other Air Force requests. This would ensure against interference from other Air Force programs. The WDD–AMC conflict over contracting authority was left much as it had been, although the Air Secretary was granted greater review authority and the AMC Commander greater flexibility.[77]

The main purpose of the Ballistic Missiles Committee was to avoid the "stumbling blocks and delaying features" of procedures dealing with military and industrial construction.[78] Under usual circumstances a specific project had to be identified eighteen months before the date funds were appropriated for construction.

The first twelve months were taken up by preliminary planning and the following reviews: Screening in Air Force headquarters by an *ad hoc* committee, Installations Board, Budget Advisory Committee, Air Council, and Air Force Secretary; then screening in OSD by the Assistant Secretaries (Comptroller) and (Properties and Installations); plus reviews in areas of special interest by other Assistant Secretaries; and finally screening by the Bureau of the Budget.[79]

To cut through this maze the Gillette Committee asked that construction funds be included in the yearly development plans to be reviewed as a lump sum. Finally, the committee recommended that the Air Force ICBM Scientific Advisory Committee also serve the Secretary of Defense.

The Gillette Report was submitted October 21, 1955. Its major proposals, which had the effect of bypassing the Air Staff

[77] An extensive review of the Gillette Committee Report can be found in *Eleventh Report*, pp. 23–27. The report, with classified portions deleted, is printed in *Organization and Management Hearings*, App. A, pp. 639 ff.

[78] The words are General Schriever's. *Organization and Management Hearings*, p. 117.

[79] *Eleventh Report*, p. 26.

on almost all matters pertaining to ballistic missiles, were for obvious reasons not favorably viewed by many elements within the Air Force. There was little that these persons could do to forestall implementation of the Gillette procedures, however, in the face of strong, united support from the Secretary of the Air Force and the Secretary of Defense. Added to this was the evident Congressional and Presidential interest. Air Force Secretary Quarles quickly approved the report and requested the Air Force Chief of Staff to execute the plan "with all possible speed."[80] On November 8, Secretary of Defense Wilson sent memoranda to the Secretary of the Air Force and the Secretaries of the Army and Navy jointly, announcing his approval.

The OSD Ballistic Missiles Committee was established the same day to serve as a single agency within the DOD for all matters relating to the ICBM-IRBM projects, particularly approvals of the development programs prepared by the Air Force Committee and the Joint Army-Navy Committee. The Deputy Secretary of Defense was appointed chairman. Members included the Assistant Secretaries of Defense for Research and Development (Vice Chairman), Applications Engineering, Properties and Installations, and Comptroller. The Budget Bureau was asked to send a representative to serve as a Committee member and help to expedite the budgetary process.

The Air Force Ballistic Missiles Committee was established by Secretary Quarles on November 14, 1955. Its membership was (as recommended in the Gillette Report) the Air Force Secretary (Chairman), the Assistant Secretary for Research and Development (Vice Chairman), the Assistant Secretary for Financial Management and Materiel, and the Assistant Chief of Staff for Guided Missiles. The office of the latter was to provide a secretariat. The committee later expanded to include the Vice Chief of Staff, the Deputy Chief of Staff for Operations, and the ARDC Commander. From 1955 through 1959 the special procedures were very effective in circumventing established Air

[80]Quarles had succeeded Talbott on August 11, 1955. Quoted phrase is from *Eleventh Report,* p. 23.

Force and DOD procedures which had before produced bottle-necks.

As noted, the procedures were not popular with the Air Staff. Nevertheless, they were accepted, however reluctantly. One reason was, of course, simply that the Secretary of Defense explicitly directed their implementation. There was another influence, however, which we have seen before.

There was yet another argument in favor of the Gillette Procedures—kept within the Air Staff—and this was the fear that Secretary Gardner might succeed in making of the Air Force ballistic missile program another "Manhattan" Project, with himself as "Czar." The Air Staff wanted ballistic missiles to evolve as strategic weapon systems and to become completely integrated into the Air Force. The Special Procedures insured that this would be so and served as a block to Gardner's ambition, real or imagined.[81]

Colonel Ray Soper, who served as Secretary of the Air Force Ballistic Missile Committee and, concurrently, as Director of the Office of the Assistant Chief of the Air Staff for Guided Missiles, and who had also been a member of the Gillette Committee, has remarked that the Gillette Procedures "worked like a charm." Following a meeting of the Air Force Ballistic Missile Committee, Colonel Soper could prepare the documents and then have them signed—or sign them himself—and send them off. This, of course, greatly speeded up the lag from decision to implementation. Colonel Soper basically operated to "bird-dog" WDD (and its successor, the Ballistic Missile Division) requests through the Pentagon.

With the formal implementation of the Gillette Proposals, the type of problems and delays that had heretofore beset the American ICBM program generally were eliminated. The ICBM had been designated the highest national priority by Presidential directive. The program was separated from the normal development channels within the Air Force and the Department

[81]Col. Ray Soper, transcript of interview conversation conducted by Harry Jordan, Division Historian, Space and Missile Systems Organization, USAF, November 29, 1966.

of Defense. An entirely new agency had been created specifically to manage the ballistic missile programs. Budget requests for the program, including even construction funds, were to be submitted in a lump sum, separately from all other service programs, and were to be approved in like fashion. The OSD Ballistic Missiles Committee would be the sole reviewing agency within OSD for all matters related to the program, including budget requests, facilities construction, and technical decisions. The Secretary of the Air Force was authorized to approve facilities requirements, construction and other contracted services, and completion dates. The line of command for ICBM Programs would be WDD to Air Force Ballistic Missiles Committee to OSD Ballistic Missiles Committee. These were striking changes in the normal mode of operations. Their effectiveness was very high and almost totally eliminated the kinds of delays, obstruction, and funding scarcity that had plagued the program in its early years. This is not to say that from this point the ICBM program enjoyed unlimited funding. It did mean that the ICBM personnel were assured of direct access to the highest civilian authorities whenever necessary. If a budget request were reduced, WDD people could immediately prepare alternative programs or arguments for the original sum and take them right back. This was a significant improvement over past procedures.

7

The Process Is
Completed

BY THE SPRING of 1954, the ICBM enjoyed, at least formally, the highest priority in the Air Force. An entirely new agency had been established to oversee its development. And by the fall of 1955, the ICBM was, by Presidential directive, the highest priority item in the national arsenal. A revolutionary, enormously simplified management chain of command had been instituted which effectively bypassed the great majority of the previous review stages, including those within the Air Staff. By late 1955, the program was strongly supported, both in personnel and funds, and was being rushed to completion.

I have been primarily concerned with the attitudes, procedures, and decisions which hindered or delayed the development of an ICBM in the United States, but now I shall briefly review events that led to the final attainment of an ICBM.

On November 8, 1955, Secretary of Defense Wilson established the OSD Ballistic Missiles Committee. Air Secretary Donald Quarles created the Air Force Ballistic Missile Committee a week later. In December 1955, the National Security Council was again briefed on the ICBM program and expressed its approval of the progress to date.[1]

By this date the WDD was also actively engaged in building an intermediate-range ballistic missile (IRBM). In November 1955 a national priority had been given to the IRBM. Two separate programs were authorized, one within the Air Force and the second a joint Army–Navy undertaking.[2]

As early as the fall of 1954, there had been serious discussion in Air Force circles about starting an IRBM project of 1,000- to 2,000-mile range. At this time the weapon was referred to as a tactical ballistic missile. General Schriever initially opposed the idea, arguing that the project would cause unnecessary duplication of technical programs and facilities, that internal Air Force competition would occur, and that within ARDC itself there would be competition for test facilities and development support. Schriever further warned that the Air Force's role in the development of ballistic rockets would be threatened. Internal Air Force conflict, with sides perhaps being taken within the Air Staff, would come to the attention of the Defense department. Doubts might be raised about the ability of the Air Force to direct the program. This situation could lead to the transfer of responsibility for one or both of the ballistic missiles to another service, or, because of their high priority, to a separate management group reporting directly to the Defense department.

These arguments had not been enough to forestall initiation of an IRBM, but they did have some weight. Their influence is obvious in the assignment of the new project directly to WDD,

[1] Interview with General Osmond Ritland. General Ritland was an immediate Deputy to General Schriever and took over Command of the Ballistic Missile Division (WDD) in 1959 when Schriever moved to the Command of ARDC.

[2] *Hearings, Study of Air Power*, p. 1118. *A Chronology of Missile and Astronautic Events*, Committee on Science and Astronautics, 87th Cong., 1st sess., p. 24.

to prevent the intra–Air Force conflict feared by Schriever.[3] The Air Force IRBM was to be handled with exactly the same management pattern as the ICBM—in other words, conducted by the WDD and run under the Gillette procedures.

A memo to the Air Force Secretary from Defense Secretary Wilson in November 1955, assigning the IRBM No. 1 to the Air Force, had included the dictum that "attainment of the earliest possible operational capability with this weapon [is] of utmost importance to national security."[4] The emphasis placed on the IRBM can be explained in part by certain findings of the Killian Committee appointed in late 1954 by President Eisenhower. After examining both long- and medium-range ballistic missiles and warning of Soviet progress in both, the Killian group determined that it would be "much easier and have much greater assurance of success" to develop a 1,500-mile missile than to rely entirely on the 5,000-mile ICBM.[5]

The IRBM was to be developed as rapidly as possible without interfering with the ICBM. In December 1955 the IRBM was granted a priority within the Air Force second only to the ICBM. This ranking was disturbed in January 1956 by a directive to the WDD assigning co-equal priority to the two programs. In the event of interference between the projects, higher headquarters was to be notified.

The WDD personnel were unhappy with these events, feeling that assigning any other project equal priority with the ICBM would inevitably slow the latter by weakening its call on materiel and personnel. The WDD people were willing to take on the added task, but were deeply involved with Atlas and preferred to concentrate on bringing it successfully to completion. These feelings were made known to the Air Staff and

[3]Similar perceptions may have motivated the strong, though unsuccessful, Air Force drive to prevent an Army–Navy IRBM.

[4]*Air Force Ballistic Missile Chronology.* IRBM no. 2 was the joint Army–Navy Jupiter. The Navy later withdrew from the program in favor of developing Polaris. The Thor-Jupiter controversy is often cited as a classic example of inter-service rivalry.

[5]*Hearings, Study of Airpower,* p. 717. The Killian group's report was finished in February 1955.

resulted in a clarification. In a letter of February 6, 1956, to General Power, General Twining, the Chief of Staff, noted that in event of conflict, the ICBM was to take priority over the IRBM.

Throughout 1956 Congressional concern about the missile programs continued to be evident. In mid-April of 1956 the Sub-committee on the Air Force of the Senate Committee on Armed Services, under the chairmanship of Senator Stuart Symington, Democrat of Missouri, opened hearings to investigate the adequacy of the "present and planned strengths of the United States Air Force."[6]

The Symington Committee "Airpower" hearings are most commonly remembered for the "bomber gap" testimony elicited from many Air Force witnesses. General Curtis E. LeMay reported, for example, that the Soviets were producing Bear and Bison aircraft "at a combined rate substantially higher than we are producing B–52s." LeMay's testimony was echoed by many others.

The committee also spent considerable time inspecting the United States strategic missile programs. The possibility of an important Soviet threat in the form of medium- and long-range ballistic missiles was widely discussed. The subcommittee members were especially interested in whether the U. S. ballistic missile programs were receiving adequate funding.

One witness who received particular attention was Trevor Gardner. In November of 1955, when President Eisenhower assigned the Air Force and the Army–Navy IRBMs equal national priority with the ICBM, Gardner had been quite upset. He felt that the ICBM was clearly the more important weapon and that this action could only slow its arrival. Gardner's position was, "We need to be more decisive and place our bets with more accuracy. Having a whole family of ballistic missile programs not only slows the programs down but it is wasteful of national funds."[7]

In planning for the fiscal year 1957 budget, Gardner felt that

[6]*Hearings, Study of Airpower*, p. 105.
[7]*Hearings, Study of Air Power*, p. 1117.

research and development should be funded more strongly than the Administration intended. On January 16, 1956, Gardner had submitted a request for an additional $250 million in R&D funds for FY 1957 and a supplemental increase of $120 million in 1956. The request was cosigned by General Twining, General Putt, Lyle Garlock (Assistant Secretary for Comptroller), General James Doolittle, Air Force scientist H. G. Stever, and the Deputy Chief of Staff, Operations, General Everest. The proposal was turned down by the Secretary of the Air Force on January 28, 1956. It was resubmitted on February 10 and was again rejected.

The letter to Secretary Quarles was the eighth attempt by Gardner since September 24, 1954, to raise the overall ceiling on research and development funding. After receiving the Quarles answer of January 28, 1956, Gardner decided to resign because he did not feel he could defend the then projected budget. Between that date and February 11, he continued to press for higher R&D funding. When his memo to Quarles of February 10 was turned down, Gardner resigned the following day.[8]

Gardner later explained that his resignation stemmed from his belief that the current R&D budget would not allow the United States to remain technically superior to the Soviets in airpower, his lack of sympathy with the Air Force organization for management of the ballistic missile program, and his fear that the total Air Force budget would guarantee an inferior Air Force in the future.

It is clear, however, that Gardner's resignation was not tied specifically to any delay in the ICBM program. In fact, at the time of his resignation, Gardner believed that the United States was probably ahead of the Soviets with the ICBM, while the latter led in IRBM development. Gardner resigned because of dissatisfaction with the overall Air Force budget and the total amount available for R&D, not because of any specific delays in the ICBM program. Indeed, one of Gardner's main complaints

[8]*Ibid.*, pp. 1135, 1143. A Gardner memo to Secretary Talbott of May 5, 1955, the memo for Secretary Quarles of January 16, 1956, Quarles' reply of January 28, and Gardner's final memo of February 10 appear on pp. 1144–48.

was that the emphasis on the ICBM, which he strongly favored, nevertheless drew funds from other valuable programs.[9]

It is important to realize that the ICBM development program was definitely not being starved at this time. General Putt was one of the signatories of the January 16 memo to Secretary Quarles asking $250 million more for R&D. In his testimony before the Committee, the General reported that the Soviet Union "appears not to worry about duplications in the development field, nor the disproportionate application of scientific and technical manpower [to] his military might." Putt noted that in general, American R&D funding had been inadequate, but went on to say that the ICBM program was adequately funded in 1955 and 1956, and that funds requested by the President for the coming fiscal year were also satisfactory. At another point, Putt stated that when the IRBM was given an equal priority with the ICBM, there was no cutback of R&D funds for the ICBM. Funds for the shorter-range missile had been found elsewhere.[10]

That funding was persistently adequate for the ICBM was supported in testimony by General Schriever, who stated at one point, "We run into problems every day and we have to find ways to solve them, but we have maintained pretty well our schedules." Senator Symington replied, "As it is going now it is going about as fast as you think it can go; is that correct?" Schriever answered, "In my opinion it is."[11]

[9]*Ibid.*, pp. 1117–1120. Gardner's views were given a wide airing after his resignation. In addition to the platform of the Air Force Hearings, Gardner wrote articles for *Look, Life,* and *The Airpower Historian,* in the period 1956–58. In these, Gardner complained of the duplication of the Thor and Jupiter, of the competition of the two with the ICBM, and of the general "maze of missile management." Secretary of Defense Charles Wilson came in for particular criticism. "Wilson has vitalized this wing-collar complacency into a procurement policy known as 'fly-before-you-buy.' It is the supreme accomplishment of men who believe in saving dollars even if you have to waste time" (*Look,* May 1, 1956). "Former Secretary of Defense Charles Wilson and Deputy Secretary Donald Quarles . . . permitted the continuance of a hopeless administrative jungle [which] has strangled scientific thinking and performance" (*Life,* November 4, 1957). See also Gardner articles in *Look,* May 15, 1956, and *The Airpower Historian,* 5 no. 1 (January 1958):3–13.

[10]*Hearings, Study of Air Power,* pp. 537, 586, 667, and 615.

[11]*Ibid.*, p. 1167. An extensive review of Administration Congressional testimony in this period which left the impression that "By and large both military

Table 7.1   Speed of Development of Various Weapons

Program	Years to First Unit Deployment	Program	Years to First Unit Deployment
B–47	7.6	Navaho	Cancelled after 9.5 years of R&D testing.
B–52	9.4	Thor	3.3 first squadron complete.
B–58	11.2	Atlas	4.9 first complex, 5.2 first squadron complete.
Snark	13.4		

[a]*Organization and Management Hearings,* p. 23. It must be noted, however, that the Thor and Atlas schedules in this are calculated from the creation of WDD and not from the program inception date used in the calculations for all other weapons in the list. If the development period for Atlas was calculated as was that for Navaho, the elapsed time would be closer to twelve years than five. The Thor number is correct but Thor was constructed basically from off-the-shelf components (except for the airframe) whose development had begun much earlier. In other words, this and other charts offered in Congressional hearings sometimes lack a consistent standard for defining program start and stop dates. As demonstrated in this study, however, Atlas' early years were minimally supported when supported at all.

People I interviewed universally believed that the ICBM program had progressed remarkably quickly following the 1954 speedup. Particularly after the institution of the Gillette procedures, those associated with the program think it moved almost as fast as it could. Certainly more money could always have been spent, and the Titan, Thor, and Jupiter programs made demands on some resources that might have been directed toward Atlas. But compared to normal procedures, progress was strikingly rapid and unfettered by excessive review.

The Gillette procedures were a truly revolutionary innovation which eliminated most of the normal Air Force review process. Table 7.1 will give an idea of the rapidity of the ballistic missile development programs. The figures are particularly notable in light of the extremely long lead times widely projected for these weapons during the period 1946–1954.

and civilian officials did agree that the United States was investing all it could profitably invest in . . . missile research and development," can be found in Moulton, "American Strategic Power," pp. 179–89.

When asked why Gardner resigned, almost all of those interviewed said that Gardner had done all that he could, that he would not have been satisfied unless he had been made Secretary of Defense at the least, and that his temperament had finally created an untenable situation.

Following the resignation of Trevor Gardner, Secretary Wilson created the post of Special Assistant for Guided Missiles, and appointed to it Eger V. Murphree, formerly of the Esso Oil Company. Murphree took office on May 27, 1956, and served until May 1957, when he was replaced by William M. Holaday. In November 1957, Holaday was named Director of Guided Missiles by Secretary of Defense McElroy. Holaday was to "direct all activities in the Department of Defense relating to research, development, engineering, production, and procurement of guided missiles."[12]

In addition to the special assistants, a number of advisory committees were formed during this period to review both the general R&D outlook and specific missile programs. The first of these, the Newbury Committee (after its chairman, Frank D. Newbury, Assistant Secretary of Defense for Applications Engineering), resulted from congressional pressure. In its report on the Defense Appropriations bill for 1955, the Senate Appropriations Committee noted the "disorganized situation relating to the guided missile program" and called for an investigation. The Newbury Committee, named by Secretary Wilson, resulted. It submitted a report February 16, 1955. As a later Congressional committee was to observe, "The Report was couched in general terms, analyzing problems and indicating the types of missile programs to be pursued in the future."[13]

A second advisory panel created within the Department of Defense in 1955 reviewed the American Space Satellite efforts.[14] Finally in 1955 a study group headed by Deputy Secre-

[12]*A Chronology of Missile and Astronautic Events,* p. 35.

[13]*Eleventh Report,* p. 13.

[14]This was the Stewart Committee, chaired by Homer J. Stewart. The Stewart Report favored the Navy Viking over the Army Redstone as a satellite launching vehicle. An Air Force proposal utilizing Atlas was actually considered best qualified for the project, but the committee feared possible interference with the ICBM program. (See *Eleventh Report,* pp. 128–92.) The whole issue of the American failure to launch a satellite before the Soviet Union is closely related

tary of Defense Reuben Robertson was named to study the time that would be needed to bring a new manned aircraft weapon system from concept to combat. The period was found to be ten years or longer.

The question of the relative positions of the Soviet Union and the United States in the development of ballistic missiles has been touched upon at several points above. During the period 1955–1957, the public picture remained quite unclear, as reputable analysts supported claims of both Soviet superiority and inferiority. In April 1955 Senator Symington had charged that the Soviet Union led in the development of the ICBM and in May warned that the Soviets might also lead in the development of missile warheads.[15]

After his resignation, Trevor Gardner also claimed that the Soviet Union led in the development of ballistic missiles, although, as noted above, his position varied between the IRBM and the ICBM. These warnings were given added weight by the findings of the Killian Committee.

Information from the Soviet Union fueled the controversy. In February 1956 Deputy Premier Mikoyan stated that the Soviet Union could deliver a thermonuclear warhead to any target on earth. In April 1957 there were reports that the USSR had created a separate rocket force equal to that of the three existing services.

Despite the claims outlined above, Eisenhower Administration spokesmen were generally optimistic about the American position. General Twining stated that the United States was a little ahead in the ICBM, although other evidence indicated that the U. S. might be behind in the IRBM. In early 1956 Defense

to the subject of this study but is nevertheless a separate matter. There is evidence that the Army Redstone group could have launched an earth satellite perhaps as early as 1956. (See *Inquiry into Satellite and Missile Programs,* pp. 283–86, 315, 317, 470–74, 509, 541, 544, 557.)

Many of the people I interviewed complained bitterly of the separation imposed by the Eisenhower Administration between the military ballistic missile programs and the earth satellite efforts. Before the Sputnik launch, military personnel were persistently told not even to use the word "space" in public. (Interviews with Krafft Ehricke, Simon Ramo, Osmond Ritland, John Sessums. On this matter see also testimony of Werner von Braun, *Inquiry into Satellite and Missile Programs,* p. 614.)

[15] *A Chronology of Missile and Astronautic Events,* p. 21.

Secretary Wilson admitted that the Soviet Union had begun to concentrate on ballistic missiles immediately after the Second World War, and that it had continued the effort to the present. The United States, on the other hand, had gone into air-breathing missiles such as the Snark and Navaho and had continued to emphasize manned bombers.

Such statements were accompanied by strong voices of reassurance, however. In November 1955 Donald Quarles expressed confidence that the United States led the Soviets in ICBM developments, although he recognized a future threat. In addition, Harold Stassen had directly answered Trevor Gardner's claims by stating that the Soviet Union trailed both the United States and Great Britain in the ballistic field.[16]

Statements of both positions could be multiplied without resolving the confusion. Whatever the relative status of the Soviet Union and the United States, it is clear that the funding of the long-range ballistic missile programs during this period was considered adequate by the Air Force personnel directly involved. This is not to say, however, that the program was immune from pressures generated by the economy-minded Eisenhower Administration. That Administration did actively attempt to hold down defense outlays throughout this period, and the ICBM program was not granted a blank check.

In July 1956 the Air Force Ballistic Missile Committee withheld approval of the Western Development Division's proposed Initial Operational Capability (IOC) attainment program pending further review. The committee at this time recommended austerity in facilities construction and proposed certain reductions in military objectives. The following suggestions were made which, given the operation of the Gillette procedures, were in effect directives or guidelines. Buildup of production facilities beyond those necessary for the program itself was to be avoided wherever possible. The limits then being applied to the IRBM production base should be applied to the ICBM. The dual approach program whereby the Titan was being developed concurrently was criticized as "over-insurance." ICBM training

---

[16]*Ibid.*, pp. 24, 25. Stassen, the former Governor of Minnesota, served from 1955 to 1958 as special assistant to President Eisenhower on disarmament problems and as U. S. representative on the UN Disarmament Commission.

launches from operational sites were not to be planned during the IOC period. Some reduction in military objectives would be considered, perhaps in IOC end dates, reaction time, or inventories. In addition, the Western Development Division was directed by the committee and Secretary Quarles to employ a ''poor man's approach'' in developing an alternate IOC program which would reflect the committee's views.[17]

By this time the ballistic missile programs were beginning to enter production phases and the costs were rapidly rising. The first static tests of an Atlas missile were conducted in late 1956. The missile was 75 feet long, 10 feet in diameter, and had 3 main rocket engines built by North American's Rocketdyne Division.[18]

Table 7.2 (p. 206) gives a clear indication of the enormous increases then occurring in missiles spending.

The huge cost increases from 1954 through 1956—and the projected jumps in 1957, 1958, and after—caused many persons within and without the Air Force to take greater notice of the missile programs.[19] General Twining expressed concern to Secretary Quarles in September 1956. At that time Twining stated an intention to watch the program carefully to determine when to eliminate second source efforts, reduce the planned production of the IRBM to eliminate production facilities, standardize on a configuration for the ICBM, simplify and reduce training equipment, and reduce spares provisioning.

Also in September General Schriever submitted a Ballistic

[17]*Air Force Ballistic Missile Chronology.*

[18]A description of the Atlas can be found in *Eleventh Report,* p. 66. The North American rocket engines were also to be employed in the Army's Jupiter IRBM. The Air Force controlled the access to the engines, however, since they resulted from an Air Force contract. For a time bitter conflict arose over these engines, with General Medaris of the Army Ballistic Missile Agency requesting the right to procure engines directly from North American, and Generals Schriever and Power of the Air Force ARDC maintaining that Army needs should be met by procurement through the Air Force. Medaris seems to have thought that the Air Force would restrict delivery to the Army on the grounds that the available engines were needed for the Atlas program. There may have been grounds for Medaris's fears. (Interview with General John Sessums.) The controversy was finally resolved when General Medaris initiated direct procurement with North American, over Air Force objections. This issue is treated at length in *Eleventh Report,* pp. 103–4.

[19]The following discussion is based on *Air Force Ballistic Missile Chronology.*

Table 7.2   Defense Obligational Program for Missile Systems
Fiscal Years 1946–60 (in millions of dollars)[a]

Fiscal Year	IR/ICBM Programs	Other Surface-to-Surface Missile Programs	All Other Missile Programs	Grand Total, All Missile Programs
1946 & prior	2.	19	51	72
1947	—	20	38	58
1948	0.3	36	45	81
1949	.1	45	53	98
1950	—	65	69	134
1951	.5	185	598	784
1952	.8	239	818	1,058
1953	3.	403	760	1,166
1954	14.	336	717	1,067
1955	159.	398	911	1,468
1956	526.	387	1,368	2,281
1957	1,401.	603	2,502	4,506
1958	2,150.	639	2,391	5,180
1959 (total)	2,946.	685	3,269	6,900
1960 (total)	3,303.	509	3,173	6,985
1961	3,424.	383	3,155	6,962

[a]Chart found in U.S. Congress, Senate, Committee on Armed Services, Preparedness Investigating Subcommittee, *Hearings: Missiles, Space, and Other Major Defense Matters.* 86th Congress, 2nd Session, 1960, p. 509. The following explanation is included: "Program data reflected in this table cover the development and capital costs involved in missile programs, *i.e.,* the cost of bringing missile systems to operational status plus the costs of procuring missiles and related equipment for operational purposes. These data include all procurement, construction and research and development programs directly associated with missile programs. These figures do not include military pay, operation and maintenance costs for operational missile units and sites, and include only those shipbuilding and aircraft costs directly associated with providing missile capability.

"Fiscal year 1960 data are preliminary estimates; fiscal year 1961 data represent projected programming."

Missile Program budget to the Air Force Ballistic Missiles Committee; it totalled $1.672 billion. Quarles disapproved this request and ordered it cut to at least $1.3 billion. At the same time he stated that the earliest IOC date was to be retained. The total IOC force, on the other hand, might be reduced. WDD was told to restudy the program.

A revised ballistic missile development program for FY 1958, based on the new ground rules, was submitted to Quarles and the Air Force Ballistic Missiles Committee in November. This program, which had the Air Staff's approval, asked for $1.335 billion. It was accepted in principle for submission to the OSD Ballistic Missiles Committee with a proviso that it might be subject to revision later if required to comply with the President's budget.

In December the $1.335 billion amount was again approved "in principle" by the OSD Committee. During later budget reduction actions taken to reduce the overall Air Force FY 1958 funds requirements, Secretaries Wilson and Quarles reduced the approved $1.335 billion to $1.135 billion. This figure was submitted to Congress.

General Schriever based his plans on the $1.135 figure. On May 21, 1957, the ARDC Headquarters issued a General Order, effective June 1, 1957, redesignating the WDD as the Air Force Ballistic Missile Division (BMD). The new name did not cause a change in budget policy. In June the Air Force Ballistic Missile Committee approved the $1.135 billion program and recommended an overtime ceiling of 8 percent as a goal.

The dictated money reductions continued through much of 1957. On August 1, the NSC approved a Defense department recommendation that the ballistic missiles program be reoriented. Thor and Jupiter production was suspended while a review of requirements was undertaken. Contractor overtime was curtailed except for flight tests. Atlas was continued at highest priority, but the Titan's priority was lowered.

The NSC action was followed in mid-August by a memo from Wilson to Quarles directing limitation of maximum production rates to two a month for Titan and four a month for Atlas. Overtime in critical production areas was to be restricted to 3 percent of the basic man-hour total, with some excess permitted for test programs. This directive had the effect of substantially reducing the Titan program.

In September 1957 the BMD submitted another revised fiscal year 1958 budget proposal reflecting the OSD directives. The total was now $944 million. The changes incorporated in this request necessitated program slippages in the Atlas of approximately four months. Titan would be delayed nine months. The following month the Secretary of Defense approved this program. Funds were allocated in the amount of $437 million for Atlas, $335 million for Titan, and $148 million for Thor. The total was $920 million, contrasted with the $1.672 billion originally requested in October 1956. General Power, then head of ARDC, had exhausted Air Force funds, and intended to confront Congress with a choice of cancelling several major weapons or providing what the Air Force considered inadequate funding. Quarles, in turn, did not believe any weapon as uncertain as a ballistic missile should be scheduled for production before it was thoroughly tested. Hence the directives to suspend production plans.

Thus, it is clear that budget cuts did take place in the ICBM Program just before Sputnik. But although the reductions in the ballistic missiles programs were sizable, they nevertheless left the missiles very well funded. The programs continued at a rapid rate and completion dates quickly approached.

Missile 4-A, the first Atlas scheduled for flight testing, was finished in the spring of 1957 and was hauled to the long-range test site at Cape Canaveral. The test was set for June 11. On that date the missile lifted off correctly, responded to control signals, and then experienced engine trouble. Less than a minute after liftoff, it was destroyed. On September 25, 1957, a second Atlas test was attempted. This effort also ended in failure.[20]

In the economy-minded atmosphere of the period, it is quite possible that further reductions might have occurred which could have resulted in slippage in the date of initial operational capability. Such an eventuality was precluded when, in the fall of 1957, the ballistic missile programs received another huge push. On August 26, 1957, Moscow radio announced the successful flight of a "super-long distance intercontinental multistage ballistic missile . . . [which] flew at a very high, unprecedented altitude . . . [and] landed in the target area."[21]

This news received little public attention. However, the next Soviet act proved impossible to ignore. On October 4, 1957, the first Sputnik was launched. A second followed on November 3.

[20]Chapman, *Atlas,* pp. 127, 133.
[21]Quoted in Moulton, "American Strategic Power," p. 197.

The psychological effect upon the American public and its leaders was profound. Despite several years of warnings, the Soviet demonstration of such advanced technology was a disturbing surprise. Its meaning was clear. If the Soviets could solve guidance and reentry problems, they could hit any point in the United States with an ICBM from Soviet soil.

In this context, the report of the Gaither Committee was an added shock.[22] This committee, which had been appointed by President Eisenhower and whose report was finished in October 1957, estimated that the United States would become a second-class power unless great changes were made. If current trends in the development of strategic weapon systems continued, the Soviet Union would be able in the future to destroy a large part of the Strategic Air Command. Even with greatly altered emphasis, the United States would trail the Soviet Union in ballistic missiles until 1960–1961. The committee recommended that SAC bombers be dispersed and that some portion be maintained on continuous airborne alert. The committee further urged that IRBM and ICBM production and deployment be accelerated, with special attention given to hardened or mobile models.[23]

Samuel Huntington has remarked that

The recommendations of the Gaither Committee might have been quietly dropped and forgotten or in part quietly adopted if it had not been for the demonstrations of Soviet prowess which accompanied their presentation to the Administration.[24]

Those demonstrations did occur, however; they affected the 1960 Presidential election and may still cause repercussions today.[25]

[22]The Gaither Committee was originally appointed to evaluate fallout shelter needs. The committee rapidly determined that civil defense could not be separated from other defense requirements. Thus, the final report became an overall judgment on the state of national defense.

[23]Morton H. Halperin, "The Gaither Committee and the Policy Process," World Politics (April 1961):360–84; Samuel P. Huntington, The Common Defense, pp. 106–9; Moulton, "American Strategic Power," pp. 201–2.

[24]Huntington, The Common Defense, p 108.

[25]Morton H. Halperin, in "The Decision to Deploy the ABM," paper presented to the 66th Annual Meeting of the American Political Science Association, Sept. 8–12, 1970, argues that President Johnson, during the ABM debates within his Administration, felt that Kennedy had scored effectively in 1960 on the missile gap issue and did not wish to face a "defense gap" charge in 1968.

Among the results were a lengthy series of hearings conducted by the Preparedness Investigating Subcommittee of the Senate Committee on Armed Services. Under the chairmanship of Senator Lyndon B. Johnson, the Subcommittee heard 70 witnesses, interviewed and received questionnaires from many times that number, and produced over 2,000 pages of testimony. Although the committee explored the whole of the American defense posture, the hearings were titled "Inquiry into Satellite and Missile Programs," and the latter received a great deal of attention. Some of the issues most often raised were the inadequacy of funding, the existence of management bottlenecks, and the efficiency of the entire program.

Almost certainly in response to the Soviet accomplishments and the resultant public and congressional criticism, the Department of Defense on November 23, 1957, removed all overtime restrictions on the Atlas and Titan programs. Any overtime necessary to meet the program objectives was authorized.[26]

Sputnik thus climaxed the effort begun by Trevor Gardner in 1953. Because of Gardner the Atlas had been given the Air Force's first priority in the spring of 1954. The three-engine configuration of the Atlas was approved in December 1954. The Thor IRBM was assigned to WDD in December 1955. The complete Thor was tested on a launch pad only thirteen months later. The first Atlas test occurred thirty months after design specification. A completely successful full-range Thor flight took place in September 1957. The first fully successful full-range Atlas flight occurred in November 1958. Thor attained IOC three and a half years and Atlas less than five years after program inception.[27]

The Titan was conceived as a backup to Atlas. It was a two-stage vehicle designed from its inception for emplacement in silos. The advanced Titan II incorporated a superior fuel, the capacity for in-silo launch from very hard sites, all-inertial guidance, and a substantially more powerful second stage. The first

[26]*Air Force Ballistic Missile Chronology.*
[27]Robert L. Perry, "The Atlas, Titan, Thor and Minuteman," in Emme, ed., *The History of Rocket Technology,* pp. 151–55.

test missile, launched on March 16, 1962, completely satisfied its range and accuracy requirements.[28]

The solid fuel Minuteman grew out of the demonstration in 1955 that large-grain, double-base solid propellants could be reliably ignited and burned. Minuteman was not initiated until 1957. The 1955 solid fuel breakthrough was also the occasion for the separation of the Navy from the Jupiter program and the initiation of the Polaris project. The solid fuel missiles benefited greatly from the substantially increased funding available after Sputnik. Nevertheless, it is interesting that

The peculiar situation of Minuteman advocates as late as 1957 was closely analogous to that of Atlas patrons half a decade earlier: essentially all the critical uncertainties of technology were reasonably well in hand and from the standpoint of national strategy there were excellent reasons for starting intensive development of the missile, but activating a full-scale development program would inevitably cause a diversion of effort from other programs to which the Air Force had commitments. Rivals to the Atlas had been the strategic bombers and the cruise missiles; for Minuteman the rivals were Atlas and Titan, only then entering their flight test stages. Before Sputnik cut the purse strings, Minuteman could have been developed only at the price of limiting expenditures on one of the larger liquid-rocket missiles.[29]

Minuteman underwent a completely successful test with all systems operating on February 1, 1962.

It seems clear that the Eisenhower Administration did not expect the Soviets to attain an ICBM (or to launch a satellite) as soon as they did. Further, it appears not to have expected that

[28]*Ibid.*, pp. 145–47, 155.

[29]Perry, "The Ballistic Missile Decisions," AIAA (1967), p. 19. It had long been recognized that solid fuels would provide significant advantages in reliability, readiness, and ease of handling. Minuteman was, however, clearly delayed because of the commitment to Atlas and Titan. Dr. Herbert York has said, "Excessive technical conservatism led us to build both the Atlas and the Titan" (*Race to Oblivion*, p. 103). The first operational Atlas (D) was extremely vulnerable and unreliable. The final Atlas (F) was able to be housed in silos but was nevertheless unsatisfactory in many ways. The improved Titan (II) offered many of the advantages of Minuteman, but was considerably more expensive. Titan II's much greater payload capacity nevertheless prompted its development and eventual deployment despite its cost. (Perry, "The Atlas, Titan, Thor, and Minuteman," pp. 145–57).

situation, if it did happen to occur, to make a great strategic difference. Accordingly, primarily for reasons of economy, the ballistic programs were slowed somewhat. But those projects were nevertheless maintained at a very high rate.

The shock of Sputnik did not noticeably accelerate the development of the first American ICBMs, although it did bring on an immediate relaxation of the funding stringencies earlier imposed and an increase in production schedules. Sputnik certainly speeded the more viable solid fuel missiles. The American reaction was ultimately to prove quite effective. After the Sputnik launch and the accompanying national uproar, the Eisenhower administration programmed approximately 1,100 missiles. Of these, 20 percent were to be first-generation Atlas and Titan, and 10 percent mobile Minutemen. Atlas was later phased out of the American arsenal. The mobile Minuteman was withdrawn from the program for technical and cost reasons.[30] Eight hundred missiles of the planned strategic ballistic force were to be the more useful Polaris and hardened Minuteman.[31]

After entering office, the Kennedy Administration undertook the largest and fastest peacetime military buildup in the history

[30]It may be recalled that early in 1954, at the time of the SMEC and RAND reports, which led to the rapid acceleration of the ICBM program, the Air Staff managed to retain both the Snark and Navaho cruise missiles despite the fact that the former in particular was thought of poorly by both the von Neumann Committee and ARDC. The Navaho was finally cancelled after more than ten years' effort and a cost of $700 million. One squadron of the Snark was actually deployed in the early 1960s. Development time was over fourteen years; costs exceeded $700 million (*Eleventh Report*, p. 64). Of the Snark, General Thomas Power was to say in 1959, "It is a subsonic missile. Let's face it, it came late. We are buying only a very few of them. They have a very limited value to SAC" (Quoted in *Ibid.*). Dr. Herbert York has stated that for several years before Snark became operational, repeated recommendations were made by the ICBM Scientific Advisory Committee that the missile be dropped. "In this case as in so many others, the momentum of the project and the politics which surrounded it made it impossible to do so" (*Race to Oblivion*, p. 80). It is possible, of course, that one factor at play in this period was a hesitancy to cancel Snark and Navaho on grounds of vulnerability because such arguments might also reflect poorly on large segments of the manned fleet.

[31]D. J. Ball, "The Strategic Missile Programs of the Kennedy Administration, 1961–1963." (Ph.D. dissertation, Australian National University, 1972), pp. vi–vii.

of the United States. The results were striking. Although the "missile gap" had apparently been a significant factor in the 1960 election, by late 1961 members of the Kennedy Administration had publicly announced that it no longer existed.[32] Early in February 1961, Secretary McNamara had committed a "slip" in denying the existence of a missile gap in a background briefing to newsmen. Although McNamara later denied he had said such a thing, a speech by Roswell Gilpatrick in October 1961 supported much the same interpretation. McNamara himself in December 1962 stated that the missile gap had been a myth.[33] The "disappearance" of the missile gap resulted from receipt of new and better intelligence on the actual complement of Soviet missiles in the field.

By 1967 the United States strategic military force had reached a total of 1,000 Minuteman, 54 Titan II, and 656 Polaris missiles. Secretary McNamara was later to state that the American missile force at the close of the Kennedy buildup was "both greater than we had originally planned and in fact more than we require."[34] Soon, missile gap was to fade from our vocabulary and be replaced by "overkill."

---

[32]The missile gap question has been the subject of much controversy. Part of the trouble has arisen from a confusion of two distinct issues. The "missile gap" usually refers to a period when the Soviet Union might have possessed a numerically greater number of ICBMs than the United States. This era was expected to occur in the early 1960s. For example, Henry Kissinger wrote in 1960, "For all the heat of the controversy, it is important to note that there is no dispute about the missile gap as such. It is generally admitted that from 1961 until at least the end of 1964, the Soviet Union will possess more missiles than the United States." [See *The Necessity for Choice* (New York: Harper, 1960), p. 15.] It is this gap that never actually materialized and was in fact soon reversed by the U.S. A second issue concerned a missile "lag," meaning a Soviet time lead in ICBM development. It is this second area that I am concerned with here.

[33]On the missile gap issue, see Edgar M. Bottome, *The Missile Gap: A Study of the Formulation of Military and Political Policy* (Rutherford, N.J.: Fairleigh Dickinson University Press, 1971) and Roy E. Licklider, "The Missile Gap Controversy," *Political Science Quarterly* (December 1970), 600–615.

[34]Quoted in *Ibid.*, p. 5.

Conclusions:
Bureaucratic Politics
and Weapons Innovation

MOST BUREAUCRATIC politics case studies explain a particular event considered to be a turning point.[1] Critics of the growing literature on bureaucratic politics most often complain about its idiosyncratic nature. The cases chosen are usually crises involving people at high levels over short periods of time. Resolution often comes within weeks, even days. This concentration on crises, say the critics, biases the sample and leaves us with a series of unconnected studies, involving changing personnel, almost always acting under strain, making ad hoc arrangements within tight time limits.[2] "So their actions aren't

[1] Many of the most interesting short case studies have been conveniently collected in Morton H. Halperin and Arnold Kanter, eds. *Readings in American Foreign Policy: A Bureaucratic Perspective* (Boston: Little, Brown, 1973).

[2] Two of the more telling critiques are Robert J. Art, "Bureaucratic Politics and American Foreign Policy: A Critique," *Policy Sciences*, 4 (December 1973):467–90; and Stephen D. Krasner, "Are Bureaucracies Important? (Or Allison Wonderland)." *Foreign Policy*, 7(Summer 1972):159–79.

always 'rational,' " the critics continue. "How could they be under such circumstances?"

The history of the ICBM, however, is a different matter. What we have seen here is not a short-term struggle between competing interests over a specific decision, but rather a decade-long pattern of nondecisions, characterized by inaction, proscrastination, selective ignorance, and an unwillingness to recognize new facts. Such a "longitudinal" study has the virtue of revealing the persistence of such patterns over considerable periods rather than basing broad claims on what might have been unusual short-run reactions. Here the actors had plenty of time, were under little strain, and had access to all relevant information. Yet organizational vested interest and an associated technological conservatism seems to have blinded them also to what is retrospectively seemingly obvious or "rational." Why was this so?

The previous chapter demonstrates that much of the harsh criticism directed at the Eisenhower Administration for not developing an intercontinental ballistic missile before Sputnik was unfair. Eisenhower unquestionably tried to hold down defense spending. The doctrines associated with massive retaliation and the "new look" assumed that defense spending could not be allowed to rise rapidly or uncontrollably. Rather, very real choices had to be made about what the nation could and could not afford. The result was that conventional war capabilities, and particularly support for ground troops, were downgraded in favor of manned strategic bombers. In the years just before Sputnik, the budget requests from the Western Development Division for ballistic missiles were significantly reduced.

Yet the real reasons for the delay in ICBM development lay primarily in the years before Eisenhower, particularly in the period from 1948 to late 1953. After 1954 the first ICBM, the Atlas, received remarkably strong and persistent support. A revolutionary management structure was implemented to speed the project, and funding, despite the cuts noted above, was consistently very high. The program did not have a blank check, but the Gillette procedures provided remarkably effective access to the budgetary process. The Gillette rules were central to the success demonstrated by the ballistic missile programs after 1955. They permitted the bypassing of much of the normal Air Force review system. For this same reason they were resisted by those bypassed. As one observer noted, "These procedures were under attack almost from their inauguration because they cut so obviously into the functional authority existing within the established organization."[3]

The observation that the "first" ICBM enjoyed strong support after 1954 was made advisedly, however. We have seen that the later solid-fuel Minuteman was delayed during the Eisenhower period. In fact, in the late 1950s the Minuteman faced the same kind of resistance that Atlas had encountered half a decade earlier, only Minuteman was slowed by Atlas not airplanes. When technology for the solid fuel Minuteman became available, it was a natural competitor with the liquid-fueled Atlas and Titan, then being developed at great cost. The

[3]W. D. Putnam, "The Evolution of Air Force System Acquisition Management," RAND Corporation, mimeo draft, May 1971, p. 13. It should be noted that the Gillette procedures finally succumbed. In May 1959 a Weapon System Management Study Group (soon known as the Anderson Committee after the Chairman, General S. E. Anderson, Commander, Air Materiel Command) was appointed within the Air Force to review the management of weapon and support systems. General Schriever had just been transferred to the Command of ARDC. He became a member of the group. The differences between AMC and ARDC approaches, which had been evident since the establishment in 1951 of the latter command, became immediately apparent. In general, the deliberations of the working group revealed "a great deal of opposition both to how the missile program operated and the ARDC—as reorganized by Schriever—in particular." (Letter to author from Harry Jordan, SAMSO Historian, November 30, 1971.)

The Anderson Committee study resulted in stalemate. Ironically, however, Schriever's move to ARDC hastened the Gillette procedures' demise because he refused to give to his successor at the Ballistic Missiles Division the freedom he had enjoyed.

The congressional scrutiny occasioned by Sputnik and the "missile gap" scare, and Air Force opposition typified by the Anderson Committee, had the effect, by 1961 at least, of modifying the Gillette procedures "to the point where the shortened decision channels characteristic of the early missile program no longer existed." (Putnam, "The Evolution of Air Force System Management," p. 29.)

Minuteman was delayed, and the Air Force personnel then working on Atlas and Titan supported that decision.[4]

The United States did not build an ICBM before the Soviet Union because the Soviets began an ICBM program in 1946 and continued it to completion, while the United States did not initiate a serious, persistent program until 1954. After that date the American performance was quite laudatory.

The initial American efforts in the missile field during and after World War II were largely reflexive. Nazi Germany had demonstrated new and potentially dangerous weapons and the American military attempted to duplicate them. After the war, when R&D funds were no longer so readily available, enthusiasm for missiles fell off.

The original postwar decision to concentrate on maintenance and improvement of forces in being, built around the soon-to-be available B–36 and the projected followon jet B–52, was rational at the time. The lesser decision in 1947 to undertake development of subsonic cruise missiles and abandon the lone long-range ballistic rocket was also reasonable. The problems facing long-range strategic missiles and particularly the ballistic proposals were thought to be in guidance, thrust, and reentry. Jet engines had only recently been developed. (The B–36 was not a jet bomber although it entered the American arsenal after the close of World War II.) Jet airplanes were the weapon of the future. Long-range missiles of any sort were widely thought to be ''Buck Rogers'' devices, destined if at all for the distant future. When the postwar funds squeeze set in, they were likely

[4]The Minuteman project initially was the idea in large part of one man, Col. Edward N. Hall of the Air Force. As early as 1954, Col. Hall was strongly suggesting the need to study solid fuels. Col. Hall was assigned to WDD and during 1955 he ''brought up the matter of the need to explore the potential of solid rockets at almost every high level meeting of R-W and the Western Development Division.'' In Col. Hall's words, there was an ''unfortunate lack of enthusiasm.'' (Colonel Edward N. Hall, ''Epitaph,'' Xeroxed, August 29, 1958; copy provided by Harry Jordan, Historian SAMSO.) Col. Hall's singleminded dedication to the idea of solid fuel rockets ultimately led to friction with his WDD bosses and he was later assigned to assist in U. K. site activation of the Thor. He subsequently resigned from the Air Force. (Interviews with Richard K. Jacobson, Robert L. Perry, Ray Soper.)

candidates for early cancellation. If any funds were to be expended, cruise missiles seemed the logical recipient. After all,
they flew at understandable speeds and in the atmosphere; with
their wings, they even looked like airplanes.[5]

The delay in the American ballistic missile program did not
result from those decisions in 1947 and 1948. It did result, however, from a refusal to alter those decisions, or the thinking that
underlay them, in the light of subsequent events. The history of
the ICBM program in the United States from 1947 until late
1953 indicates that cultural resistance within the Air Force and
elsewhere to the idea of long-range ballistic rockets was at least
as important as the state of the relevant technology in dictating
the choices made. The early postwar decisions to subordinate
missiles to manned aircraft (most importantly jets) and ballistic
missiles to air-breathing versions were justified at the time. That
justification became increasingly weak, however, as years
passed and technology developed. As early as 1949, Air Force
R&D personnel and the RAND Corporation were stressing ballistic possibilities. The next four or five years are a study in
resistance and neglect, culminating in the strongly worded slowdown direction dictated from the Air Staff in mid-1953 just as
Trevor Gardner was becoming frightened by American missile
shortcomings and only a few months before the dramatically
opposite recommendations of the Strategic Missiles Evaluation
Committee.

I do not claim that ballistic missile technology was on hand in
1949, or that the United States should have leaped into production of the first ballistic design presented. What I do say is that
the weapon was of potentially enormous significance and that a

[5]These decisions were made, however, in the face of persistent predictions
that subsonic missiles would likely be extremely vulnerable to defensive measures as early as 1952—as indeed would subsonic aircraft. The subsequent history
of the turbojet Snark and ramjet Navaho were to disprove totally the assumptions about the relative ease of producing a cruise missile. On the other hand,
one Air Force officer with wide experience in the missiles program stated in
1958 that "the degree of complexity of a ballistic missile is not so great as that of
a modern bomber or even most modern fighters" (Col. Edward Hall,
"Epitaph").

serious research and development effort should have been initiated and supported. This was not done.

The argument most often used against ballistic missiles in the
period 1949–1954 was that the technology was not available.
Other arguments sometimes heard were that there was no requirement for such a weapon; in other words, no relevant threat.
Contrary evidence to each of these claims was increasingly
available during this period. Much of the needed technology
either existed or was within reach. What seems often to have
happened is that the Air Force devoted little time or money to
long range ballistic research, therefore produced few results,
and then used the lack of results to demonstrate that the necessary technology was unavailable, even impossible.

Some indication of the state of the requisite technology can be
seen in Wernher von Braun's later statement before a Senate
investigating subcommittee that, ''I am convinced that, had we
continued our operation at Peenemünde with the same momentum that developed during the war, we could have produced an
ICBM in 1950.''[6] The even more optimistic judgment that the
A–10 transatlantic rocket could have been operational by 1946 if
its development had continued in Germany after the outbreak of
war has been attributed to Walter Dornberger.[7]

The history of the German V–1 and V–2 weapons is quite
instructive. It appears that a clause in the Versailles Treaty
which forbade Germany to possess or develop conventional
military aircraft first inspired some German planners to consider
the possibilities of long-range missiles.[8]

The V–2 ballistic missile was begun first. It was handled by
the Dornberger–von Braun group at Peenemünde under the
auspices of the Ordnance Department of the German Army.
After the Battle of Britain, however, when it appeared that the

[6] Hearings, *Inquiry into Satellite and Missile Programs*, p. 584.
[7] Joseph W. Angell, ''Guided Missiles Could Have Won,'' *Atlantic*, 188, no. 6
(December 1951), 62.
[8] *Ibid.*, p. 30. It must be remembered, however, that Germany also undertook
the secret creation of forbidden forces. See *E. H. Carr, German-Soviet Relations between the Two World Wars, 1919–1939* (Baltimore: Johns Hopkins
Press, 1951).

Peenemünde weapon might be relied upon extensively, the Luftwaffe, "unwilling that Germany should be saved entirely by efforts of the Army," called for a " 'retaliation weapon' that would outshine, if possible, the massive, complex, and costly V–2."[9] The result was the pulse jet V–1, "buzz bomb."

As one analyst of the German effort has noted,

The German war machine, already overburdened with factional conflict and lacking adequate centralization, suffered severely from the ensuing struggle between advocates of the two new weapons. . . . They had an entirely new and revolutionary weapon, but those who had the say did not know what to make of it until it was altogether too late.[10]

It is intriguing, both as an historical sidelight and in the context of the postwar missile skepticism in the United States, to recall the judgment of President Eisenhower, one uniquely placed to evaluate the German weapons:

It seemed likely that if the German had succeded in perfecting and using these new weapons six months earlier than he did, our invasion of Europe would have proved exceedingly difficult, perhaps impossible. I feel sure that if he had succeeded in using these weapons over a six-month period . . . OVERLORD might well have been written off.[11]

Fortunately, interservice rivalry, among other factors, helped prevent this result.

So much for the state of missile technology. The no-requirement argument lodged against the ICBM was also strange insofar as Air Force studies from the earliest postwar period persistently demonstrated that manned subsonic bombers would soon be highly vulnerable to enemy defensive measures. This possibility greatly jeopardized strategic bombardment and might have been expected to call attention to the "invulnerable" ballistic missile. The parallel claim of no Soviet threat is also confusing. On the one hand, it is not clear why Soviet actions should have necessarily dictated the American response.

The argument need not be countered in this manner, however.

[9] Angell, "Guided Missiles Could Have Won," p. 33.

[10] *Ibid.*, pp. 33–34.

[11] Dwight D. Eisenhower, *Crusade in Europe* (Garden City, N.Y.: Doubleday, 1948), p. 260.

Through this period, and particularly in the early 1950s, reports of Soviet missile activity were common in the public press and in Air Force intelligence. The actual overall Air Force intelligence assessment is not easy to determine. Certainly the Air Force's actions in the period indicate that the picture was not particularly worrisome. Yet I have noted the existence of persistent reports to the contrary. It is possible that such reports were ignored.[12]

Whatever the reasoning, there was in the highest levels of the Air Force R&D hierarchy opposition to the accelerated development of long-range ballistic missiles and an apparent failure to appreciate technological unpredictability or even to recognize technological advances.[13]

Before the recommendations of the Strategic Missiles Evaluation Committee in 1954, the Air Staff was interested in long-range strategic missiles only when they perceived a threat from an enemy or from a sister service. And of the two, threats from the Army or Navy seemed to motivate the Air Staff more. Army and Navy proposals to develop long-range missiles were persistently opposed by the Air Force, which strongly defended its sole claims to the strategic role. Throughout the late 1940s and early 1950s a series of agreements was reached between the three services allocating roles and missions. In the fields of guided missiles the Air Force consistently claimed the strategic role and abandoned other missile projects in exchange for reciprocal cessation of long-range projects by the other services. The documentation provided here makes it clear that this was a conscious effort.

[12]Support for this latter assessment has been provided by T. F. Walkowicz, a former executive secretary to the Air Force Scientific Advisory Board. Walkowicz stated in 1956 that, "The Democrats kept our ICBM program on the back burner for many years, even when it was becoming more and more apparent that the Soviets were concentrating a major effort on their own program." T. F. Walkowicz, "The Race for the ICBM," in J. F. Loosbrock and Richard M. Skinner, eds., *The Wild Blue* (New York: G.P. Putnam's Sons, 1961), p. 575.

[13]This analysis is supported by Robert Perry, "The Ballistic Missile Decisions," pp. 25–28.

Throughout this period the Air Force agreed that ballistic missiles were of potentially great importance—that they were the weapons of the future. Further, the Air Force consistently claimed that it was the obvious choice to develop and employ the weapons and that it was conducting so thorough a research and development program that no parallel efforts by the other services were necessary. After each debate and resultant "treaty," the Air Force, having gained the long range ballistic responsibility, proceeded generally to ignore the weapon until the next challenge to its control.

The events of 1953–54, in which Trevor Gardner played such a major role, did not necessarily have to take place then. The advent of Gardner was a unique and in some ways chance event. Gardner was exceedingly strong-minded, obstinate, and forceful. If he (or someone like him) had not been brought into the Defense Department, or had he not been convinced by the ICBM proponents of that weapon's importance (an entirely possible scenario, given the economy-minded, anti-defense-spending approach of the Republicans) the ICBM turnaround could have occurred a year or two later. Events did conspire to make Gardner's chosen task somewhat easier, but he accomplished things that other persons would not have.

Similarly, if the crash ICBM development program had been initiated in, say, 1951, rather than 1954, there is every reason to assume that an Atlas-type missile could have been available in perhaps 1955–1956. The follow on missiles might then have also appeared earlier. The requisite technology was available or could have been produced (as it later was) by a crash effort. This is not to say that we ought all to be warmongers, madly producing any and all weapons we can dream up. Rather it says much the reverse. But a serious research and development effort could have been initiated and sustained at minimal cost compared to the enormous potential significance of the end result. This effort was not made for some very questionable reasons.

One of the most interesting findings of this study is that within the Air Force planners' own perspectives their actions with regard to ballistic missile development were neither consistent nor rational. As has been noted, air planners consistently predicted that surface-to-air antiaircraft missiles would become available during the early 1950s and that these weapons would be particularly effective against subsonic aircraft. These same planners agreed that ballistic missiles were, within any conceivable technology, unstoppable. Yet, development of these vehicles was persistently delayed. Enormous efforts were put into developing the B–52 as a follow on to the B–36. In addition, during the 1950s, the Air Force strongly promoted the B–70, a supersonic long-range heavy bomber designed to follow the B–52.[14]

As noted, much money was also invested in the Snark, the least efficient of the contemplated long-range missiles. The Snark and the B–52 were broadly comparable weapons, but the Snark always lacked accuracy and reliability and never developed operational capability.[15] The suspicion remains that the Snark may have been supported in some quarters precisely because it did *not* constitute a real threat to the B–52 or any follow on bomber. During the same period, the Air Force hierarchy devoted significant efforts to standoff missiles, which were considered vital to the health and effectiveness of the manned bomber fleet. The cultural identification with manned airplanes and the cultural resistance to ballistic missiles seems obvious.[16]

[14]The B–70 was first conceived in 1953 as a 2,200 mph long-range heavy bomber to be ready as early as mid-1964. (In its current form, as the B–1, it is still in the works and still strongly promoted by the Air Force.) A good summary of the early history of this airplane can be found in the 1962 CQ Almanac, pp. 416–19. Another aircraft concept which received strong Air Force support in the 1950s was the ill-fated nuclear plane. For a review of its rise and fall, see Herbert York, *Race to Oblivion.* pp. 60–74.

[15]The Snarks fired from Cape Canaveral were persistent failures. The average miss distance was over 1,000 miles. At least one came down in the wrong hemisphere, disappearing somewhere in the interior of Brazil.

[16]Robert L. Perry was the first to point out to me that the Air Staff consistently promoted the development of bomber-launched standoff missiles, in the face of continued statements from R&D personnel that the required technology was as difficult as that for the long-range surface-to-surface ballistic missile. See chapters 3 and 5. Perry has observed that the development of air-launched weapons, even when they were plainly based on technology in which the ballistic missile agencies were most competent, was entrusted to the aircraft industry under the Air Materiel Command. (Perry "The Ballistic Missile Decisions," p. 27.)

There is further contradiction in the Air Force position in this period. Before 1951, long-range ballistic missiles were dismissed because they wouldn't fly; if they did, it was argued that they couldn't possibly hit a useful target. After 1951, when the R&D staffs had managed to resurrect a low-effort ICBM program, the performance requirements were set at extremely difficult levels. CEP was 1,500 feet; warhead weights were between 5,000 and 10,000 lbs. Yet this was precisely the period of the closest Air Force adherence to the theories of massive strategic bombardment and "city busting" with nuclear weapons. Clearly, for this purpose strict accuracies were not important. What was important was to ensure delivery of the nuclear payloads, and for this ballistic missiles would seem to be perfect. They were considered invulnerable. If the nuclear stockpile was assumed to be low, better to entrust the valued bombs to an invulnerable delivery vehicle than hope the right bombers got through. If the nuclear stockpile was larger (as it certainly was expected to be as early as 1949), accuracy requirements became even less important.

The irony grows even greater in light of the subsequent history of the Atlas. After the acceleration of the Atlas program in 1954—occasioned primarily by the SMEC recommendations —Atlas performance goals were set at 5,500 nautical miles range, one megaton explosive yield, and five miles CEP.[17] These characteristics were considerably closer to the Air Force concepts of strategic warfare. Yet, by the time the Atlas was becoming operational, American planners had drawn back from the implications of this strategy (and of the "massive retaliation" popularized by Secretary of State Dulles) and were beginning to speak in terms of graduated response and counterforce options. The Atlas of 1954 was hardly appropriate to these concepts. On the other hand, the extremely high accuracies demanded of the 1951–53 ICBM would have been quite useful, indeed nearly vital.[18]

[17]York, *Race to Oblivion*, p. 88.
[18]Again I am indebted for assistance in this analysis to Robert L. Perry (interview). See also Perry, "The Ballistic Missile Decisions," p. 15.

Note, too, that Atlas specifications were chosen, according to Dr. Herbert York, because "Draper . . . said he could foresee much better CEP's than five miles, and we simply took that figure as a conservative estimate; . . . 5,500 miles is . . . precisely one-fourth of the earth's circumference . . . and . . . one million is a particularly round number in our culture." York adds that "We picked a one-megaton yield for the Atlas warhead for the same reason that everyone speaks of rich men as being millionaires and never being tenmillionaires or one hundred thousandaires."[19]

All this may surprise you if you expect defense policy, and particularly weapon configuration calculations, to result from rational, consistent, technically informed analysis. The fault may lie, however, in such an expectation. Samuel Huntington has observed that "Military policy is not the result of deductions from a clear statement of national objective. It is the product of the competition of purposes within individuals and groups and among individuals and groups. It is the result of politics, not logic."[20] Other analysts have made similar points. David W. Tarr, for instance, has noted that

Defense policies are formulated within a framework of competing groups, interests, and values, and the decisions precipitated are usually the product of the vigorous bargaining efforts of the participants. It should not be surprising, therefore, that the product of the process is often not clearly related to the foreign policy objectives it is supposed to serve.[21]

Indeed, the results may prove internally inconsistent or contrary to the purposes of current strategy.

In short while strategies and weapons systems compete in the policy-making arena, the clash tends to be resolved through military bargains that produce "mixes" of military forces and hardware which are com-

---

[19] York, Race to Oblivion, p. 89. "Draper" was Stark Draper, director of the Instrument Laboratory at M.I.T. and an expert in inertial-guidance systems, who worked closely with the Strategic Missiles Evaluation Committee.

[20] Samuel P. Huntington, The Common Defense, p. 2.

[21] David W. Tarr, "Military Technology and the Policy Process," Western Political Quarterly, 18 (March 1965):135.

patible with the basic views of all three military services but may represent contradictory elements in the overall strategic picture.[22]

Other commentators have noted that the "mixes" will usually include at least what is considered most vital by each service. Morton Halperin and Leslie Gelb have reduced this concept to a bureaucratic strategy aimed at providing the essence of what each actor in a given decision situation desires. They call this the practice of supporting "Option B," a form of consensus between two undesirable alternatives, Options A and C, which works because everyone is given the central element of what he wants. The fact that the various pieces of Option B may be inconsistent or even contradictory makes little difference.

Option B solves a lot of problems for the bureaucrat. Bureaucrats do not like to fight with each other. Option B makes everyone a winner (by letting everyone do the essence of what he wants), preserves the policy consensus, and provides ultimate comfort to the bureaucrat—deference to his expertise and direct responsibility.[23]

Elsewhere Halperin has observed that

Air Force officers agree that the essence of their program is the development of a capability for combat flying, particularly involving the delivery of nuclear weapons.[24]

It is worth noting that the strategic bombardment function has

---

[22]*Ibid.*, p. 141. These ideas, and indeed much of the recent literature on "bureaucratic politics," all owe a great debt to the work of Charles E. Lindblom. See, for example, David Braybrooke and Charles E. Lindblom, *A Strategy of Decision: Policy Evaluation as a Social Process* (New York: The Free Press, 1963), parts 1 and 2.

[23]Leslie H. Gelb and Morton H. Halperin, "The Ten Commandments of the Foreign-Affairs Bureaucracy," *Harpers* (June 1972), p. 30.

[24]Morton H. Halperin, "Why Bureaucrats Play Games," *Foreign Policy*, no. 2 (Spring 1971):79. This formulation of "essence" is broader than the Gelb-Halperin use just above. Here Halperin employs it to denote the core of the Air Force's self-image.

The concept of organizational "essence" is developed more fully in Arnold Kanter, "Presidential Power and Bureaucratic Compliance: Changing Organizational Objectives" (paper presented to the Annual Meeting of the American Political Science Association, Chicago, September 1971). See pp. 4–11, for a discussion of Air Force "essence."

been the central element of the Air Force from the very earliest period.[25] One historian of the strategic bomber, Robert Krauskopf, in discussing the experience of General Trenchard's Independent Force in the British effort in World War I, has observed that "from this very early beginning the concept of strategic air warfare was closely related to the idea of the independent air force, and the long-range or "strategic" bomber came to be looked upon as the basic tool of independent air operations."[25]

Krauskopf also notes that, following the creation of a General Headquarters Air Force in the United States in 1935, "The Army airman was, thereafter, more than anything else, a champion of the long-range bomber and centered his aspirations around the potentialities of that type of aircraft."[26]

Without referring to the phenomenon as illustrative of an "essence," Samuel Huntington has made some relevant comments. "Appointments to the top positions within a service tended to reflect the relative importance of functions within the service. . . . Service spokesmen often attempted to identify the entire service with the functional doctrine most important to the service at the moment."[27]

The results of this perspective, in addition to the effect on the missile programs, are that most Air Force officers do not see close combat support or a strong transport capability as the essence of their organization. One seeming contradiction among many in this situation is that the Air Force nevertheless insists on performing the troop transport and close air support role—to keep the Army out of the airplane business.

The stand of bureaucrats on a policy issue is influenced by its impact on the ability of their organization to pursue its essential programs and

[25] It should be noted that through much of the 1930s, conflict existed within the Army Air Forces between the advocates of long-range strategic bombers and those of tactical air. Claire Chennault was the most notorious of the latter. Henry Arnold headed the bomber faction and was ultimately responsible for the flowering of bombardment aviation.

[26] Robert W. Krauskopf, "The Army and the Strategic Bomber, 1930–1939," *Military Affairs*, 22, no. 2 (Summer 1958): 83–90. The second half of this article is found in *ibid.*, no. 4, (Winter 1958–59): 208–15.

[27] Huntington, *The Common Defense*, pp. 406, 409.

missions. They resist most strongly efforts to take away these functions or to share them with other organizations. They also resist proposals to reduce funds for these programs or missions. Autonomy is most precious as it affects the essence of the organization.[28]

Halperin has observed that organizations with missions attempt to maintain or further their autonomy, organizational morale, organizational essence, and their roles and missions.[29] One of the interesting aspects of the ballistic missile story is, of course, that the missiles placed several of these organizational goals in conflict. Ballistic missiles obviously were among the most important Air Force functions. Were they to go to another service, the Air Force's autonomy, and indeed its purpose, would be threatened. However, the missiles also challenged the organizational essence and thus the Air Force's morale. The result was the ambivalent approach the Air Force followed until, and even after, the dictates of the SMEC. On the one hand, missiles were dismissed or derided, while on the other, they were consistently claimed as *Air Force* weapons and missile efforts by the other services were strongly resisted. This pattern, of course, also explains the Air Force drive to gain control of the medium-range missile after first attempting to kill the program.

Robert L. Perry, a perceptive analyst and sympathetic critic of the Air Force, has succinctly stated the bomber–missile issue:

Without going deeply into the sociology or psychology of the phenomenon, it is plain that the people who had grown with manned bombers before and during World War II and who mostly stayed with them through the next decade developed an abiding affection for them, an affection based in some degree on what aircraft meant as a way of life, a symbol, a means of performing their military assignment. With minor exceptions, those who sought to bring on change had no such commitments; they were primarily engineers and scientists of one sort or another and only secondarily airplane commanders. It is not really important whether the opponents of change, or its supporters, consciously recognized the possibility that the adoption of the ballistic

[28]Halperin, "Why Bureaucrats Play Games," p. 80.
[29]*Ibid.*, p. 76.

missile as a primary means of delivering nuclear weapons would cause the decline or even the disappearance of the strategic bomber. It is important, however, that they sometimes acted as if they foresaw that possibility.[30]

Explanation of the Air Force's actions is not difficult. Indeed, the concurrent internal neglect of and external struggle for ballistic missiles was the obvious solution to the dilemma. Autonomy, morale, roles and missions, and organizational essence were all preserved.

Although there is no need to detail here the Navy structure and "essence," it is worth noting that the Navy Polaris program met some of the same resistance that the ICBM faced in the Air Force. The Polaris development was managed in ways similar to the Western Development Division operations. The Navy created a Special Projects Office under Admiral William Raborn, and the project was given a separate funding line. As Raborn has observed,

This made the rest of the Navy very happy because now they were going to keep we [sic] upstarts in our own ballfield. We couldn't come poaching on their money, and so they went along with it very readily and we were happy because we didn't have anybody poaching on us which they later tried to do when we got to be better funded.[31]

Morton Halperin has observed that "most senior naval officers have tended to view the Polaris missile-firing submarines as a service to the nation, extraneous to the Navy's 'essential' tasks."[32] It should be noted, however, that neither the Army nor the Navy suffered the internal strains and bitterness that beset the Air Force during the development and introduction of ballistic missiles. The most immediate explanation is simply that the missiles did not threaten any established Army or Navy weapon. Without harming the central purposes of either service, ballistic missiles offered the opportunity of broadening their

[30]Robert L. Perry, "The Ballistic Missile Decisions," pp. 26–27.

[31]Admiral William F. Raborn, speech to the AIAA, Panel on Rocketry in the 1950s, October 28, 1971, Washington, D.C. For a brief review of the development of Polaris, see Wyndham D. Miles, "The Polaris," in Eugene M. Emme, *The History of Rocket Technology,* pp. 162–88.

[32]Halperin, "Why Bureaucrats Play Games," p. 79.

roles. The Army, indeed, from their earliest days showed continuing although sporadic interest in the weapons and bitterly
resisted the transfer of operational responsibility of the Jupiter
IRBM to the Air Force.

The early history of the strategic bomber also illustrates the
potential dangers of organizational self-interest and resultant
blindness. During the earliest years of military aviation, Army
ground commanders consistently saw its purpose as defense
against hostile airplanes, reconnaissance, and artillery sighting.
Airplanes were considered appendages to ground warfare, subordinate to the main business of fighting. Just as consistently,
the new air officers extolled the possibilities of independent operations, particularly bombardment. The conflict associated with
General Billy Mitchell has become a part of American folklore
and need not be recounted here. It is intriguing, however, that
the history of the strategic bomber in the Army in many ways
parallels that of the ballistic missile a generation later.

As late as the first Franklin Roosevelt Administration, a Secretary of War felt the urge to denounce the idea of mass bombing as the "phantasy of a dreamer," while calling for adherence
to the principles of traditional defense rather than trying to
"purchase freedom with gadgets."[33] The similarity of this language to that later employed to dismiss the ballistic missile is
striking; and the parallels in the histories of the two weapons do
not cease there. As Robert Krauskopf has observed, even after
the establishment of the Army Air Corps, "The significance of
offensive aviation was still unrecognized and the organizational
structure that would allow it to be concentrated for the performance of an independent mission was not provided." Furthermore, "Even in later years, after the swift progress of technology had caught up with the most advanced ideas on air power,
this skepticism and unsympathetic attitude persisted."[34]

Resistance did not come solely from within the Army. The
early bomber, after all, could fly over water as well as over land,

[33] George H. Dean, quoted in Krauskopf, "The Army and the Strategic
Bomber." The discussion here of the advent of the strategic bomber draws
heavily on Krauskopf's analysis.

[34] Krauskopf, "The Army and the Strategic Bomber," p. 84.

and it also encountered opposition from the Navy. As Krauskopf has noted,

> Although there had always been a role in coastal defense for the Army
> and its aviation, the Navy was strongly averse to seeing its normal
> functions unsurped or interfered with. The concept of the land-based
> bomber as a weapon of defense over the high seas, at great distances
> from the coastline, was, therefore, consistently opposed by the Navy.[35]

Thus it happened that in 1937 when the Air Corps utilized the
recently acquired B-17's to intercept the Italian liner *Rex* 600
miles out in the North Atlantic in a well publicized exercise,
"the Navy's reaction was swift and emphatic, and the War
Department promptly issued an order prohibiting army aircraft
from executing flights more than 100 miles beyond the
coastline."[36]

Krauskopf has also revealed that the General Staff in the late
1930s concluded that no requirement for a long-range heavy
bomber existed in the national defense program, a determination
that was later to be repeated in the case of the ballistic missile.[37]
The General Staff even opposed the heavy bomber at one point
in 1936 on the grounds that it was "a weapon of aggression
which a peace-loving power should not possess." A different
but similar argument was later employed in the Navy in the
B-36–supercarrier controversy when that service's representatives said the bomber was not only militarily unsound and obsolete, but also that the strategy on which it was based was im-
moral. This situation finally came full circle when the Air Force
later said that the Navy Polaris strategy which included "city-
busting" was both militarily unneeded and morally abhorrent.[38]
The central issue in both the supercarrier and Polaris situations
was of course the Air Force demand for a monopoly over the
strategic retaliatory role.

[35]*Ibid.*, p. 87.

[36]*Ibid.*, p. 88.

[37]*Ibid.*, p. 93. Krauskopf states that this internal War Department controversy
significantly hampered the procurement of heavy bombers prior to World
War II.

[38]See David W. Tarr, "Military Technology and the Policy Process,"
Western Political Quarterly, 18 (March 1963): 141.

Elting E. Morison has provided other studies of military be-havior that closely parallel the Air Force reaction to ballistic missiles. Continuous aim gunnery (in which the gun can move to counteract the rolling of the ship) was introduced into the American Navy at the turn of the century. The results in im-proved accuracy were extraordinary. It has been reliably re-ported that gunnery accuracy increased in the British and American Navies by 3,000 percent in six years. Yet the changes were strongly and effectively resisted for years, despite the fact that the proposed reform would greatly and demonstrably in-crease the combat effectiveness of the Navy. Indeed, the situa-tion was not changed until a very junior but very persistent naval officer managed to interest President Theodore Roosevelt in the issue.

Morison details the official naval response to the original sug-gestions of reform as passing through three stages. First, there was no response at all; the reports of the new techniques were simply ignored. After this no longer proved effective, a form of blindfolded rational rebuttal was employed, wherein despite ir-refutable evidence of continuous aim gunnery's success, the evidence was denied. Finally, the reaction degenerated to ad hominem attack. Throughout this period there was "deeply rooted, aggressive, persistent hostility" from the Navy au-thorities.

Morison explains the reaction in this manner.

The opposition, where it occurs, of the soldier and the sailor to such change springs from the normal human instinct to protect oneself, and more especially, one's way of life. Military organizations are societies built around and upon the prevailing weapons systems. Intuitively and quite correctly the military man feels that a change in weapon portends a change in the arrangements of his society.

He adds,

It is very significant that they [the Navy] withstood it until an agent from outside, outside and above, who was not clearly identified with the naval society, entered to force change.[39]

[39]Elting E. Morison, *Men, Machines, and Modern Times* (Cambridge: M.I.T. Press, 1966), pp. 36–37.

A second case offered by Morison concerns a steam vessel, the *Wampanoag*, introduced into the American Navy in 1868. This ship handled beautifully in all weather, steamed with great economy at high speed, and was "the most remarkable man-of-war in the world and . . . put the United States Navy a full generation ahead of all other navies."

A year after her appearance the *Wampanoag* was inspected by a board of naval officers appointed by the Secretary of the Navy to report on naval steam ships. The board determined that the ship was "a sad and signal failure, and utterly unfit to be retained in the service," and that it would be a "happy riddance." No changes would salvage her. She was "too much of an abortion."[40]

The board appears simply to have employed past perception in determining what was "likely" to happen or "reasonable" to infer. Thus the board claimed that the vessel would be unstable, liable to great rolling, very difficult to maneuver or maintain in place, and unsuitable to the use of sail. These findings were the more remarkable in that they were in all particulars save the last totally incorrect. Furthermore, the vessel had been in service for a year and had openly proved its excellence. It handled well in all weather and was in fact remarkably "steady," "efficient," and "easy." The naval board denied these claims despite clear and overwhelming evidence. As a result the *Wampanoag* was laid up for a year, retired from active patrol, and finally sold out of the Navy.

A final section of the report of the naval board which inspected the steam vessels probably explains the board's strange conclusions better than anything else.

Lounging through the watches of a steamer, or acting as firemen and coal heavers, will not produce in a seaman that combination of boldness, strength, and skill which characterized the American sailor of an elder day; and the habitual exercise by an officer of a command, the execution of which is not under his own eye, is a poor substitute for the school of observation, promptness, and command found only on the deck of a sailing vessel.[41]

[40]*Ibid.*, pp. 111, 115.
[41]*Ibid.*, p. 144.

The naval gunnery innovations were finally implemented after intervention by President Theodore Roosevelt. The steam vessel *Wampanoag* was designed and promoted by an engineer, Benjamin F. Isherwood, whose ideas concerning ship building and naval strategy were rejected by the professional naval officers of his day. Likewise the ICBM was virtually ignored by the Air Staff until the efforts of the Strategic Missiles Evaluation Committee and its mentor, Trevor Gardner, forced a change. Commenting upon such phenomena, Harry Howe Ransom has offered the hypothesis that "major changes occur in military organization and doctrine only upon the impetus of major or compelling external pressures, usually of a political—rather than professional military—nature."[42]

Another analyst has specifically mentioned the ICBM in discussing the general problem of military adjustment to technological innovation. Edward Katzenbach observed in 1958:

Lag time, that lapsed period between innovation and a successful institutional or social response to it, is probably on the increase in military matters. Moreover, as the tempo of technological change continues to quicken, it is likely that lag-time will increase as well. This is understandable: the kind of readjustment in terms of doctrine, organization and training that the ballistic missile will demand of those who have flown manned aircraft from land and sea simply shocks the imagination.[43]

The strategic bomber and the ICBM both illustrate that a revolutionary new weapon may be subordinated to outdated doctrine or outdated methods if it is not assigned to an agency designed to foster it. The bomber was promoted by the Air Corps during its early years, but was persistently opposed by the Army General Staff in favor of combat support and reconnaissance. The ICBM was developed by a totally new organization, the Western Development Division, in large measure because Trevor Gardner and the members of SMEC feared that it would be delayed, if not actually sabotaged, if left to the normal

[42] Harry Howe Ransom, "The Politics of Airpower—A Comparative Analysis," *Public Policy* (1958), p. 87.

[43] Edward L. Katzenbach, Jr., "The Horse Cavalry in the Twentieth Century: A Study on Policy Response," *Public Policy* (1958), p. 120.

operations of the Air Force. Polaris too was developed by a "Special Projects Office." It is worth pointing out that in the Soviet Union ballistic missiles were first developed under the artillery arm where they were strongly promoted and later a separate service was organized for their operational use.

Edward Katzenbach has offered excellent insight into the problem of organizational innovation:

At first there would seem to be a paradox here. As weapons systems have become more complex, the lead-time needed to bring them from the drawing board to the assembly line has become markedly longer. On the basis of the longer lead-time one might hypothesize that the institutional lag might lessen inasmuch as prior planning would seem eminently more possible. It might even be surmised that the institutional response might be made to coincide with the operational readiness of new weapons. To date, however, military institutions have not been able to use this lead-time effectively because real change has so outdistanced anticipated change. Moreover, there is not the urgency that there should be in the military to make major institutional adjustments in the face of the challenge of new weapons systems, if for no other reason than that the problem of testing is so difficult. Just as in the academic world it is well-nigh impossible to *prove* that any change in curriculum would enable future leaders to think more clearly than those with a classical education, so in the military it is quite impossible to *prove* that minor adjustments in a traditional pattern of organization and doctrine will not suffice to absorb technological innovations of genuine magnitude.[44]

John Steinbruner has attempted to relate the role, organizational, and individual factors involved in foreign policy decision making through a model of cognitive processing employed by the individual human mind during situations of uncertainty.[45]

[44]*Ibid.*, pp. 120–21.

[45]John D. Steinbruner, "The Mind and Milieu of Policymakers: A Case Study of the MLF" (Ph.D. dissertation, M.I.T., 1968). Steinbruner builds in particular upon the work of Graham Allison. See Allison, *Essence of Decision: Explaining the Cuban Missile Crisis* (Boston, 1971). He takes Allison's third model a considerable step further, however, by systematically utilizing organization theory and the literature of theoretical and experimental cognitive psychology. His position is that the interaction of organization roles and cognitive processes has an important effect on policy outcomes. The policy process must be studied at both the organizational and psychological levels.

Steinbruner holds that: "Roles in the foreign policy bureaucracy are not so clearly constrained independently of the person occupying them that we.can

In his study of the multilateral force Steinbruner found that the organizational process model did not provide sufficient explanation under conditions of "structural uncertainty."[46] In particular, Steinbruner found that the policy makers he studied employed transformational and impossibility inferences to protect a belief system to which they were committed. The "impossibility inference" is especially relevant to the study of the ICBM. In brief, it refers simply to the process of denying the existence or possibility of an idea that would otherwise require considerable restructuring of belief patterns.

> The impossibility inference, as the name implies, consists in a belief that something is impossible (and therefore can be removed from consideration). . . . The grounds for which this type of inference is advanced are typically deductive rather than inductive, meaning that belief strength for such inferences derives not from empirical information but rather from their position in established belief structures.[47]

The impossibility inference appears to have been present in the early history of the ICBM. Most Air Force personnel at the Air Staff level (and probably elsewhere) simply denied that an "accurate" long-range rocket was possible, at least in the foreseeable future. The ballistic rocket was at least implicitly a competitor to the manned strategic bomber. The bomber was (and indeed still is) the central focus of identification within the Air Force. To conceive of a new weapon that might someday perform its primary task much more efficiently would require

ignore cognitive processing as a constant in the process. Indeed, as we have seen repeatedly, the organizational phenomena which occur seem to be based on cognitive processing phenomena. Though the theoretical perspective from the organizational level cannot obviate the necessity of the more complex and difficult cognitive processing model, neither can the latter wholly replace the former" (p. 493).

[46]Steinbruner's organizational behavior model is based on Richard Cyert and James March, *A Behavioral Theory of the Firm* (Englewood Cliffs, New Jersey: Prentice-Hall, 1963). This model postulates local rationality (each subunit will proceed according to its own established goals), problemistic and sequential search (acting in the face of problems, beginning a search with the nearest variant of current policy, and addressing major objectives sequentially), and uncertainty avoidance through short-term feedback. See Steinbruner, pp. 250–53, 508. This model closely resembles the theories of incremental decision-making described by Charles Lindblom and others.

[47]*Ibid.*, p. 301.

great restructuring of beliefs. The literature of cognitive psychology, as well as most people's everyday experience, makes it clear that such restructuring is a difficult, unpleasant task. The normal reaction is to reject the disturbing new element. The Air Force's behavior in the early days of the ICBM followed this pattern. The Krauskopf and Morison studies noted above show the same pattern at work at other times in the Army and Navy.

It is worth remembering that Air Force planners in 1947–48 did not expect even long-range supersonic bombers to be operationally available before 1957. Since the Air Force officers not only understood bombers and knew they worked but often equated their own personal usefulness and well-being with that weapon, it is not surprising that long-range supersonic missiles were placed even further into the future. On the one hand, experience would dictate that building an improved airplane would be easier than creating a revolutionary "ultimate" weapon. Reinforcing this outlook would be the personal, organizational, and psychological resistance to a challenger to the central role of the bomber.

Such problems are neither unexpected nor uniformly harmful. There may be real difficulties in testing a weapon's effectiveness in the absence of war. Just as the weapon itself is difficult to test—particularly a revolutionary strategic weapon—so too the viability and flexibility of the military organization itself is difficult to judge.

Adding to the tendency to preserve what is familiar is a desire to avoid risk. Analysts of organizational behavior have long described risk aversion as a primary organizational or bureaucratic goal. The normal practice of risk aversion is necessarily heightened by the nature of the military, which requires secure procedures and equipment. Naturally, the military relies on tested, well understood weapons. Unproven revolutionary concepts or devices may be dangerous to the national security. Thus, the very nature of the military role heightens the effects of the organizational and cognitive processes here discussed.

Of course, any new weapons system is bound to compete with already existing commitments simply because it is new and has therefore never had a budget line of its own. Similarly, *all* of the budget will already be allocated to the existing functions. There is unlikely to be a convenient "slush fund" to pay for the new ideas that may appear. This may seem simplistically obvious, but it is important to remember. There is a built-in and inevitable resistance to new ideas that will cost money unless additional outside funding appears available. But such funding is unlikely, particularly for a seemingly revolutionary development, until after the item has proven its worth.

At first, there was not so much strong opposition to ballistic missiles as simple inattention or dismissal. The long-range ballistic missiles were virtually ignored at the highest levels of the Air Force, as the minimal funding and statements of knowledgeable personnel make clear. The concept of the self-fulfilling prophecy consistently operated during this period. If the decision is made that something cannot be developed because of technological impossibility, and then that judgment is used to justify a refusal to provide development funds, the item will not be developed and the judgment will appear true.[48] Hence the circular ICBM history. No money was made available; so no research was done. No research was done; so no missiles were produced. No missiles were produced; so no demonstration of usefulness and capability was made. No demonstration of usefulness was made; so no money was made available. Control of money was always

---

[48]This circular bind was recognized at the time by the ballistic missile proponents. Discussing the cancellation of the Convair MX–774 rocket project on grounds of infeasibility, one rocket advocate observed, "The foregoing represents an opinion which might have been rendered 3 or 4 decades ago regarding a similar proposal for an airplane. The only possible means for building up a background of experience and 'know-how' in the relatively new field of missile design is by the actual construction and test of those various categories of missiles for which tactical or strategic needs have been determined to exist. . . . Various studies, i.e., project Rand Rpts. . . . have shown that rocket power can most efficiently deliver a missile to targets at range of 4,000 miles and above. In the opinion of this office, therefore, the rocket type missile definitely has a place in the USAF G.M. program" ("Evaluation of CVAC 1,000 mile range missile," by chief, Guided Missiles Section, Engineering Div., AMC. Feb. 28, 1949. File "MX 774." Box "MX–774." HQ USAF, DCS/D, GM Branch, National Archives).

vital to this process. Whatever faction controlled the money tended to control the choice of weapons and thus to determine overall organizational doctrine. Once the missile people got their own budget, the bomber people were in trouble.

A contributing problem in the early years was that the Air Research and Development Command was a new organization with less prestige and less clout than the longer established commands. Its interests and responsibilities, including ballistic missiles, consequently suffered.

Hindsight, of course, is a particularly satisfying faculty. The self-interest, misperceptions, blind spots, and rigidities of those under inspection stand out brightly. The temptation to identify and chastise the villains of any particular case is strong. Certainly the board of naval officers that inspected the steam vessel *Wampanoag* appear to have simply been stupid. The resistance to ballistic missiles in the Air Force and the seeming necessity to force their development on that service seems like blind pigheadedness.

I have tried to explain and even justify some of this inertia, if only by the somewhat disheartening means of describing its widespread occurence elsewhere. Many of the problems I have discussed may be unavoidable. Large organizations may develop and adhere to standard operating procedures and traditional norms for the sensible reasons of economy and efficiency. Military agencies may by necessity be particularly reliant on such operations. On the other hand, large organizations need the capacity to change and adapt. Armed forces may have a special need for such qualities. There is an apparent dilemma between adherence to procedure and the capacity for change, but it is not one that should be left to solution by temporary random compromise.

The whole history of the American ICBM is one of attempts by the missile's advocates to generate interest in the weapon in the existing organizations or to create alternative (and more favorably disposed) organizations. The RAND Corporation was conceived of as a means of incorporating advanced political, strategic, and scientific thinking in military weapons planning. RAND was to provide this function because it was thought the military would not on its own—that it might be too conservative, shortsighted, or tradition-bound.

The Air Research and Development Command was promoted because the Air Materiel Command was not judged to be doing an adequate job. It was too tied to manned aircraft and maintenance and incremental improvement of forces in being. The von Neumann Committee strongly recommended the establishment of a separate agency to oversee the crash ICBM development because the established Air Force agencies were not expected to push the program properly. My contention is that each of these efforts was helpful in accomplishing its stated purpose and that the perspective behind each new organizational innovation was probably correct.

The ICBM might have been developed earlier than it was had an agency free of Air Force perspective existed, had it enjoyed access to all relevant information, and had it been heeded. Such an agency, were it to exist at present, might serve the purpose which was originally conceived for RAND, provided it were not funded by the military and thus not dominated by any particular service or doctrine. Such an agency would need not only independence, but adequate funding and organizational clout. A part-time Scientific Advisory Committee, which was rapidly socialized by the parent service and ignored to the extent it produced unpopular ideas would not suffice. At present Congress is not competent to perform this function, although it might be made so. A technologically respected independent agency with access to all necessary information would, in any event, be very useful to congressional deliberations.

Certainly, some form of institutionalized weapons evaluation is not an idea unique to this study. It has often been suggested before, and, in fact, organizations have existed or presently exist which were designed to a greater or lesser degree to provide this service. Candidates that come to mind are the nonprofit Federal Contract Research Centers (FCRC's) such as

RAND, the Center for Naval Analyses (CNA), and Research Analysis Corporation (RAC).[49] There are also "in-house" agencies, which were intended to perform certain evaluative services. Two of the most obvious examples are the Advanced Research Project Agency (ARPA) and the Weapons System Evaluation Group (WSEG), although similar responsibilities fall within a wide area of jurisdictions, including the Systems Analysis section of the Department of Defense.

However, neither the semi-autonomous FCRC's nor the in-house agencies such as ARPA or WSEG have adequately fulfilled the function here prescribed. There are several reasons for this failure, but the missing key factors are independence and authority. The Defense-oriented think tanks do in certain cases provide critical evaluation, but they operate from a precarious position, as is evident in their recent history. As long as their budgets are healthy and unchallenged, the FCRCs are able to exercise notable independence. In the late 1960s, however, the think tanks entered upon harder times as both Congress and academia challenged their usefulness and legitimacy. Budgets were significantly slashed in several cases. The results were easily predictable. As budgets fell, so did independence. Faced with a sudden need for allies the FCRCs hastened to ensure the support of their primary sponsors. But an embattled petitioner is hardly in a position to demand and exercise independence. Since the crunch of the late 1960s, the FCRCs have indulged in markedly less disagreement with their parent services.

Clearly the potential for such problems always existed. If the major portion of one's funding comes from one sponsor with specified policy interests, the tendency must be to support that source's objectives or at the least avoid open conflict. The solution, then, might be to have the technologically-able evaluative agency located under the Secretary of Defense, thus placing the function under an office that is not committed to any doctrine,

[49]The Research Analysis Corporation, which was until the late 1960s in a proprietary relationship with the Army, has since been phased out of its favored position and is now simply a piece of the General Research Corporation, forced to compete for contracts in the open market.

service, or weapon type and that nevertheless possesses appropriate authority.

The Secretary of Defense would appear to be an ideal client. His office is supposedly not closely associated with any particular service or doctrine, he is charged with coordinating the national defense (presumably in the most efficient and effective way), and he is (again presumably) in a position to enforce his decisions. This reasoning leads us to the Advanced Research Project Agency and the Weapons System Evaluation Group.

These agencies are under the office of the Defense Secretary and they deal with technological evaluation. They have not, however, been successful in providing the function called for here. Both ARPA and WSEG are located under the Director of Defense Research and Engineering (DDR&E). ARPA is staffed primarily by civilians and its director is consistently a well respected civilian scientist. ARPA is, however, mainly a contracting agency whose primary function is to let and monitor outside contracts aimed at inspecting basic technologies for the very long run. Its jurisdiction is the technological feasibility of basic ideas, not the evaluation of proposed new weapons systems. ARPA looks at the possibility of pieces of a potential weapons system, not the usefulness of the whole animal.

WSEG, which is also formally under DDR&E, is in fact inseparable from the Institute for Defense Analysis (IDA). WSEG's personnel are all active military officers. The civilians associated with WSEG are employees of IDA assigned to the Weapons System Evaluation Division of IDA. WSEG was originally intended to provide support to the Secretary of Defense and the Joint Chiefs of Staff in the broad areas of force mix and force effectiveness. It was meant to give impartial, objective advice on these issues and to monitor and evaluate weapons systems—precisely those responsibilities projected for the evaluative agency suggested here. Unfortunately, WSEG has not always proved effective and its weapons monitoring and evaluating functions have in many ways fallen by the wayside. The problem is that WSEG is made up of active military officers and is, in many respects, a committee on which the three services are represented equally. Such bodies, despite their best intentions, will not be able to provide the strong, critical role needed. Rather, they will tend to revert to "backscratching," trading off support for someone else's project for support for their own. Compromise positions recommending support of everybody's positions will tend to be the rule. The gradual abandonment of WSEG's evaluative role would seem to support this contention.

What is called for is the combination of ability, independence, and authority. WSEG and the FCRCs have at times lacked independence. ARPA lacked the proper mandate. Outside critics have lacked authority. Ability must be sought and paid for but it is available. Independence will not occur if an agency's budget is dependent upon one client with strongly delineated preferences. Independence must also be guarded; it cannot be assumed or the risk of gradual domination by an interested group will be increasingly great. Authority will not accrue naturally to the organization with the "best" ideas. It must be granted and ensured by a source competent to do so.

One possible source would seem to be an able Secretary of Defense (with an able staff) with clear Presidential support. It is simply unrealistic to expect a military service (or any organization) to monitor itself if such monitoring requires judgments contrary to its own perceived self-interest. That function can only come from outside. The Systems Analysis office of the Secretary of Defense might be able to fill this need, but it does not at present appear to be doing so in many instances. Furthermore, the matters discussed in this study will involve continual conflicts. Organizations will tend to act as described herein. If that behavior appears mistaken to an outsider, he will have to struggle to change it, and the struggle will be never ending. The effort is not only worthwhile, however. It is necessary.

Again, this study does not advocate building any weapon military or civilian scientists can dream up. Indeed, it says precisely the opposite. A well funded and independent review agency with high-level support and full technological and political access should produce more efficient and economical choices. Not only might unusual technological or strategic concepts receive a more objective hearing, but old and potentially outmoded weapons and doctrines might also face valuable scrutiny. The B–1 bomber, large and numerous aircraft carriers, gilt-edged tanks, and sophisticated fighters, for example, may indeed be vital to American security. But their merit might receive a more valid judgment outside the councils of the service that advocates them.

One important point to remember is that the influence of the weapons available on both the formulation of strategy and the choice of military action is great—too great to be left to the kind of institutional procedures here detailed. Military commanders and their political superiors will be constrained by the weapons they possess. If such weapons allow only a certain range of actions, response will be necessarily limited to that range regardless of political or strategic analysis.

Graham Allison has stated that President Kennedy was originally strongly attracted to the use of a "surgical" air strike against the missile emplacements in Cuba and withdrew from the idea only after the Air Force claimed such a strike was not feasible—that only a saturation raid would assure destruction of all the sites.[50] Similar incidents could be recounted.[51]

The interrelationship of politics, strategy, and weapons choice must be recognized. The nature of the weapons possessed by a nation can strongly influence its strategic thinking and political–military actions. Current strategic doctrine should not totally constrain research and development efforts, just as current technology should not determine the full range of strategic

---

[50]Allison, *Essence of Decision,* pp. 59–60, 123–26, 197–210. Allison also shows that the Air Force was not accurate in its statements to Kennedy. The Air Force wanted to perform a massive saturation strike and told Kennedy a lesser effort would be ineffective—this "fact" was not true. Kennedy recoiled from that option and further deliberation finally resulted in the choice of the naval blockade.

[51]The reader is urged to read the Brookings Institution study, *Bureaucratic Politics and Foreign Policy,* by Morton H. Halperin, which bolsters its insightful theoretical analysis with a wealth of illustrations.

speculation. If either or both phenomena occur, a process of reinforcement may inevitably follow whereby doctrine restrains research and research then only supports the prevalent doctrine. This is not the best solution. If war is too important to be left to the generals; so too may be the choice of weapons which may determine whether or not you get into a war and how you fare once there.

Bibliography

A NOTE ON SOURCES

In the Introduction, I briefly described the procedure whereby Air Force records were declassified for use here. Under the ground rules there detailed, research was undertaken at the Historical Office, Air Force Systems Command, Andrews Air Force Base, Maryland; the Air Force Historical Archives, Maxwell Air Force Base, Montgomery, Alabama; and the National Archives, Washington, D.C.

These three institutions each contained a wealth of material, and many individual documents have been cited throughout. I shall not list each record here; certain items do, however, deserve individual mention.

Two particularly useful sources were Ethel M. DeHaven, *Aerospace—The Evolution of USAF Weapons Acquisition Policy, 1945–1961,* published by the United States Air Force, DCAS Historical Office, 1962, and Mary R. Self, *History of the Development of Guided Missiles, 1946–1950,* published by the USAF, AMC Historical Office, 1951. Both were read at Andrews Air Force Base. Even more useful than the works themselves, which were often general or overly decorous, were the large document collections appended to each. The De-Haven collection was read at Andrews Air Force Base. The three volumes of Self documents were found at Maxwell Air Force Base in Alabama.

Two other Air Force studies with document collections proved helpful. These were Robert L. Perry, *The Development of the Snark Guided Missile, 1945–1953* (USAF, WADC, 1956) and J. Allen Neal, *The Development of the Navaho Guided Missile: 1945–1953* (USAF, WADC, 1956). Both these items, and the document collections, were read at Andrews Air Force Base. Strangely, there is no Air Force history of the Atlas development program, despite that weapon's much greater importance. Air Force historical personnel cannot explain this shortcoming except to note that during General Schriever's tenure at WDD/BMD/ARDC little emphasis was placed on maintaining accurate, detailed historical records. Another source, which proved particularly helpful in chapter 7, was the *Air Force Ballistic Missile Chronology 1946–1957* (USAF, BMD, 1957).

The National Archives in Washington, D.C., contain two valuable collections of Air Force records, those of the Guided Missiles Branch, Directorate of Research and Development, Deputy Chief of Staff/Development, and those of the Guided Missiles Division, Assistant for Guided Missiles, Deputy Chief of Staff/Operations. These files proved enormously helpful in piecing together the story of the earliest years. Unfortunately, the records end in 1949, at which point the various Air Force commands began writing semiannual "histories" of their operations. General records were then discarded (presumably after a few years). These "histories" are available, upon declassification, at the Air Force Archives, Maxwell Air Force Base. Those I inspected were not particularly useful. They are often short, bland discussions of promotion policy, organizational structure, and major areas of responsibility. Extensive document collections are included only in a few instances; in many cases no documents are appended at all.

Two collections of papers were consulted within the Library of Congress—those of Curtis E. LeMay and Hoyt S. Vandenberg. In both cases the same rules applied as had governed the other Air Force documents inspected. Access had to be granted first by the Air Force and all notes had to be cleared by that service. Unfortunately, neither collection yielded anything but general or peripheral references to long-range missiles.

The Harry S. Truman and Dwight D. Eisenhower Libraries were also consulted. The Truman Library yielded two interesting notes which have been incorporated in chapter 4. The Eisenhower Library was unable to add anything of significance to the substance of Chapters 6 and 7. On the issues that most needed further illumination, for example the appointment of Trevor Gardner and the events leading to the von Neumann Committee Report, nothing was available. Similarly, there was no additional information on the NSC briefing in the summer of 1955 and the subsequent presidential directive assigning first national priority to the ICBM.

Note was taken in the Introduction of the difficulties encountered by those interviewed in trying to recall events of two and even three decades ago. The problems were considerable. On the other hand, it is quite likely that had a more recent subject been chosen, public release of previously classified records would have been difficult, despite the Air Force procedures and the Freedom of Information Act.

One intriguing phenomenon helped to make this so. Perhaps three quarters of those interviewed offered large periods of their time. Two hours was a common interview and some lasted three and four. Furthermore, the respondents were normally friendly, enthusiastic, and cooperative. The reason seems to have been (and this judgment was suggested by several of those interviewed) that the ICBM crash development period from 1954 until, say, 1959 was the most exciting period in their lives. Work was feverish and the participants felt a part of a great and urgent national effort. Adding to this feeling was the scientific stimulation inherent in the work and a sense of intense and vital competition with the Russians. Thus, a typical interviewee, upon hearing of my interest, would call for coffee, lean back, say, "ask me anything," and begin to tell stories. This would continue, as noted above, in many cases for hours. This occurred not only with respondents now retired but also with executives in the aerospace firms, who were interrupted during their work day. Although the enthusiasm did not always manage to clear away the clouds of time, it was nevertheless helpful.

Two final sources deserve mention. Robert L. Perry, who has worked both at the RAND Corporation and within the Air Force's historical effort, has been often cited herein. He consented to several interviews during the early stages of this book and provided useful direction and needed moral support. As work progressed, short, lucid Perry articles were discovered intermittently. The numerous citations indicate their value. Finally, Mr. Perry read the entire manuscript and offered detailed, friendly criticism. I am grateful. Mr. Harry Jordan, historian with the Space and Missile Systems Organization, responded to my queries with two lengthy, thoughtful letters. Subsequently, he read and commented upon the completed manuscript. Mr. Jordan's analysis was sharp and direct. Many of his insights found their way into this study and unquestionably improved the end result.

PUBLIC DOCUMENTS

U.S. Congress. House of Representatives.

———— Committee on Appropriations, Subcommittee on Defense Appropriations. *Hearings, The Ballistic Missile Program.* 85th Cong., 1st sess., 1957.

———— Committee on Armed Services. *Hearings, Investigation of National Defense Missiles.* 85th Cong., 1st sess., 1958.

———— Committee on Government Operations. *Air Force Ballistic Missile Management: Formation of Aerospace Corporation.* 87th Cong., 1st sess., 1961.

———— Committee on Government Operations, Subcommittee on Military Operations. *Hearings, Organization and Administration of the Military Research and Development Programs.* 83rd Cong., 2nd sess., 1954.

———— Committee on Government Operations, Subcommittee on Military Operations. *Hearings, Organization and Management of Missile Programs.* 86th Cong., 1st sess., 1959.

———— Committee on Government Operations, Subcommittee on Military Operations. *Hearings, Organization and Management of Missile Programs.* 86th Cong., 2nd sess., 1960.

———— Committee on Government Operations, Subcommittee on Military Operations. *Organization and Management of Missile Programs.* 86th Cong., 1st sess., 1959.

———— Committee on Science and Astronautics. *Basic Scientific and Astronautic Research in the Department of Defense.* 86th Cong., 1st sess., 1959.

———— Committee on Science and Astronautics. *A Chronology of Missile and Astronautic Events.* 87th Cong., 1st sess., 1961.

———— Committee on Science and Astronautics. *Hearings, Missile Development and Space Sciences.* 86th Cong., 1st sess., 1959.

———— Committee on Science and Astronautics. *Hearings, Progress of Atlas and Polaris Missiles.* 86th Cong., 1st sess., 1959.

———— Committee on Science and Astronautics. *Progress of Atlas and Polaris Missiles.* 86th Cong., 1st sess., 1959.

———— Committee on Science and Astronautics. *Space, Missiles, and the Nation.* 86th Cong., 2nd sess., 1960.

———— Committee on Science and Astronautics. *Status of Missile and Space Programs.* 86th Cong., 1st sess., 1959.

U.S. Congress. Senate.

———— Committee on Aeronautical and Space Sciences, Subcommittee on Governmental Organization for Space Activities. *Hearings, Investigation of Governmental Organization for Space Activities.* 86th Cong., 1st sess., 1959.

———— Committee on Armed Services, Preparedness Investigating Subcommittee. *Hearings, Inquiry into Satellite and Missile Programs.* 85th Cong., 1st and 2nd sess., 1958.

———— Committee on Armed Services, Preparedness Investigating Subcommittee. *The United States Guided Missile Programs.* 86th Cong., 1st sess., 1959.

———— Committee on Armed Services, Preparedness Investigating Subcommittee and the Committee on Aeronautical and Space Sciences. *Joint Hearings, Missile and Space Activities.* 86th Cong., 1st sess., 1959.

———— Preparedness Investigating Subcommittee of Committee on Armed Services and Committee on Aeronautical and Space Science. *Joint Hearings, Missiles, Space, and Other Major Defense Matters.* 86th Cong., 2nd sess., 1960.

———— Subcommittee on the Air Force of the Committee on Armed Services. *Study of Airpower.* 84th Cong., 2nd sess., 1956.

———— Committee on Foreign Relations. *United States Foreign Policy: Developments in Military Technology and Their Impact on United States Strategy and Foreign Policy.* 86th Cong., 1st sess., 1959.

U.S. Library of Congress.

Legislative Reference Service. *United States Defense Policies Since World War II.* Washington, D.C.: Government Printing Office, 1957.

———— *United States Defense Policies in 1958.* Washington, D.C.: Government Printing Office, 1959.

First Report of the Secretary of Defense, 1948. Washington, D.C.: Government Printing Office, 1948.

Second Report of the Secretary of Defense and the Annual Reports of the Secretary of the Army, Secretary of the Navy, and Secretary of the Air Force for Fiscal Year 1949. Washington, D.C.: Government Printing Office, 1950.

Semiannual Report of the Secretary of Defense and the Semiannual Reports of the Secretary of the Army, Secretary of the Navy, and Secretary of the Air Force: January 1 to June 30, 1950. Washington, D.C.: Government Printing Office, 1950.

———— *January 1 to June 30, 1951.* Washington, D.C.: Government Printing Office, 1951.

———— *January 1 to June 30, 1952.* Washington, D.C.: Government Printing Office, 1952.

———— *January 1 to June 30, 1953.* Washington, D.C.: Government Printing Office, 1953.

———— *January 1 to June 30, 1954.* Washington, D.C.: Government Printing Office, 1955.

———— *July 1 to December 31, 1954.* Washington, D.C.: Government Printing Office, 1955.

———— *January 1 to June 30, 1955.* Washington, D.C.: Government Printing Office, 1956.

———— *July 1 to December 31, 1955.* Washington, D.C.: Government Printing Office, 1956.

——— *January 1 to June 30, 1956.* Washington, D.C.: Government Printing Office, 1957.

——— *January 1 to June 30, 1957.* Washington, D.C.: Government Printing Office, 1957.

Survival in the Air Age. A Report by the President's Air Policy Commission. Washington, D.C.: Government Printing Office, 1948.

BOOKS AND MONOGRAPHS

Allison, Graham T. *Conceptual Models and the Cuban Missile Crisis: Rational Policy, Organization Process, and Bureaucratic Politics.* Santa Monica, California: The RAND Corporation, August 1968.

——— *Essence of Decision: Explaining the Cuban Missile Crisis.* Boston: Little, Brown, 1971.

Alsop, Joseph and Stewart. *The Reporter's Trade.* New York: Reynal & Company, 1958.

Armacost, Michael H. *The Politics of Weapons Innovation: The Thor-Jupiter Controversy.* New York: Columbia University Press, 1969.

Army Air Forces Scientific Advisory Group. *Toward New Horizons: A Report to General of the Army H. H. Arnold.* Washington: 1945.

Arnold, Henry H. "Air Power and the Future." In Walter Millis (ed.), *American Military Thought.* Indianapolis: Bobbs-Merrill, 1966.

——— *Global Mission.* New York: Harper and Bros., 1949.

Art, Robert J. *The TFX Decision: McNamara and the Military.* Boston: Little, Brown, 1968.

Baar, James J., and William E. Howard. *Combat Missileman.* New York: Harcourt, Brace, 1961.

——— *Polaris!* New York: Harcourt, Brace, 1960.

Baldwin, Hanson W. *The Great Arms Race: A Comparison of U.S. and Soviet Power Today.* New York: Praeger, 1958.

Ball, D. J. "The Strategic Missile Programs of the Kennedy Administration, 1961–1963." Ph.D. dissertation, Australian National University, 1972.

Bottome, Edgar M. *The Missile Gap: A Study of the Formulation of Military and Political Policy.* Rutherford, New Jersey: Fairleigh Dickinson University Press, 1971.

Braybrooke, David, and Charles E. Lindblom. *A Strategy of Decision: Policy Evaluation as a Social Process.* New York: The Free Press, 1963.

Brodie, Bernard. *Strategy in the Missile Age.* Princeton: Princeton University Press, 1959.

——— and Eilene Galloway. *The Atomic Bomb and the Armed Services.* Public Affairs Bulletin No. 55. Washington, D.C.: Government Printing Office, 1947.

Bush, Vannevar. *Modern Arms and Free Men*. Cambridge: M.I.T. Press, 1968.

Caidin, Martin. *Countdown for Tomorrow*. New York: E. P. Dutton, 1958.

Caraley, Demetrios. *The Politics of Military Unification: A Study of Conflict and the Policy Process*. New York: Columbia University Press, 1966.

Carr, E. H. *German-Soviet Relations between the Two World Wars, 1919–1939*. Baltimore: Johns Hopkins University Press, 1951.

Chapman, John L. *Atlas: The Story of a Missile*. New York: Harper and Brothers, 1960.

Congressional Quarterly Service. *Congress and the Nation, 1945–1964: A Review of Government and Politics in the Postwar Years*. Washington, D.C.: Congressional Quarterly, 1965.

Cox, Donald W. *America's New Policy Makers: The Scientist's Rise to Power*. Philadelphia: Chilton Books, 1964.

Cyert, Richard, and James March. *A Behavioral Theory of the Firm*. Englewood Cliffs, New Jersey: Prentice-Hall, 1963.

Dinerstein, H. S. *War and the Soviet Union*. New York: Frederick A. Praeger, 1959.

Eisenhower, Dwight D. *Crusade in Europe*. Garden City, New York: Doubleday, 1948.

Emme, Eugene. *The History of Rocket Technology*. Detroit: Wayne State University Press, 1964.

———— (ed.) *The Impact of Air Power: National Security and World Politics*. Princeton: Van Nostrand, 1959.

Enthoven, Alain C., and K. Wayne Smith. *How Much is Enough? Shaping the Defense Program, 1961–1969*. New York: Harper, 1971.

Gantz, Kenneth F. (ed.). *The United States Air Force Report on the Ballistic Missile*. Garden City, New York: Doubleday, 1958.

Garthoff, Raymond. *Soviet Strategy in the Nuclear Age*. New York: Frederick A. Praeger, 1958.

Gavin, James M. *War and Peace in the Space Age*. New York: Harper & Bros., 1958.

Gilpin, Robert. *American Scientists and Nuclear Weapons Policy*. Princeton: Princeton University Press, 1962.

Goddard, Esther C. (ed.), with Edward Pendray. *The Papers of Robert H. Goddard, 1882–1945*, Vols. I, II, III. New York: McGraw-Hill, 1970.

Goldberg, Alfred (ed.). *A History of the Air Force: 1907–1957*. New Jersey: D. Van Nostrand, 1957.

Hammond, Paul Y. *The Cold War Years: American Foreign Policy Since 1945*. New York: Harcourt, Brace and World, 1969.

————— *Organizing for Defense: The American Military Establishment in the Twentieth Century*. Princeton: Princeton University Press, 1961.

————— *Resource Limits, Political and Military Risk Taking, and the Generation of Military Requirements*. Santa Monica, California: The RAND Corporation, Pubn. P–3421–1, September, 1966.

Heflin, Woodford Agee (ed.). *The United States Air Force Dictionary*. Princeton: D. Van Nostrand, 1956.

Hewlett, Richard G. and Oscar E. Anderson. *A History of the United States Atomic Energy Commission*. Volume II. University Park, Pa.: Pennsylvania State University Press, 1962.

Hilsman, Roger. *The Politics of Policy Making in Defense and Foreign Affairs*. New York: Harper and Row, 1971.

————— *To Move a Nation*. New York: Delta Books, Dell Publishing Company, 1964.

————— and William W. Kaufmann (eds.). *Military Policy and National Security*. Princeton: Princeton University Press, 1956.

Holley, I. B., Jr. *Ideas and Weapons*. New Haven: Yale University Press, 1953.

Hubler, Richard G. *SAC: The Strategic Air Command*. New York: Duell, Sloan and Pearce, 1956.

Huntington, Samuel P. *The Common Defense: Strategic Programs in National Politics*. New York: Columbia University Press, 1961.

Janowitz, Morris. *The Professional Soldier: A Social and Political Portrait*. Glencoe, Ill.: The Free Press, 1960.

Johns, Claude, Jr. "The United States Air Force Intercontinental Ballistic Missile Program, 1954–1959: Technical Change and Organizational Innovation." Ph.D. dissertation, University of North Carolina at Chapel Hill, 1964.

Johnson, Ellis. "The Lead-Time Problem and Technological Waste." In Walter F. Hahn and John C. Neff (eds.). *American Strategy for the Nuclear Age*. New York: Doubleday, 1961.

Kaufmann, William W. *The Requirements of Deterrence*. Princeton: Princeton University Press, 1954.

Kinter, William R. *Forging a New Sword*. New York: Harper & Bros., 1958.

Kissinger, Henry A. *The Necessity for Choice*. New York: Harper, 1961.

Laird, Melvin R. *A House Divided: America's Strategy Gap*. Chicago: Henry Regnery Company, 1962.

Lapp, Ralph E. *Arms Beyond Doubt: The Tyranny of Weapons Technology*. New York: Cowles Book Company, 1970.

Lapp, Ralph E. *Man and Space: The Next Decade*. New York: Harper and Bros., 1961.

——————— *The Weapons Culture.* New York: W. W. Norton, 1968.

Ley, Willy. *Rockets, Missiles and Space Travel.* New York: The Viking Press, 1952.

Lindblom, Charles E. *The Intelligence of Democracy.* New York: The Free Press, 1965.

——————— *The Policy-Making Process.* Englewood Cliffs, New Jersey: Prentice-Hall, 1968.

Lowe, George E. *The Age of Deterrence.* Boston: Little, Brown, 1964.

MacCloskey, Monro. *The United States Air Force.* New York: Praeger, 1967.

Malina, Frank J. "Origins and First Decade of the Jet Propulsion Laboratory." In Emme (ed.). *The History of Rocket Technology.* Detroit: Wayne University Press, 1964.

Medaris, John B. *Countdown for Decision.* New York: G. P. Putnam's Sons, 1960.

Miles, Wyndham D. "The Polaris." In Eugene Emme (ed.). *The History of Rocket Technology.* Detroit: Wayne State University Press, 1964.

Millis, Walter (ed.). *American Military Thought.* Indianapolis: Bobbs-Merrill, 1966.

——————— *Arms and Men.* New York: Putnam, 1956.

——————— *The Forrestal Diaries.* New York: Viking Press, 1951.

Millis, Walter, H. Mansfield and H. Stein. *Arms and the State.* New York: Twentieth Century Fund, 1958.

Morgenstern, Oskar. *The Question of National Defense.* New York: Random House, 1959.

Morison, Elting E. *Men, Machines, and Modern Times.* Cambridge: M.I.T. Press, 1966.

Moulton, Harland B. "American Strategic Power: Two Decades of Nuclear Strategy and Weapon Systems, 1945–1965." Ph.D. dissertation, University of Minnesota, 1969.

Neal, Roy. *Ace in the Hole: The Story of the Minuteman Missile.* Garden City, New York: Doubleday and Company, Inc., 1962.

Neustadt, Richard E. *Alliance Politics.* New York: Columbia University Press, 1970.

——————— *Presidential Power.* New York: Wiley, 1960.

Nieburg, H. L. *In the Name of Science.* Chicago: Quadrangle Books, 1966.

Parson, Nels A. *Guided Missiles in War and Peace.* Cambridge: Harvard University Press, 1956.

Peck, Merton, and Frederick Scherer. *The Weapons Acquisition Process.* Cambridge: Harvard University Press, 1962.

Perry, Robert L. "The Atlas, Thor, Titan, and Minuteman." In Eugene Emme. *The History of Rocket Technology.* Detroit: Wayne State University Press, 1964.

——— *System Development Strategies.* RAND (unpublished draft).

Rees, Ed. *The Manned Missile: The Story of the B-70.* New York: Duell, Sloan and Pearce, 1960.

Reinhardt, George C. *American Strategy in the Atomic Age.* Norman: Oklahoma University Press, 1955.

Roberts, Chalmers M. *The Nuclear Years: The Arms Race and Arms Control, 1945–1970.* New York: Praeger, 1970.

Rockefeller Brothers Fund. *International Security: The Military Aspect.* New York: Doubleday, 1958.

Rosen, Milton W. *The Viking Rocket Story.* New York: Harper, 1955.

Rothstein, Robert L. *Planning, Prediction, and Policymaking in Foreign Affairs.* Boston: Little, Brown, 1972.

Schilling, Warner R., Paul Y. Hammond, and Glenn H. Snyder. *Strategy, Politics, and Defense Budgets.* New York: Columbia University Press, 1962. (Contains three studies, one by each contributor.)

Schriever, Bernard A. "The USAF Ballistic Missile Programs." In Kenneth F. Gantz (ed.). *The United States Air Force Report on the Ballistic Missile.* Garden City, N.Y.: Doubleday, 1958.

Schwartz, Urs. *American Strategy: A New Perspective.* London: Heinemann, 1967.

Schwiebert, Ernest G. *A History of the U.S. Air Force Ballistic Missiles.* New York: Frederick A. Praeger, 1965.

Smith, Bruce L. R. *The RAND Corporation.* Cambridge: Harvard University Press, 1966.

Smith, Perry McCoy. *The Air Force Plans for Peace.* Baltimore: The Johns Hopkins University Press, 1970.

Spanier, John. *American Foreign Policy Since World War II.* New York: Frederick A. Praeger, 1965.

Stanley, Timothy. *American Defense and National Security.* Washington, D.C.: Public Affairs Press, 1956.

Stein, Harold (ed.). *American Civil–Military Decisions: A Book of Case Studies.* University, Ala.: The Inter-University Case Program, University of Alabama Press, 1963.

Steinbruner, John. "The Mind and Milieu of Policymakers: A Case Study of the MLF." Ph.D. dissertation, M.I.T., 1968.

Sturm, Thomas A. *USAF Scientific Advisory Board: Its First Twenty Years, 1944–1964.* Washington, D.C.: Government Printing Office, 1967.

Swenson, Loyd S., James M. Grimwood, and Charles C. Alexander. *This New Ocean: A History of Project Mercury.* Washington, D.C.: Government Printing Office, 1966.

Taylor, General Maxwell D. *The Uncertain Trumpet.* New York: Harper and Bros., 1960.

Thomas, Shirley. *Men of Space*. Vol. I. Philadelphia: Chilton Co., 1960.

Truman, Harry S. *Memoirs*. 2 Vols. New York: Doubleday, 1956.

Ulanoff, Stanley. *Illustrated Guide to U.S. Missiles and Rockets*. Garden City, N.Y.: Doubleday, 1962.

Von Karman, Theodore, with Lee Edson. *The Wind and Beyond*. Boston: Little Brown, 1967.

Von Neumann, John. "Can We Survive Technology." In Walter F. Hahn and John C. Neff (eds.). *American Strategy for the Nuclear Age*. New York: Doubleday, 1960.

Walkowicz, T. F. "The Race for the ICBM." In J. F. Loosbrock, and Richard M. Skinner (eds.). *The Wild Blue*. New York: G.P. Putnam's Sons, 1961.

Williams, Beryl, and Samuel Epstein. *The Rocket Pioneers on the Road to Space*. New York: Julian Messner, Inc., 1958.

York, Herbert F. *Race to Oblivion: A Participant's View of the Arms Race*. New York: Simon and Schuster, 1970.

Zaehringer, A. J. *Soviet Space Technology*. New York: Harper & Bros., 1961.

ARTICLES AND PAPERS

"Across the Atlantic in 30 Minutes." *U.S. News and World Report*, January 20, 1956, pp. 21–4.

"Air Force Ballistic Missile Division." *Air Force*, 41 (March 1958):78.

"Air Force Ballistic Missile Organization." *Air Force*, 41 (March 1958):77.

"Air Force Cover-Up." *The New Republic*, July 29, 1957, pp. 5–6.

Allison, Graham T., and Morton Halperin. "Bureaucratic Politics: A Paradigm and Some Policy Implications." *World Politics*, 24 (Special Issue, 1971):40–79.

——— "Conceptual Models and the Cuban Missile Crisis." *American Political Science Review*, 63 (September 1970):689–718.

Alsop, Joseph. "After Ike, the Deluge." *Washington Post*, October 7, 1959, p. A–17.

——— "Facts about the Missile Balance." *Washington Post*, September 25, 1961, p. 10.

——— "McNamara and the Chiefs." *Washington Post*, May 10, 1963, p. 8.

"AMC Responsible for Management Methods in Weapons Manufacture." *Aviation Week*, April 11, 1955, pp. 17–18.

Angell, Joseph Warner. "Guided Missiles Could Have Won." Part I. *Atlantic Monthly*, 188 (December 1951):29–34.

——— "Guided Missiles Could Have Won." Part II. *Atlantic Monthly*, 189 (January 1952):57–63.

Baldwin, Hanson W. "A Military Policy for the Missile Age." *New York Times Magazine,* November 3, 1957, pp. 13ff.

Brodie, Bernard. "Military Demonstration and Disclosure of New Weapons." *World Politics,* 5 (April 1953):281–301.

———— "Nuclear Weapons and Changing Strategic Outlooks." *Bulletin of the Atomic Scientists,* 13 (February 1957):56–61.

———— "Some Notes on the Evolution of Air Doctrine." *World Politics,* 7 (April 1955):349–70.

———— "Strategic Bombing: What It Can Do." *The Reporter,* 3 (August 14, 1950):28–31.

————"Strategy as a Science." *World Politics,* 1, no. 4 (July 1949): 467–88.

———— "War Department Thinking on the Atomic Bomb." *Bulletin of the Atomic Scientists,* 3 (June 1947):150–55.

Buchan, Alastair. "The Age of Insecurity." *Encounter,* 20 (June 1963):34–43.

Burke, Arleigh A. "Missiles and the Defense Organization." *Vital Speeches,* 24 (February 1958):244–47.

Burns, Arthur Lee. "From Balance to Deterrence: A Theoretical Analysis." *World Politics,* 9 (July 1957):494–529.

Butz, J. S., Jr. "Rivalry Intense in Soviet Weapon Design." *Aviation Week,* November 24, 1958, pp. 91–104.

"Civilian Managers Grow Sour on System." *Aviation Week,* June 24, 1957, pp. 29–31.

Connery, Robert H. "Unification of the Armed Forces—The First Year." *American Political Science Review,* 43, no. 1 (February 1949):38–52.

"Corporations: Builder of the Atlas." *Time,* January 20, 1958, pp. 76–82.

Cottrell, Alvin J. "Military Security and the New Look." *Current History,* 38 (April 1960):193–239.

———— and James E. Dougherty. "Nuclear Weapons, Policy and Strategy." *Orbis,* 1 (Summer 1957):138–160.

Dawson, Raymond H. "Congressional Innovation and Intervention in Defense Policy: Legislative Authorization of Weapons Systems." *American Political Science Review,* 56 (March 1962):42–57.

"Debate Over Missiles." *Commonweal,* 69 (February 20, 1959):532.

Demler, Marvin C. "Problems and Pitfalls in Guided Missile Research." *Air Force* (September 1956):114–17.

De Seversky, Alexander P. "A Lecture on Air Power." *Air University Quarterly Review,* 1 (Winter 1947):23–40.

Dinerstein, Herbert. "Revolution in Soviet Strategic Thinking." *Foreign Affairs,* 36 (January 1958):241–52.

Dulles, John Foster. "Challenge and Response in United States Foreign Policy." *Foreign Affairs,* 36 (October 1957):25–43.

————— "Policy for Security and Peace." *Foreign Affairs*, 32 (April 1954):353–364.

Emme, Eugene M. "Some Fallacies Concerning Air Power." *Annals*, 299 (May 1955):12–24.

Finletter, Thomas K. "New Look at Air Policy." *Atlantic Monthly*, 192 (September 1953):25–30.

Ford, Corey, and James Perkins. "Boss of the Missilemen." *Saturday Evening Post*, 231 (August 23, 1958):30 ff.

Fox, William T. R. "Civilians, Soldiers, and American Military Policy." *World Politics*, 7 (April 1955):402–18.

Gardner, Trevor. "But We Are Still Lagging: Reasons Why, What We Can Do about It." *Life*, November 4, 1957, pp. 30–33.

————— "How We Fell Behind in Guided Missiles." *Airpower Historian*, 5, no. 1 (January 1958):3–13.

————— "Our Guided Missile Crisis." *Look*, May 15, 1956, pp. 48–52.

Gelb, Leslie H., and Morton H. Halperin. "The Ten Commandments of the Foreign Affairs Bureaucracy." *Harpers*, June 1972, pp. 28–37.

Glasser, Otto J. "Atlas ICBM Weapon System." *Air Force*, 41 (April 1958):72–74.

"Guided Missile Preview: A New Arsenal for U.S." *United States News and World Report*, March 31, 1950, p. 20.

"Guided Missiles: AAF Forms 1st Experimental Group to Work Out Tactics, Technique of Guided Missile Operations." *Air Force*, 29, no. 3 (March–April 1946):22–23.

Hall, Colonel Edward N. "Epitaph." August 29, 1958. (Photocopy).

Halperin, Morton H. "The Decision to Deploy the ABM: Bureaucratic Politics in the Pentagon and White House in the Johnson Administration." *American Political Science Association*, September 1970. Convention paper.

————— "The Gaither Committee and the Policy Process." *World Politics*, April 1961, pp. 360–84.

————— "Choosing Our Weapons." *The New Republic*, October 2, 1961, pp. 34–36.

————— "The President and the Military." *Foreign Affairs*, 50, no. 2 (January 1972):310–24.

————— "Why Bureaucrats Play Games." *Foreign Policy*, no. 2 (Spring 1971):70–90.

Healey, Denis. "The Sputnik and Western Defense." *International Affairs*, 34 (April 1958):145–56.

Hilsman, Roger. "American Military Policy: The Next Phase." *Current History*, 33 (October 1957):208–15.

————— "Congressional–Executive Relations and the Foreign Policy Consensus." *American Political Science Review*, 52 (September 1958):725–44.

_____ "The Foreign Policy Consensus: An Interim Research Report." *Conflict Resolution,* 3 (December 1959):361–82.

Hoag, Malcolm. "Some Complexities in Military Planning." *World Politics,* 11 (July 1959):553–576.

Hotz, Robert. "ARDC Shuffles Weapons Systems Pattern." *Aviation Week,* February 22, 1954, p. 12.

_____ "Facts and Fiction on the ICBM." *Aviation Week,* September 2, 1957, p. 21.

_____ "Firing of 900-Mile Russian Missile Spurs U.S. Changes." *Aviation Week,* February 20, 1956, pp. 26–27.

"How Far Have Guided Missiles Come?" *Business Week,* October 25, 1952, pp. 108–20.

Huntington, Samuel P. "Equilibrium and Disequilibrium in American Military Policy." *Political Science Quarterly,* 76 (December 1961):481–502.

_____ "Radicalism and Conservatism in National Defense Policy." *Journal of International Affairs,* 8 (1954):206–22.

_____ "Strategic Planning and the Political Process." *Foreign Affairs,* 38 (January 1960):285–99.

"If Russia Wins Missile Race." *United States News and World Report,* January 20, 1956, pp. 25–26.

Jackson, Henry M. "The Increasing Threat of Ballistic Missiles." *Bulletin of the Atomic Scientists,* 12 (March 1956):90–92.

_____ "Toward a Superior Force in Being." *New York Times Magazine,* May 20, 1956, pp. 17 ff.

Jacobs, Paul. "Pilots, Missilemen, and Rockets." *The Reporter,* February 8, 1958, pp. 14–21.

Kanter, Arnold. "Presidential Power and Bureaucratic Compliance: Changing Organizational Objectives." *American Political Science Association* (September 1971). Convention Paper.

Katzenbach, Edward L., Jr. "The Horse Cavalry in the Twentieth Century: A Study on Policy Response." *Public Policy* (1958): pp. 120–49.

_____ "The U.S. Missile Muddle." *The Reporter,* October 3, 1957, pp. 12–16.

Kennan, George F. "The Illusion of Security." *Atlantic Monthly,* 194 (August 1954):31–34.

Klass, Philip. "AF Tries 'Weapons System' Plan." *Aviation Week,* June 22, 1953, pp. 16–17.

Krauskopf, Robert W. "The Army and the Strategic Bomber, 1930–1939." *Military Affairs,* 22, no. 2 (Summer 1958):56–64; and 22, no. 4 (Winter 1958):48–55.

Larrabee, Eric. "The Politics of Strategy." *Bulletin of the Atomic Scientists,* 17 (March 1962):16–21.

Lavine, Harold. "What Arms Policy to Prevent World War III?" *Commentary,* 18 (November 1954):434–39.

Lee, Ben S. "Missiles Super-Agency Fast Taking Shape." *Aviation Week,* October 30, 1950, pp. 12–14.

Licklider, Roy E. "The Missile Gap Controversy." *Political Science Quarterly,* 85, no. 4 (December 1970):600–15.

Lindblom, Charles E. "The Science of 'Muddling Through.' " *Public Administration Review,* 19 (Spring 1959):79.

Lindsay, Richard C. "How the Air Force Will Use Its Missiles." *Air Force,* 39, no. 9 (September 1956):98–102.

Livingston, J. Sterling. "Decision-Making in Weapons Development." *Harvard Business Review,* 36 (January–February 1958):127–36.

Loosbrock, John F. "The USAF Ballistic Missile Program." *Air Force,* 41 (March):84–95.

Murphy, C. J. V. "America's New Strategic Position." *Fortune,* 50 (August 1954):70–1 ff.

——— "America's Widening Military Margin." *Fortune,* 56 (August 1957):94 ff.

——— "The Atom and the Balance of Power." *Fortune,* 48 (August 1953):97 ff.

——— "Blowup at Hughes Aircraft." *Fortune,* 49 (February 1954): 116–18.

——— "The Budget and Eisenhower." *Fortune,* 56 (July 1957): 96–99.

——— "Defense and Strategy." *Fortune,* 48 (July 1953):35–40.

——— "Defense: The Converging Decisions." *Fortune,* 58 (October 1958):119 ff.

——— "Defense: The Revolution Gets Revolutionary." *Fortune,* 53 (May 1956):101 ff.

——— "The Eisenhower Shift." *Fortune,* 53 (January 1956):83–87, 206–8.

——— "Eisenhower's Most Critical Defense Budget." *Fortune,* 54 (December 1956):112 ff.

——— "The New Air Situation." *Fortune,* 52 (September 1955): 86–87.

——— "Strategy Overtakes Mr. Wilson." *Fortune,* 49 (January 1954):80 ff.

——— "The U.S. as a Bombing Target." *Fortune,* 48 (November 1953):118–21.

——— "The White House Since Sputnik." *Fortune,* 57 (January 1958):98–101 ff.

Nitze, Paul H. "Atoms, Strategy and Policy." *Foreign Affairs,* 36 (January 1956):188–98.

Norris, John G. "New Deterrent Weapons and Space Vehicles."

Washington Post, May 7, 1959, p. A–21; May 8, 1959, p. A–9; May 9, 1959, p. A–6; May 10, 1959, p. A–12; May 11, 1959, p. A–7.

————— "No Missile Gap Exists, Defense Study Shows." *Washington Post,* February 7, 1961, pp. 1, 36.

"Now U. S., Too, Has Supermissiles." *United States News and World Report,* December 27, 1957, p. 31.

"$100 Million Missile Program under Fire." *Aviation Week,* April 24, 1950, pp. 12–13.

Ostrander, Donald R. "Who Is Doing What in Ballistic Missile Research." *Air Force,* 39, no. 9 (September 1956):107–11.

Page, Jerry D. "Tooling Up for the Ballistic Missiles Training Program." *Air University Quarterly Review,* 10, no. 4 (Winter 1958–59):6–20.

Parry, Albert. "Why Should We Have Been Surprised?" *The Reporter,* 17 (October 31, 1957):13–15.

Perkins, Donald T. "Dropping the Pilot." *Annals of the American Academy of Political and Social Science,* 299, (May 1955):128–33.

Perry, Robert L. "The Air Force and Operations Research: A Commentary on I. B. Holley's Paper." 1969 (photocopy).

————— "The Ballistic Missile Decisions." Paper prepared for fourth annual meeting of American Institute of Aeronautics and Astronautics, October 1967.

————— "The Mythology of Military R&D." May 1966 (photocopy).

Phillips, Thomas R. "The Atomic Revolution in Warfare." *Bulletin of the Atomic Scientists,* 10 (October 1954):315–17.

————— "The Growing Missile Gap." *The Reporter,* 20 (January 8, 1959):10–16.

Power, Thomas S. "SAC and the Ballistic Missile." *Air University Quarterly Review,* 9 (Winter 1957–1958):2–30.

Putman, W. D. "The Evolution of Air Force System Acquisition Management." Santa Monica, California: RAND Corporation, May 1971. Xerox draft.

Radford, Arthur W. "Defense for the Long Haul." *Vital Speeches of the Day,* 20 (January 1, 1953):171–73.

"Ramo-Wooldridge, ARDC Groups Act as Missile System Managers." *Aviation Week,* February 20, 1956, p. 28.

Ransom, Harry Howe. "The Politics of Airpower—A Comparative Analysis." *Public Policy* (1958): pp. 87–119.

Raymond, Jack. "Kennedy Defense Study Finds No Evidence of a Missile Gap." *New York Times,* February 7, 1961, pp. 1, 18.

"Report Spells Out Guided Missile Plan." *Aviation Week,* March 6, 1950, pp. 12–13.

Rollefson, R. "Why So Many Missiles?" *Bulletin of the Atomic Scientists,* 13 (October 1957):295–301.
"SAC in Transition: Special Report on Strategic Air Command." *Aviation Week,* 72 (June 20, 1960):101–144.
Schilling, Warner R. "The H-Bomb Decision: How to Decide Without Actually Choosing." *Political Science Quarterly* (March 1961): 24–46.
––––––– "Science, Technology, and Foreign Policy." *Journal of International Affairs,* 13, no. 1 (Winter 1959):7–18.
––––––– "Scientists, Foreign Policy and Politics." *American Political Science Review,* 56, no. 2 (June 1962):287–300.
Schriever, Bernard A. "AFBMD: Catching Up with the Soviets." *Missiles and Rockets,* 4 (July 28, 1958):pp. 53–58.
––––––– "Development and Status of the Air Force Guided Missile Program." *Western Aviation,* 37, no. 2 (February 1957):27–30.
Schwiebert, Ernest G. "USAF's Ballistic Missile—1954–1964: A Concise History." *Air Force and Space Digest,* May 1964, pp. 51–113.
"Senator Blasts Air Force Management." *Aviation Week,* July 20, 1953, p. 13.
Sides, John H. "Ten Years of Missile Progress." *Astronautics,* 2 (September 1957):24–26.
Simpson, Mary M. "The Race for Missiles." *Bulletin of the Atomic Scientists,* 13 (1957):302–8.
Smith, C. H. Jr.; M. W. Rosen, and J. M. Bridger. "Super Altitude Research Rocket Revealed by Navy." *Aviation,* 46 (June 1947): 40–43.
Stone, C. B. "USAF Seeks More Efficient Management." *Aviation Week,* April 4, 1955, p. 17.
Symington, Stuart. "The Intercontinental Ballistic Missile." *Vital Speeches of the Day,* 20, no. 23 (September 15, 1954):711–16.
––––––– "Where the Missile Gap Went." *The Reporter,* 26 (February 15, 1962):21–23.
Tangerman, E. J. "Can We Catch Up in Rocket Research?" *Aviation,* XLV (June 1946):40–41, 148–50.
Tarr, David W. "Military Technology and the Policy Process." *Western Political Quarterly,* 18 (March 1965):135–48.
"The Truth about Missiles: What Went Wrong." *United States News and World Report,* December 27, 1957, pp. 35–41, 64.
"USAF Ballistic Missile Milestones." *Air Force,* 41 (March 1958): 80–84.
Van Riper, Paul P. "A Survey of Materials for the Study of Military Management." *American Political Science Review,* 49 (September 1955):828–850.

"WDD Directs ICBM, IRBM Development." *Aviation Week,* August 6, 1956, pp. 101–5.

Witze, Claude. "AMC Develops Missile Support System." *Aviation Week,* August 19, 1957, p. 16.

————— "Classified Report Says Soviets Can Neutralize SAC by 1960." *Aviation Week,* December 1, 1957, p. 24.

Wohlstetter, Albert. "The Delicate Balance of Terror." *Foreign Affairs,* 37 (January 1959):211–34.

Wolfers, Arnold. "Superiority in Nuclear Weapons: Advantages and Limitations." *The Annals of the American Academy of Political and Social Science,* 299 (November 1953):7–15.

Wolk, Herman S. "The Strategic World of 1946." *Air Force,* 54, no. 2 (February 1971):40–43.

Wood, Robert H. "Overselling the Missile." *Aviation Week,* July 31, 1950, p. 46.

York, Herbert F. "Military Technology and National Security." *Scientific American,* 221, no. 2 (August 1969):12, 17–29.

CORRESPONDENCE RECEIVED

Karel Bossart. December 9, 1971. Convair Aircraft.

William Gould Dow. December 30, 1972. Rocket and Satellite Research Panel.

Harry Jordan. November 30, 1971 and January 4, 1972. Historian, Space and Missile Systems Organization (USAF).

Lester K. Murray. December 29, 1971. Convair Aircraft.

Donald L. Putt. February 16, 1972. Air Research and Development Command; Deputy Chief of Staff/Development (USAF).

Herbert F. York. December 1, 1971. Second von Neumann Committee; Atlas Scientific Advisory Committee (Office of the Secretary of the Air Force).

INTERVIEWS, WITH MOST RELEVANT IDENTIFICATION

Arnold Anchordoguy. August 11, 1971. Redondo Beach, California: Thompson-Ramo-Wooldridge (TRW).

Bruno Augenstein. August 5, 1971. Santa Monica, California: RAND Corporation.

Franklin Collbohm. August 21, 1971. Los Angeles: RAND Corporation.

Richard DeLaurer. August 10, 1971. Redondo Beach: TRW, Inc.

Edward Doll. August 11, 1971. Redondo Beach: TRW, Inc.

Krafft Ehricke. August 9, 1971. Los Angeles: Convair Aircraft.

William Graham. August 9, 1971. Santa Monica: RAND Corporation.

Arnold Horlick. August 5, 1971. Santa Monica: RAND Corporation.

Richard K. Jacobson. August 17, 1971. Huntington Beach, California: Western Development Division (USAF).

Thomas Lanphier, Jr. August 24, 1971. La Jolla, California: Convair Aircraft.

Curtis E. LeMay. August 16, 1971. Newport Beach, California: USAF (Commander SAC, Chief of Staff).

John Kenneth Mansfield. December 21, 1971. Washington, D.C.: Staff, U.S. Congress, Joint Committee on Atomic Energy.

Reuben Mettler. August 10, 1971. Los Angeles: TRW, Inc.

William Patterson. January 3, 1972. Washington, D.C.: Convair Aircraft.

Robert L. Perry. August 6, 7, 9, 1971. Santa Monica: Air Force Historical Office; RAND Corporation.

Robert Piper. August 6, 1971. El Segundo, California: Historian, Space and Missile Systems Organization (SAMSO) (USAF).

William Putnam. August 12, 1971. Santa Monica: RAND Corporation.

Simon Ramo. August 9 and 20, 1971. Los Angeles: TRW, Inc.

Osmond Ritland. August 12, 1971. Huntington Beach: Western Development Division (USAF).

Alfred Rockefeller. August 6 and 17, 1971. El Segundo: Western Development Division (USAF).

Bernard Schriever. March 12, 1974. Washington, D.C. (USAF).

Howard Seiver. August 11, 1971. Redondo Beach: TRW, Inc.

John W. Sessums. August 19, 1971. Redlands, California: Air Research and Development Command (USAF).

Ray E. Soper. August 23, 1971. San Diego, California: Air Staff, Office of the Special Assistant for Guided Missiles (USAF).

Charles Terhune. August 18, 1971. Pasadena, California: Western Development Division (USAF).

Dean E. Wooldridge. August 13, 1971. Santa Barbara, California: TRW, Inc.

John Zoekler. August 16, 1971. Redondo Beach: Western Development Division (USAF).

Index